THE MAN WHO WON
THE BATTLE OF BRITAIN

THE MAN WHO WON
THE
BATTLE OF BRITAIN

Robert Wright

CHARLES SCRIBNER'S SONS · NEW YORK

CONTENTS

ACKNOWLEDGMENTS

Since this book is essentially a personal one in its style, I am taking the opportunity of retaining that in offering my thanks to all those—the list is a long one—who have been so helpful in providing expressions of their views on various aspects of the story that has now been placed on record. They are named in this book, and through that many of them have become members of what Lord Dowding has called, with warm gratitude, 'the band of loyalists'. On the other hand, it must be understood that, unless otherwise stated the opinions that have been expressed are mine, and they do not represent, in any way whatsoever, any official views.

It is with pleasure that Lord Dowding and I would like to acknowledge the facilities that were provided for research by Louis Jackets, the Head of the Air Historical Branch of the Ministry of Defence. As always, he was most helpful, as was Tom Gleave, another old and valued friend. They both went out of their way with kindness and consideration to be of help whenever they were asked for it.

For quotations from various published sources, I wish to thank the following authors and publishers: Maurice Ashley, *Churchill as Historian*, Charles Scribner's Sons; Anthony Eden, *The Reckoning*, Houghton Mifflin; Sir John Wheeler-Bennett, *et al.*, *Action This Day*, Macmillan Ltd. of London; Andrew Boyle, *Trenchard*, W. W. Norton; Paul Brickhill, *Reach for the Sky*, W. W. Norton; Sir Winston Churchill, *History of the Second World War*, Houghton Mifflin; Ronald W. Clark, *The Battle for Britain*, Harrap; Basil Collier, *The Defense of the United Kingdom*, Her Majesty's Stationery Office; John Connell, *Wavell*, Collins; the *Daily Telegraph;* Air Commodore Alan C. Deere, *Nine Lives*, Hodder & Stoughton; Sholto Douglas, *Combat and Command*, Simon & Schuster; Air Chief Marshal Lord Dowding, *Twelve Legions of Angels*, Jarrold; Lord Dowding's Official Despatch, *The Battle of Britain* (a supplement to the *London Gazette*), Her Majesty's Stationery Office; Group Captain T. P. Gleave, *I Had a Row with a German*, Macmillan Ltd. of London; C. G. Grey, *History of the Air Ministry*, Allen & Unwin; Sir Basil Liddell Hart, *et al.*, *Churchill Revised*, Dial Press; Sir Basil Liddell Hart, *The New Cambridge Modern History*, *Vol. XII*, Cambridge University Press; Air Vice Marshal J. E. Johnson, *Full Circle*, Ballantine Books; Air Chief Marshal Sir Philip Joubert de la Ferte, *The Third Service*, Thames & Hudson; the *Observer;* General Sir Frederick Pile, *Ack-Ack*, Harrap; Walter Raleigh, *The War in the Air*, Vol. I, Oxford University Press; D. Richards and Hilary St. G. Saunders, *Royal Air Force 1939-45*, Her Majesty's Stationery Office; D. Robertson, *George Mallory*, Faber & Faber; Marshal of the R. A. F. Sir John Slessor, *The Central Blue*, Frederick A. Praeger; A. J. P. Taylor, *English History 1914-1945*, Oxford University Press; Telford Taylor, *The Breaking Wave*, Simon & Schuster; Viscount Templewood, *Nine Troubled Years*, Collins; H. R. Trevor Roper, ed., *Hitler's War Directives 1933-45*, Sidgwick & Jackson; *Trial of German Major War Criminals: Proceedings of the Military Tribunal at Nuremberg*, Her Majesty's Stationery Office; Derek Wood and Derek Dempster, *The Narrow Margin*, McGraw-Hill; Air Marshal Sir Peter Wykeham, *Fighter Command*, Putnam; Field Marshal Lord Wavell, *Other Men's Flowers*, Jonathan Cape.

Official documents are reproduced by kind permission of the Controller of Her Majesty's Stationery Office.

FOREWORD

The truism that no man can see himself for what he is as fairly and squarely as those who have served under him is particularly apt when it is applied to those who have occupied any high public office or an appointment of high command in time of war. An appreciation of that is one of the reasons why I have always been hesitant about assisting in the writing by others of any accounts which deal with my time in the Royal Air Force. I know the need to be on one's guard.

When I look back over the many years of my service in the R.A.F., which culminated in the Battle of Britain, it would seem that not a little of what I did and said, particularly at the end of that career and quite apart from what I thought, has given rise to repeated gusts of controversy. Since such controversy has never been of my choosing, I have been purposely reticent about discussing publicly personal views and experiences of mine which seem to have excited so much curiosity. I have no strong objection to controversy, provided that it is at least intelligent and well-informed and about matters that are of importance; but I have no time for idle curiosity, and no wish whatsoever to be contentious.

After so many years of a silence on my part that, for several reasons, has been self-imposed, the time has now come, mainly through the resurgence of interest in the Battle of Britain, to speak about matters in which there is a public interest. Yet again there are those questions about my views and my actions —with an accompanying speculation about the part that I played—in one of the great periods of our history: the fighting of the Battle of Britain.

This situation has also brought home to me, in a way that is deeply moving, the nature of the position that I appear to occupy in the hearts and minds of those of that time of 1940 with whom I had the closest contact: the men and women who fought with me in that battle. Of late, again through circumstance, I have become very aware of that, and nothing could make me feel prouder than that it should come from, among others, those pilots and air-crews who, in serving under my command, have been referred to as my 'chicks'.

For personal reasons, upon which I need not dwell, it became necessary to find some way in which I could say what I wanted to say, and for that to be placed on record by someone whom I felt understood and shared, with discretion, my views on my career in the Royal Air Force. The one man whom I knew that I could rely upon in this somewhat delicate situation was Robert Wright, an old and trusted friend.

In the Second World War Robert Wright served in the R.A.F. as a navigator in night fighters. During the whole of the Battle of Britain he was on the staff at the Headquarters of Fighter Command, and for a short time during the battle he was my Personal Assistant. Over the years that have passed since then, Wright and I have become close friends; and we have discussed at great length—at times with sorrow and at other times with an enjoyable and understanding humour as well as an intense interest—the experiences that were mine.

The curiosity that Robert Wright and I came to feel about several of the more obscure aspects of those personal experiences, some of which have always mystified me, led us to examine them in every light possible, and in great depth. Our discoveries, and Wright's own experiences, have enabled him to work in a manner that is agreeable to me without being dominated or controlled by me. While in the broad view this book is to some extent a collaboration, there are views of his own that he had to be free to express about me and my thoughts and actions which I could not and would not wish to venture to comment upon myself. These interpretations are from Wright's point of view, and they have to be recorded in order that we should make known with as fair an appreciation as possible a story that is not generally known.

My various personal papers and files, all of which I placed in the hands of Robert Wright for his exclusive use, my official despatch, a small book of my own that was published over twenty years ago, and a short biography that came out twelve years ago together contain some record of my Service career and the Battle of Britain. But even that record is not complete. It does not give the details of certain personal aspects of my experiences. These are what have now been thoroughly examined in the painstaking research that has been done, and with the assistance of information from other sources, and vitally important material which has only recently been made available, we have been able to complete the story.

The examination that has been made of these more personal aspects of my experiences—which occurred during what was, I suppose, the most important period of my life—reveals some points that have never been made known to the public. I have agreed to that being done with the hope that it will put an end to all further speculation. Out of it there has come this book. In his approach the author has been fair and faithful, endeavouring to render a full account, from both the personal and the historical point of view, of all that I should like to have placed on record.

DOWDING

Tunbridge Wells,
Kent

INTRODUCTION

ALL those who lived and worked in Britain as well as those who fought in the skies over this country during the summer of the year of 1940 experienced a time of heroic proportions. It was also, for those concerned, a time of emotional involvement. The fate of the free world teetered on the brink of disaster, and for the few who were trying to maintain some degree of balance there was a terrible anxiety about the outcome of the tipping of the scales. After the strange and at times terrifying struggle that took place in the air, the essential freedom about which we are so given to boasting, perhaps a little too glibly, was finally preserved for us. It was done by a small band of men, many of whom were very young, who were probably the most highly skilled that the world had ever known in the profession of the bearing of arms.

It has been said of those young men that they were 'the gayest company who ever fired their guns in anger.' There can be no question about the truth of that, even if, when it came to the actual moment of the firing of those guns, the pursuit was in such deadly earnest. None can speak with greater feeling about that than the enemy; and none will speak with greater admiration for the high endeavour of those who fought than the men and women on the ground whose task it was to sustain the men in the air. For all the gaiety of its irrepressible youth, so far as Fighter Command of the Royal Air Force was concerned the Battle of Britain was a matter of living or dying.

In the eyes, and at times the ears, of the public who watched and listened there was reflected, and readily accepted, from those who did the fighting this almost indefinable light-heartedness that can be so typical of the British way of life. Everybody on the ground was involved, but so far as they could know at the time it was scarcely more than a struggle that was taking place in the skies over their heads. Few knew that it was the first—nobody knew that it was to be the last—great battle fought solely in the air. For those on the ground it had to be in an alien element. And how could anyone know, then, that the outcome of that battle was to decide the whole course of the second great world war that had come in less than thirty years?

For the British that great conflict in which the Royal Air Force repulsed the onslaught of the German Luftwaffe has left the name of the Battle of Britain proudly adorned with a lustre which time will never tarnish. There has been amply recorded in history a full accounting of the facts of the actual waging of the battle. What has never been fully recorded is the story of what happened in the affairs of the man who led the fighters of the Royal Air Force to that victory. He was no longer young when he did that; and he had already waged a strenuous fight for preparedness, and his sense of responsibility and his deep feeling for those who were fighting in the air brought for him a particularly intense emotional involvement.

Before and during the Battle of Britain, Air Chief Marshal Sir Hugh (now Lord) Dowding, the excessively reticent Englishman who was Air Officer Commanding-in-Chief of Fighter Command, conducted himself in a manner that bore the hall-mark of great leadership. For that alone his name deserves its place among those of Britain's most illustrious commanders. But, one has to ask, how well is that understood by all those whose way of life Dowding helped so much to preserve? And how much is it appreciated that, after achieving what he did, a burden was placed on his shoulders that he should never have had to bear?

Such general recognition as now exists of the name of Dowding is, at most, less than appropriate. For reasons that have been obscured by controversy, such recognition as there is has come about years after the event, almost forcing its way unaided through obscurity out into the light of reason. Now we know that at the time, in the moment of a great victory, Dowding was pushed aside in a fashion that was of no credit to those in whose hands there rested his good name. Moreover, it was most unusual, and almost exactly the opposite of the time-honoured custom that the British have always observed in acknowledging the success of their armies on the land and their fleets at sea. For too long Dowding has been left to stand alone in the shadows: a silent figure about whom some people speak, about whom many ask questions, and for whom a few have felt a deep sympathy and a sense of injustice over the treatment that was meted out to him at the time of victory. The price of that silence of his has been a high one.

Many years ago Sir Winston Churchill made the statement: 'It is always dangerous for soldiers, sailors or airmen to play at politics. They enter a sphere in which the values are quite different from those to which they have hitherto been accustomed.' Whether that comment was intended to be as cynical as it sounds is difficult to judge. Churchill knew at first hand all about the bitter quarrelling and sordid intrigue that bedevilled the relationships between the political and the military leaders during the First World War. It has been said that because of his knowledge and experience of that he was determined that there should be no repetition of it under his leadership in the war of 1939–45. He was not always successful. Political forbearance from intrigue is an ideal of a very high order.

From long before the time when, in September, 1939, Britain went to war with Germany, Dowding had been carrying on his shoulders a load of responsibility that was probably greater, in the military sense, than that accepted by any other single individual. He was a thorough-going professional military airman, and he knew nothing about politics. The responsibility that was his was the defence of the United Kingdom. For fourteen months after the outbreak of war he continued to shoulder that responsibility, and at the same time he had to endure political pressures that were well-nigh intolerable. It is small wonder that at times his patience became a little frayed; and when one learns to appreciate the fortitude that he displayed it becomes possible to understand why, when the final blow fell, he retired into silence.

For many years the name of Dowding was allowed to remain in those shadows that were created for him by lesser men. From time to time some lip-service was paid to his achievements; but a truly equitable recognition of what Dowding achieved at the time of the gravest peril to our way of life has never been fully accorded him. In some respects he brought upon himself a few of the shadows in which he had stood because of his refusal to say anything about what had happened to him. In his own words, he has always been 'extremely anxious to avoid any statements on contentious matters'.

The distress that was caused Dowding by the actions of others before, during and after the Battle of Britain was so acute that for many years he found the subject well-nigh impossible to discuss even with close friends. During that time he once wrote to me saying: 'If you ever "did" the *Aeneid* at school you may remember one of the opening lines: "Infandum regina jubes renovare dolorem." "You ask me, oh queen, to resuscitate an intolerable grief." Pretty well everyone who writes a book covering the period of the Battle of Britain sends to me for a foreword or for comments of some kind. Always I am dragged back into the atmosphere of devastating strain when I was fighting the Germans and the French and the Cabinet and the Air Ministry and now and again the Navy for good measure . . .'

But time was to bring into a better perspective the vital importance of the great air battle of 1940; and it was only time that could ease the restraint that for so long had inhibited Dowding from being able to examine with sufficient objectivity the precise reasons for the distress that had been caused him. It was then, only some three years ago, that he began to feel that his own long silence might be broken, and in another letter to me he was able to write that he thought that 'a more accurate appreciation of the situation seems to have leaked through to the public by a form of osmosis.' He added:

'I am little concerned with public opinion about me and my conduct in preparation for, and during, the Battle; although I sense a considerable swing of public sentiment in my favour since the termination of the Battle (which the general public in England did not even recognize as a separate operation of war, because of the continuance for the time being of the night bombing, which was a completely different operation with a different objective). Also, it seemed to me that the Ministry itself did very little to inform the public, largely because the same confusion existed in the minds of senior officers in the Ministry.'

Nearly thirty years have passed since the fighting of that memorable battle. As loyal as ever to his sense of what is appropriate in the views that he held then and the stand that he made, Dowding revealed in that one statement the reason why, today, he is held in such high esteem by all those who had the good fortune to work with him, and particularly under his command, during the time of his highest endeavour. There is also in it the reason why so many now feel very strongly that the time has come to speak up on Dowding's behalf.

This book is not a history of the Battle of Britain. That factual story has been dealt with already, in detail, by many historians. This is the story of what happened to one of the men who took part in that battle, and it is intended that it should be placed alongside the many other personal accounts that have been written by or about other participants in it. The fact that it deals with the personal story of what happened to their leader will help, perhaps, to round out the overall picture of those times.

ROBERT WRIGHT

Chichester,
Sussex

CHAPTER ONE

THOSE PROUD IDEALS

DURING the years of the latter half of the eighteen-nineties, as the old century and an old world gave way to the beginning of the onslaught of our own troubled times, two boys in their teens named Archibald P. Wavell, the son of an army officer, and Hugh C. T. Dowding, the son of a school-master, were together at Winchester, one of England's most famous schools. Only a few years later another boy named Charles F. A. Portal was among those who attended this school.

Nearly fifty years later, shortly after the end of the second great world war of the first half of this twentieth century, there was published privately the war service record and roll of honour of the boys of that school. During the half century that had passed since Wavell, Dowding and Portal had been at Winchester, their successes in life had marked them out as three of the foremost Wykehamists of their time; and jointly over their names they contributed the preface to this school record. By then, in the correct style created for them after the time-honoured fashion to which the British have clung in honouring the achievements of those who have served their country well, their names had become Field Marshall Earl Wavell, P.C., G.C.B., G.C.S.I., G.C.I.E., C.M.G., M.C., Air Chief Marshal Baron Dowding of Bentley Priory, G.C.B., G.C.V.O., C.M.G., and Marshal of the Royal Air Force Viscount Portal of Hungerford, K.G., G.C.B., O.M., D.S.O., M.C.

In a sense esoteric, and in the eyes of some perhaps a little fulsome, such honours and awards are the hallmarks which indicate the public recognition that was accorded Wavell, the soldier and fine scholar, Dowding, the airman and great humanitarian, and Portal, the airman and outstanding administrator. Such was the measure of the acknowledgement of what these boys had become after their years of endeavour.

In that preface to the record of their school, these three men whose names had become world-famous referred to themselves as having been 'fortunate enough to hold high command in the late war'. But that was scarcely more than a comment that was made in passing. What they stressed, together and with very genuine feeling, was their conception of 'the two proudest ideals' of all those who have ever been to the school. The first of these ideals they gave as 'Service to our King and Country.' Of the second they said that 'the other ideal is Manners.'

Naming the war that had only recently come to an end as 'the greatest and most ruthless example in world history of man's inhumanity to man,' these three distinguished military leaders suggested that 'Service and Manners . . . both quiet and unobtrusive but genuine . . . if practised between nations as well as between individuals, are perhaps the two qualities best calculated to bring some rest and promote prosperity and happiness in our present distracted world.'

Such was the view that was held in maturity by these men who, in their earlier years, were of the generation that had seen at first hand such brutal service in fighting in the First World War, and who were, with that harsh experience forever in mind, to become great leaders in the Second World War.

From the beginning of their service in these high appointments it was inevitable that all three men should come to know only too well what it meant to be forced into an involvement in that political sphere which Winston Churchill had described as 'dangerous' for men such as these. Of the three, Dowding was to achieve the greatest single triumph: the victory under his command in the Battle of Britain. But despite that triumph, and almost in the moment of its realization, he was to learn that the political values were indeed, in Churchill's words, 'quite different from those to which' he had been accustomed. That was particularly true in Manners, which were violated in a decision being reached, under Winston Churchill's leadership, that was so largely the result of 'playing at politics'.

The strange hand of chance had brought Wavell and Dowding and Portal together as military leaders of equal importance in the service of their country at that critical time in 1940. It also led to Wavell—who was himself having a difficult enough time at the hands of the politicians—being the one who warned Dowding in the summer of that year of the political dangers that were in store for him. And, stranger

still, it even led to Portal having to be the one who had
to implement, towards the end of the year, a decision
that amounted to a questioning of Dowding's conduct as a
Commander-in-Chief and of his handling of his Command
during the Battle of Britain.

The lack of Manners that was exhibited by others in this
matter must have been distasteful enough for Portal. For
Dowding, it was the last straw in the treatment that he had
been subjected to for altogether too long. In the very moment
of his great triumph, he had imposed upon him an indignity
that was intolerable; and after a lifetime of proud 'Service to
our King and Country' he had to endure, through a violation
of that precious ideal of Manners, an injustice that was
inexcusable. Dowding had indeed been 'fortunate enough to
hold high command,' and for a long time; but in the end he
was also unfortunate enough to incur displeasure. Political
values, it seemed, made no allowance for the ideals which were
to such a marked degree a part of his whole outlook on life.

Hugh Caswall Tremenheere Dowding was born on 24 April
1882, into a world that was vastly different from that in which
he was to have to make his way. If ever there was a man who
had to face with resolution and integrity the dangers of that
world, and its tortuous games in which the values are quite
different from those of Service and Manners, that man was
Dowding. They were not games of his choosing, and the stand
that he made in his life was all the more notable because of his
acute distaste for much of what he became involved in, and
against which he had to stand in a distracted world.

At the time when, many years later, Dowding finally brought
himself to start making the effort to put on paper some record
of his views about the experiences that had been his, he made
a comment about himself that is typical of his way of thought
and his style in expressing himself. He said: 'Since I was a child
I have never accepted ideas purely because they were orthodox,
and consequently I have frequently found myself in opposition
to generally accepted views. Perhaps, in retrospect, this has not
been altogether a bad thing.'

While the forthright clarity of that view is essentially a part of the nature of the man, there is much in it that can be attributed to the influence of Dowding's parents. Their honesty and sincerity and the happiness of his early life under their guidance are aspects of that life which have always enabled him to express for his mother and father the greatest admiration and respect. The simple integrity that was instilled into him from the beginning was to make it all so much more difficult for him when he had to face the reality of association with men and women of less rectitude. For Dowding the quality of integrity has always been of the utmost importance, and it has always been the outstanding trait in his own character.

As with a surprising number of other military leaders of his time, Dowding's family was, as he has put it, 'mainly clerical and scholastic'. His grandfather, Benjamin Charles Dowding, was a clergyman, and his grandmother, Maria Caswall, was the daughter of a clergyman. 'I don't think I had any very distinguished ancestors.' There was an uncle who became an Admiral in the Royal Navy, and who explored the sources of the Amazon and the Orinoco in South America; another uncle was a chaplain in the Royal Navy; and yet another uncle was stroke of the Oxford crew in his time, and then lived and died in India.

The family had roots deep in the West Country. Dowding's father, Arthur John Caswall, was born in Southbroom, near Devizes. He won a scholarship which took him to Winchester, where, as a leader, he became Prefect of School. He went on to New College, Oxford, where he met his future wife, Maude Tremenheere, the sister of a friend, and the daughter of a general in the Indian army, who was also at one time Governor of Aden.

'After leaving Oxford my father became an assistant master at Haileybury, and later at a preparatory school at Slough,' Dowding said of the man who was to exert a great influence in his life. 'After a few years of that he started, in partnership with another man, a preparatory school, which they named St Ninian's, at Moffat, in Dumfrieshire.'

It was there that Dowding was born, and since that just happened by chance to be in Scotland he has been quite often and quite incorrectly referred to as 'a dour Scotsman'. Hugh Dowding was the first of four children, the others being his sister Hilda, and his two brothers, Arthur and Kenneth. He received his early education at St Ninian's, and from there he went to his father's old school, Winchester.

Of his time at Winchester, Dowding has said that it was 'very uneventful'. He was there for four years. In his book *Other Men's Flowers*, Wavell recalled: 'A contemporary of mine at Winchester, who has risen to great eminence and leadership in the youngest of the three Services, once told me that he adopted a military career simply because joining the Army Class was the only way in which he could escape having to learn Greek.' That contemporary was Dowding, and joining the Army Class was what, as he has put it, 'decided my career'. He passed the necessary examination and entered the Royal Military Academy, Woolwich—'The Shop'—in September, 1899.

Owing to the Boer War that was then being fought in South Africa, the course at Woolwich that would normally have lasted two years was shortened to one year. 'I had passed in high enough to get a commission in the Royal Engineers,' Dowding commented on the first steps that he took in his chosen career. 'I would have got it if I had kept my place, but I failed through laziness.'

The advice then given to Dowding was that he should choose to join the Garrison Artillery in preference to the Field Artillery —'wrongly, I thought later'—and he was commissioned as a gunner on 18 August 1900, at the age of eighteen and a half. On a Second Lieutenant's pay of five shillings and seven pence a day—'with one's mess bill coming to about three and six'— Dowding started his Service career in Gibraltar, which he disliked. A year later his company was transferred to Ceylon, which he found more congenial and where he had an opportunity to learn to play polo.

'After less than a year in Ceylon we were moved to Hong Kong, which was a delightful station,' Dowding has said, recalling that he enjoyed plenty of polo and racing. 'I bought a beautiful little Waler which I got cheap because it was a confirmed buck-jumper. I don't know how many times he had me off before we came to terms with one another.' Hong Kong was very different from what it is today. Then, in 1903, there were no roads round the island, and no motor-cars; and such were the social customs that even mixed bathing was frowned upon and indulged in only by the more daring.

Just before the Russo-Japanese war of 1904–5—yet another war in an age that now seems so long ago—Dowding and a brother officer spent two months of their leave in Japan. During the time that he had been on duty in Hong Kong the Russian fleet, that was later to be destroyed by the Japanese, had sailed past, and Dowding has recalled that there was 'considerable apprehension among the authorities in Hong Kong lest the fleet should attempt to seize the place as a base of operations against Japan'.

While still in Ceylon, Dowding had applied for a transfer to the Mountain Artillery in India. In the spring of 1904 his posting to Rawalpindi came through, and he heard that there were prospects of an expedition into Tibet. But the place that should have been his was taken by a more senior subaltern. Of the experiences that were to be his from that time on, Dowding commented: 'Perhaps I was unlucky, but the Staff Officers with whom we had dealings in India mostly seemed to us to be somewhat amateurish.'

That alone was a comment which, while justified, could perhaps be said to have had in it a fuse that, after long-delayed action, was to trigger off an explosion nearly forty years later, and to create a situation that was to cause Dowding so much trouble. In his young days he had had to learn the hard rules of Service discipline, and how to live with them, and it was this which caused him later to feel strongly about infringements of that discipline.

From the very beginning, Dowding had shown marked tendencies towards forthright expressions of his own views, but he learnt to contain them and to express them only at the right time and to the best effect. He has commented that most people dislike being cursed at whether the fault was theirs or not. 'I never much minded being cursed,' he has remarked of the time he spent as a subaltern, very much under the thumb of a stern discipline.

As a subaltern, Dowding had his full share of difficulties with those who were senior to him, including a refusal by his

Commanding Officer to allow him to put his name down for the Staff College course at Camberley which it was so necessary any young officer should attend if he wished to make any progress in his career in the Army. 'He thought that I didn't take life as a soldier seriously enough,' Dowding has surmised. 'The only thing to do then was to get out of his Battery.' He applied to join a Native Battery. By then, Dowding had been in India three years. His request was granted, and he was sent to a hill station in northern India which he has described as 'the best station at which I ever served. The polo was excellent, the shooting was very good and varied, and there was plenty of social life. And finally we were blessed by the absence of any Headquarters with its complement of brass hats.'

In describing his new Commanding Officer of that time, Dowding defined, perhaps without realising it, the qualities which he considered should go into the making of such an officer up to any level of command. He spoke of him as '. . . one of the best officers I ever served under, kindly and humorous but not slack, and intolerant of slackness in others. He had his own methods of discipline.' Those methods were very largely unspoken.

'What I liked about my time in a Native Battery,' Dowding has added, 'was the responsibility which came the way of the subaltern, so different from the lot of the junior officer in an infantry regiment.'

It was this chance to accept responsibility that was to lead Dowding, in 1909, to a meeting with a man who was to play a vitally important role in his life in the Battle of Britain, thirty-one years later. Dowding was detailed to take part in an exercise in which the enemy was represented by the famous Gurkhas. With his Section, he was to form part of a retreat. But by starting the day's manoeuvres at four o'clock in the morning instead of six o'clock, Dowding caught the 'enemy' Gurkhas still having breakfast, and technically they were annihilated. The officer commanding the Gurkhas was a young subaltern named Cyril Newall.

After six years' service in India, Dowding returned to England to attend the Staff College course at Camberley, which was to last two years. Although there was much about it that he liked, Dowding once made a comment in some notes: 'I was always irked by the lip-service that the Staff paid to freedom of thought, contrasted with an actual tendency to repress all but conventional ideas.' Since he chose to think of himself as a nonconformist, and he was by nature a stern realist, he was surprised to find how many men there were in their thirties who appeared to be clever enough but who could become, under the existing system, so adolescent in their outlook.

It was this experience of his while at Camberley, and the prospect of the very slow rate of progress in promotion which he had to face, that made Dowding begin to feel a dissatisfaction with the Army, and even to dislike it. But a new field was opened up for him in a way that was quite unexpected, and it was of a particularly stimulating interest. He became aware of the developments that were taking place in the use of the air.

In the very conventional nature of their Army training in 1912, it was not altogether surprising that the air was, as Dowding has put it, 'sedulously avoided in almost all our exercises'. But when the time came, after waiting for over a year, for him to become a commander in one of the Staff College exercises, Dowding found that he 'actually had six aeroplanes in my imaginary command'. He made prompt use of all of them for reconnaissance, and found the information they could supply proved his point. From that he quickly came to the conclusion that it would be of distinct value to his career if he were to learn to fly.

The Royal Flying Corps had come into existence only the year before, in April 1912. But those who wanted to become pilots in the R.F.C. had to pay the cost themselves of learning to fly at civilian training schools, with the promise of a refund from the government if they managed to qualify. The next step for all pilots after that was to go to the Central Flying School of the R.F.C. at Upavon in Wiltshire; but the Royal Aero Club certificate, or 'ticket', as it was called, was 'an essential prerequisite' for entry to the school.

Through being at the Staff College, Dowding was acceptable enough for this later training. In an exercise of his own judgment that was typical of his hard-headed realism, he made an arrangement with a flying school at Brooklands whereby he would pay for his tuition in the elementary training after he got his ticket and the official refund. Time was also in his favour because all flying in those days of 1913 was done in the early morning, before the heat of the day disturbed the air currents. That gave him the opportunity to leave Camberley by car while it was still dark, have his instruction in flying at Brooklands, and be back in time for the start of the day's work at the Staff College.

After a total of one hour and forty minutes in the air—as a passenger, under dual control, and going solo—Dowding took his test, passed, and received his Royal Aero Club certificate which entitled him to fly and carry passengers. That was early in the morning of his last day and the final passing-out inspection at Camberley. The next day Dowding went with his family for a holiday in Switzerland.

'It was my third season in Switzerland, and skiing had become the principle recreation of my life,' Dowding has recalled. 'My youngest brother Kenneth and I were both deeply bitten by the sport, and we became good enough in those happy-go-lucky days to share third place in the British Championship.' Apart from the years of the First World War, Dowding went to Switzerland for the skiing very nearly every season between the years of 1911 and 1939. At one time he was President of the Ski Club of Great Britain.

Before any holder of the Royal Aero Club certificate to fly could qualify for his wings in the Royal Flying Corps, it was necessary for him to complete the course at the Central Flying School at Upavon, which had been established only some eighteen months before Dowding went there. 'We learned to fly biplanes of a slightly more advanced type than the "box-kite" on which I had got my ticket at Brooklands,' Dowding recorded in his early notes.

At Upavon early in 1914 Dowding was to meet for the first time most of those who were to become famous, as founder members, in the history of the Royal Air Force. The foremost of these was Major Hugh Trenchard, who was then already just over forty years of age. He was second in command at the flying school, having found his way into the R.F.C. almost as the last resort after an undistinguished career in the Army. One of Dowding's instructors, a man just a year older than he was who became noted for both his ability and charm, was Captain J. M. (later Marshal of the R.A.F. Sir John) Salmond.

'My sojourn was uneventful,' Dowding's notes record of his time at Upavon; and at the end of the course in the spring of 1914 he received his wings as an accredited pilot in the Royal Flying Corps. By this time he had reached the rank of captain and was thirty-two years of age. 'My original idea in learning to fly was to increase my value as a Staff Officer,' Dowding has said. After becoming a pilot he felt, as others had, that he would rather plan for a future wholly in the new air arm. But the controlling influence in his life was that which had been exerted all along by his father. It had always been very strong, and it still compelled Dowding to pay more attention to his father's views than might have been expected of him even in those days, and he had to give up the thought of flying as a career.

It is perhaps a commentary on the way of life of such people at that time that they could be ruled by such firm parental control, even in their careers in adult manhood. It was accepted by Dowding without question because all their lives the Dowdings had been a particularly well-disciplined and united family. 'It was the only thing in my life that I ever held against my father,' Dowding has said. 'He wouldn't let me go into the Royal Flying Corps as soon as I got my ticket because he thought flying was much too dangerous an occupation.'

That put an end to any thoughts that Dowding had had about a life in the air, and he was placed on the Royal Flying Corps Reserve. After that setback he had to pick up the threads of his service in the Garrison Artillery. But he did not have to return to India. Instead, he was posted to a company stationed at Sandown, on the Isle of Wight. But then there came the event that was to change the whole course of the world's history, and to alter Dowding's life in such a way that, as he has put it, 'my father could not do a thing about it.' The Great War—the First World War of 1914–18—snapped the bonds containing a system that had for too long remained static, and let loose the latent forces of distraction which even now are still bedevilling us.

When one considers the progress that Dowding was to make in his career from the time of the outbreak of war in August 1914, and the importance of the part that he was to come to play so quickly as one of the foremost of the professional military airmen, his start in the Royal Flying Corps was a singularly modest one. But the timing was right, even if he was no longer a particularly young man; and his character was of a nature that was suited, despite his reserve, to this new Service.

The Royal Flying Corps needed men who were above all else individualists, and without exception all the early birds were just that. Some of them were mad; some were eccentrics; some were looking for a new way of life or self-expression. They were all men of distinct originality. The madmen fell by the way-side, and the eccentrics added colour if nothing else. It was those who were trying to find a way of self-expression who gave to the infant Service that quality of independence which, in a remarkably short time, provided what was to become the Royal Air Force, a Service with a metal of its own, and its own tradition.

While at the Staff College at Camberley, Dowding had been dubbed with the nickname of 'Stuffy' that was to stay with him for the rest of his life. His fellow students at Camberley found that he had a strong inclination to stand apart from the usual boisterous antics of men of their type. It was not that he disapproved of them or of what they got up to. He did not. But he could not bring himself to become whole-heartedly one of them or their way of expressing themselves. He was too critical of his own behaviour, and he had been brought up in too rigid a style, to be able to join in any rough and tumble.

For one thing, Dowding drank very little, and that was unusual in Army circles. He once said that so far as he could recall he had only been drunk twice in his life, and he had not enjoyed it. Although he observed the rules, Dowding was never particularly interested in the social aspects of the life of a young Army officer, and that was another reason why he became 'Stuffy' to those with whom he worked. At first it was merely a nickname. Later he became more generally known as 'Stuffy', without the reason for that being understood, and over the years the name has come to be used with an increasing affection and with no questions about its origin.

So far as Dowding was concerned, the nickname was accepted in the spirit of that brand of humour for which he was to become so well-known to his intimates. For all the imperturbability of his appearance, that humour was shrewd, dry, and quick. It amused him that he should be thought of as stuffy, and it was, at least in his own mind, original. There was also in it a hint that was possibly quite unintentional of what he was later to become: a rebel without appearing to be one. In that he was distinctly one of the first of the few.

'I was called up as a R.F.C. Reservist within a few hours of the outbreak of war,' Dowding recalled with relish. He was sent to Dover as Commandant of the temporary camp and airfield which were organised there for the launching of the first squadrons of the Royal Flying Corps that were to be sent across the Channel to France as part of the British Expeditionary Force. Twenty-six years later there stood near that site the R.D.F., or radar, station at Dover which was to figure prominently in the Battle of Britain.

Among those who flew off to France during the next few days were men whose names were later to make Air Force history. Dowding watched them go, wondering how he could find his own way to join them. The chance soon came, and with it there also came the first of the clashes that Dowding was to have with Trenchard during the years that lay ahead. He was posted to Farnborough, which was by then commanded by Trenchard, to join a new squadron being formed there. 'Here all was impatience among those left behind,' Dowding once wrote about those anxious days, 'thinking as we did that the war would be over before we crossed the Channel. I used to go and worry Trenchard about twice a week about getting out to France.'

Since Trenchard was anxiously trying to arrange for his own posting to France, Dowding was rather asking for the sharp retort that he eventually got. He was posted to France as an observer. 'It was by way of being a fearful insult to send out a qualified pilot as an observer, but I was well enough content.'

The first flying that Dowding did when he got to France in 1914 was with No. 6 Squadron, and it was over much the same area that was to see the last of the fighting before the evacuation from Dunkirk in 1940. Following that, he was flying in the beginning of the fighting near Ypres, and he was one of the early few, he has recalled, who, in contact with the enemy in the air, 'would shoot at one another with carbines or automatic pistols while our ammunition lasted'. Writing of his own activities in that, he has added: 'I had a Mauser pistol with a shoulder stock. It was quite a good weapon for the purpose, but I never hit anything.'

An early introduction for Dowding to the more technical aspects of the Service in which he was later to become so competent came as soon as the beginning of 1915. He was posted as a Flight Commander to what was called the Wireless Squadron. After some experience of that work in France, Dowding was sent back to England to form a Wireless Experimental Establishment at Brooklands, and he was a step further on the way towards becoming one of the pioneer airmen in the work of communication with aircraft through the use of radio, including, as far back as 1915, air-to-ground telephony.

'I was the first person, certainly in England if not in the world, to listen to a wireless telephone message from the air,' Dowding has claimed. 'We could have fixed up two-way communication too if we had not received a directive from the War Office that radio-telephonic communication between air and ground was not considered to be practical.' Dowding had early enough experience of the ever-ready inclination of bureaucracy to resist looking forward with eagerness and imagination; and it was to plague him throughout his Service career.

In the summer of 1915, Dowding returned to France to command No. 16 Squadron. It was a relief for him to get back to the front and to active service flying. 'It is a strange thing,' he once wrote, 'but, though I served for twenty years in the

Army, I never really identified myself with it. Soldiers with a capital S were on one side and I was on the other.' Quite a few of those who had been in the Army and had found their way into the Royal Flying Corps felt exactly the same way.

By this time Trenchard was also out in France, a Lieutenant-Colonel commanding the Wing of which Dowding's squadron was a part. No. 16 Squadron was stationed at Merville, on the banks of the River Lys, and they took part in one of the early engagements: the Battle of Loos. They were equipped with a mixed bag of what would now be considered very primitive aircraft, and they spent their time in artillery observation, photography and bombing. Dowding has recalled that they were also 'given two single seater "Scouts", which were the fore-runners of the specialist "Fighters" '.

In actual combat in the air at this time, No. 16 Squadron brought down only one enemy aircraft. It landed safely enough behind the British lines. 'The pilot and observer were then shot in cold blood by some passing soldiers,' Dowding has said of this incident, which still angers him. 'I collected such of their personal belongings as were not required by the Intelligence Staff and had them dropped by an improvised parachute over the lines with a note stating where they had been buried.'

One of the few mementoes that Dowding has saved is the message bag that was dropped by the Germans a day or so later containing an acknowledgement of his message. Some forty years later, long after even the Second World War, Dowding received a letter from Germany about this incident: Apparently the message that he had sent to the Germans had become somewhat garbled, and, he was told, it came to be understood by the German air force that if it was believed that any of their men who had become prisoners were not being properly cared for all that had to be done was to drop a message addressed to Major Dowding who would immediately remedy the situation.

While still in command of the squadron in Trenchard's Wing, Dowding had another 'unpleasantness', as he has called it, with Trenchard, this time over a technical matter. 'I had some Maurice Farmans with eighty horse-power engines, and I was sent some propellers for seventy horse power-engines.' Unable to get any help over replacements out of Wing Headquarters,

Dowding rang up Trenchard and asked him to sort it out. Trenchard merely replied that the same propeller was suitable for both engines, but when Dowding pointed out that it was not so Trenchard gave him an order to bore holes in the propellers that he had and make them fit.

Since the boring of such holes would seriously weaken the propeller and possibly cause it to break up, Dowding obeyed the order to the extent of doing the test flight himself. Fortunately the propeller held together, but before Dowding could make a full report Trenchard told him, by telephone, that he had been misinformed, that they were the wrong propellers, and that he was making sure that the right ones were being sent to him.

'Not only had he taken the word of some half-baked motor salesman against mine,' Dowding commented, 'but he had not cancelled his orders to me directly he found that he had been wrong.'

By the time the war entered its second year, Dowding had known almost every conceivable experience in flying. He had crashed in a single-seater Bleriot, and that, and similar crashes by other pilots, had led to the discovery that through a fault in cockpit design the pilots were breathing in gases from the engine exhaust. He had experience of the use of wireless, of all kinds of co-operation with the army on the ground, of bombing, elementary though it was, and of operational flying in all sorts of weather. Coping with the weather alone led him to 'the first time I ever experienced, or even heard of, icing **up**,' which, on that occasion, led to his getting 'well and truly lost'.

Promotion in the new Service was accelerating, and at the end of 1915 Dowding became a Lieutenant-Colonel and was posted to command the Administrative Wing at Farnborough. The only impression that remains in his mind of that time was his failure to get from the headmasters of the better-known public schools the response he hoped for when he tried to get them 'to secure suitable applicants for commissions in the Royal Flying Corps'. Even his own school was not at all helpful. 'The fact was that, in modern argot,' he has ruefully commented, 'the Royal Flying Corps was distinctly non-U.'

'My only other outstanding recollection of my time at Farnborough,' Dowding recalled, 'was flying to Brooklands over the rifle ranges at Bisley and finding a bullet hole in the tail fin of my aeroplane when I returned.'

In the spring of 1916 Dowding superintended the formation of No. 70 Squadron with the new Sopwith 1½ Strutters, and in mid-summer he flew with them to France. He had been posted back to the front to command the Fighter Wing that was working directly under R.F.C. Headquarters. This brought Dowding, as he put it, 'under the immediate eye of Trenchard', who was by then a Major-General commanding the whole of the Royal Flying Corps in France.

'We were told confidentially that we were to prepare for the great offensive of the Somme,' Dowding recalled. 'The method of securing command of the air was to fly continuous patrols of aircraft over the enemy lines from dawn to dusk.' He found that the rate of casualties in the squadrons from these operations were, to his mind, too high, and although there were orders that officers of the rank of Lieutenant-Colonel and above were not to fly on operations, he found his way around that and led a formation across the lines to find out for himself what conditions were like.

'I was flying a B.E.2c,' Dowding said of what then happened. 'My observer was in the front seat, and we were armed with a Lewis gun which he could fire only backwards or sideways. We were well across the lines when we were attacked by a large German formation. My observer was kneeling on his seat facing backwards, and I was flying straight and level to give him an easy shot at a German flying behind and to the left of us.'

Superiority in aircraft performance was a see-saw throughout the war, first one side and then the other gaining the upper hand. But Dowding's B.E.2c was no match for the latest German fighters, particularly the Fokkers.

'We were getting shot up all the time,' Dowding continued, 'and yet my observer did not fire. A bullet came in under my arm and went between my hands and just nicked my knuckles, but it made a big splash of brass when it hit the joy-stick, and some of my instruments were smashed. Then I saw that my observer's face above me was streaming with blood.'

Believing that his companion had been shot through the head, or pretty badly wounded, Dowding spun down out of the fight, and at ground level headed back for his airfield. After he landed he found that his observer had not been badly injured at all. 'One of the first bullets had gone through the brass casing of the recoil cylinder of the Lewis gun,' Dowding explained, 'and it had splashed fragments of brass into his face, causing copious bleeding but no serious injury. Luckily nothing got into his eyes. His gun was jammed. My hand was painful for a week or so, but soon recovered.'

That one experience gave Dowding cause to make the comment: 'I don't suppose I should have survived many flights at that time in a B.E.2c, not against those Fokkers.' The control column, or joy-stick, of his aircraft with the splash of the bullet hole through it is another memento that he still has of his days as an operational pilot.

Looking back on that time of the battles of the Somme, Dowding has said that 'not many amusing things happened during that grim period.' But, he added, 'life's seldom entirely destitute of humour.' He has recalled walking along the main street of Fienvillers one evening 'when an extraordinary roaring emanated from one of the lighted windows of R.F.C. Headquarters.'

'What on earth is that?' asked the man with Dowding, who was an Army staff officer only recently posted to them.

'Oh . . . that's only Boom talking to some Wing Headquarters or other,' Dowding replied.

'Good heavens,' the other man said, 'why doesn't he use the telephone?'

After the intensity of the fighting on the Somme died down, Dowding tried to get some relief for his own hard-pressed squadrons. The strain of the continuous flying and fighting was telling heavily on the pilots. But orders from R.F.C. Head-quarters were that, even though the fighting on the ground had eased off, they were to maintain the pressure in the air by continuing with their offensive patrols.

'I thought it very reasonable that squadrons engaged in intensive operations should be periodically relieved, as was done in other branches of the Service,' Dowding has said of this; 'and I asked Trenchard if this could be done.' But this only brought about a further unpleasantness with Trenchard. 'He was very angry,' Dowding added.

'Criticized even then,' Andrew Boyle, Trenchard's biographer, has written, 'Trenchard has been condemned since for refusing to relax the pressure on his pilots, especially those engaged, day in day out, irrespective of weather or alternative tactical needs, in offensive sweeps. . . . Few of his subordinates were more upset by the early losses on the Somme than Dowding.'

As a result of this, Trenchard, it was reported, began to feel uneasy about Dowding's 'being obsessed by the fear of further casualties'. He referred to Dowding as a 'dismal Jimmy', and stated that he proposed to replace him.

Many years later a distinguished R.A.F. leader who knew both men well stated: 'Though normally a good judge of men, Trenchard was liable at times to be misled by his own prejudices: and then, as in this case, he could be unjust.'

There was no placating Trenchard, and he had Dowding posted. 'Almost at once I was promoted to the rank of Colonel, sent home, and never employed in the field again during the war,' Dowding said of the incident.

At the time when, the year before, Dowding had been in command of No. 16 Squadron, the Commanding Officer of No. 12 Squadron, which was flying from an airfield only a few miles away, was Major Cyril Newall, formerly of the Gurkhas. He now took Dowding's place in command of the Headquarters Wing on the Somme.

CHAPTER TWO

THE EARLY BIRDS

In his new command back in England, with his Headquarters in Salisbury, Dowding was responsible for the training of the Royal Flying Corps in an area stretching from Cheshire to the New Forest. Of what he found in this, the Southern Training Brigade, he has said: 'I at once saw the results of Trenchard's policy of intensive flying at all times, irrespective of peaks or lulls in ground activity. If the output of pilots was insufficient for his needs he demanded that the flying instructors should be sent.'

As a result of that, Dowding discovered, several training squadrons under his command had only one qualified pilot on their strength in addition to the Commanding officer. 'This was killing the goose which laid the golden eggs with a vengeance,' Dowding commented.

In the experiences that he had had with officialdom, and which by now were quite extensive, Dowding had come to feel a deep distrust. That was only increased when he tried to get the authorities at R.F.C. Headquarters in London to call a halt to the drain of instructors so that he could at least rebuild his depleted staff. They were of no help whatsoever.

'Eventually I wrote a personal letter to Trenchard's Senior Personnel Staff Officer,' Dowding said. 'I asked him to use his influence as and when possible to enable us to restore an adequate flow of properly trained pilots.'

It was a fair and legitimate enough effort on Dowding's part to correct a situation that was also causing many others the gravest of concern. But the officer to whom Dowding addressed his letter took a step beyond what Dowding had expected, or asked, of him. 'He at once took my letter and showed it to Trenchard,' Dowding added, 'and that finished me with Trenchard till the end of the war and for eight years afterwards.'

It was from the time of the battles on the Somme during 1916—that grim period of the First World War which has been written so indelibly into our nation's history as one of appalling sacrifice—that Dowding began to feel acutely concerned over the problem of casualties in action. That concern was to remain with him, increasing as the years passed, and in time it was to present itself to him yet again and in an even more formidable shape.

By 1917 Dowding had attained a rank and acquired a reputation which, for all that his views in certain quarters may have been regarded with disfavour, could not be denied. He had also rapidly become a recognised authority on training. That led to his promotion in the summer of that year to the rank of Brigadier-General. He was then thirty-four years of age.

'I had served for thirteen years as a subaltern,' he has recalled, 'and then in less than four years I had become a Brigadier-General. Thereafter, with the exception of a few months, I remained a General or Air Officer for twenty-six years. It was a strange lopsided record.'

But there was an understandable enough reason for that. Dowding was part of a vast and necessarily rapid expansion of an entirely new Service. By the end of the First World War, in November of the following year, the Royal Air Force had become the largest and most powerful air force in the world. The figures of its composition alone are indicative of its astonishing growth. In August 1914 the British had only 56 military aircraft and the R.F.C. and R.N.A.S. consisted of a handful of enthusiastic pioneers. At the end of 1918, the R.A.F. had a strength of over 22,600 aircraft—3,300 of which were classified as first line—and 103 airships. There were over 130 squadrons serving overseas, and over 50 at home, at 400 airfields at home and just over 270 overseas. All this absorbed some 27,000 officers, and over 250,000 men in the other ranks; and there were 25,000 members of the Women's Royal Air Force. From such an infinitely small beginning in 1914, the new air force had become, in the short period of four years, a very great Service.

That last year of the Great War was spent by Dowding entirely in England; and early in the year he was to have his first taste of what it was like to find his career suddenly at the mercy of the whims of the transient political head of the Service, and to be helpless in doing anything about it.

The Air Minister, later to be the Secretary of State for Air, was at that time Lord Rothermere. Dowding was summoned to the War Office. He had only just received from that august body 'a letter that was warmly appreciative of my work during 1917'. Now he was told abruptly by Rothermere that he was to be relieved of his command and replaced by an officer who was well known for his good ideas about training, and who was at that time a major.

'I never knew the ins and outs of what happened,' Dowding recalled, 'but this man had captured Lord Rothermere's ear and was promoted immediately from major to brigadier-general. But just as suddenly it developed that it was not my job they were after, and they decided to leave me alone. One of the other Training Brigade Commanders was displaced. And only shortly after that the new brigadier-general was himself caught up in the political manoeuvering and found himself back in the rank of major with a suddenness equal to that of his advancement.'

From his Brigade Training Command Headquarters in Salisbury, Dowding went north to York in the spring of 1918 to take up an appointment as Chief Staff Officer to the Senior Administrative Commander of the R.A.F. in that area. It was further good experience for him, and opportunity was offered in that for advancement in his career. But while those such as Trenchard, Salmond, Newall, Dowding and some others were learning the ropes in the higher ranks for the benefit of their new Service, opportunity in a more practical sense had been providing, during the whole of the four years of the Great War, the foundations for others who were to become intimately involved in Dowding's story over the next twenty odd years.

Among the younger men, there was Charles F. A. Portal, who was to equal the name of Trenchard in R.A.F. history. Portal had been in such a hurry to get into the war in 1914 that he had gone from Oxford straight out to France as soon as it broke out. He began his career as a despatch-rider in the Royal Engineers, was later commissioned, and then learnt to fly in the R.F.C. Portal's record as a reconnaissance pilot with long service on the Western Front was a particularly distinguished one.

Another of those who went straight from Oxford out to France almost immediately after the outbreak of war was Sholto Douglas, the son of a clergyman and art historian. Of the same age as Portal, he was born in Oxford, had gone to school at Tonbridge, and up at Oxford was a subaltern in the gunners, from which he transferred to the Royal Flying Corps after getting out to France. He became a noted fighter pilot. Somewhat younger than Portal and Douglas, Harold Balfour had gone from school to France to serve as a subaltern in the notorious trenches on the Western Front while he was still only seventeen years of age. He also found his way into the Royal Flying Corps as a fighter pilot.

Starting out from New Zealand, where his father was a university professor, Keith Park served as a gunner at Gallipoli, and in 1916 he was severely wounded in the heavy fighting on the Somme. While still burdened with a medical category of being totally unfit for any further military service, all the documents on Park's medical history were lost. He quickly took advantage of that and joined the R.F.C. and also became a well-known fighter pilot.

The young officer of those times who was to play the most curious part in Dowding's later story was Trafford Leigh-Mallory. Born at Mobberley, Cheshire, he was the youngest son of the rector of the parish, whose father had also occupied the same position. There were four children: two girls and two boys. Of the latter, the one who first became well-known, while he was still young, was George Mallory, the famous mountaineer who died near the summit in climbing Mount Everest in 1924. In their youth the brothers climbed together in Wales.

It has been written of George Mallory that his 'instinct always was to look for things that would be difficult to do and then to do them', and that ' "impossible" was a word that acted as a challenge to him.' Much the same could be said of his brother, Trafford; and one of their sisters is credited with saying that 'I think we were rather exceptionally unruly children.' George Mallory was at Winchester—going there immediately after Dowding left to go into the army, and some five years before the time that Portal was there—but Trafford

Leigh-Mallory (the father adopted the hyphenated name in 1914) went to school at Haileybury, where he was a boy with the present Marshal of the Royal Air Force Sir John Slessor.

While still young, Trafford Leigh-Mallory had come to know, through his brother's close friendship with them, people in a distinctly intellectual sphere. Rupert Brooke, Robert Graves, Geoffrey and Maynard Keynes, James and Lytton Strachey, Clive and Vanessa Bell and the Huxleys were among them. But the Great War interrupted what might have been for him the more academic interests, and he went straight into the army from school, also seeing service first in the trenches on the Western Front. In 1916 Leigh-Mallory transferred to the Royal Flying Corps, and as a pilot he specialised in army co-operation, in which he was soon to become, and to remain, an expert.

In November, 1918, Trafford Leigh-Mallory was in command of No. 8 Squadron. His brother, George, was in the gunners and also out in France, and at the end they met near Cambrai. In a letter to his wife about their meeting, George Mallory wrote: 'I was delighted to see T. He was in tremendous form, happy and gay and full of life. He gives me the impression of success, not merely from the fact that he affects magnificence, rushing about in a splendid Crossley car and giving orders with the curt assurance of an Alexander the Great, or Lord North-cliffe or Rockefeller, but because he so evidently enjoys every detail of successful action and has such a wonderful singleness of forward-looking conviction . . .'

It was an early insight into what was to come, and in 1924, only a few months before his death on Everest, George Mallory wrote to his sister Mary about their brother, saying: 'T. looks forward without a doubt to success and promotion in the future, and is quite sure he is at the heart of Imperial Defence at present; I daresay he does his job very well.'

By the end of the war in 1918, when Dowding was a Brigadier-General, Harold Balfour was a Captain, and Portal, Sholto Douglas, Keith Park and Leigh-Mallory were all Majors in command of squadrons. Cyril Newall was also a Brigadier-General, and one of the leaders in the use of bombers.

During this early period of his life, on into his middle

thirties, Dowding had always made his home with his father, latterly in his house in Wimbledon. In the Service he had become thought of as a confirmed bachelor. But in February, 1918, he married a cousin of a brother officer whom he had first come to know at Farnborough during the first year of the war. A year later his son, Derek, was born.

With the ending of the Great War, Dowding became one of the senior officers in the newly formed Royal Air Force and was deeply involved in the problems of mass demobilization. To his astonishment, this also presented to him a most unexpected personal problem. 'I received a letter informing me that my services would not be required in the Royal Air Force,' Dowding has explained, 'and that I was to return to the Royal Artillery.'

It has always been taken for granted that this was a further step in the disapproval felt for Dowding by Trenchard, who had become the Chief of the Air Staff. It reflected no credit whatsoever on Trenchard, and there was some little feeling in the Service that Dowding was being treated most unfairly. One of the early senior Service officers who became attached to the new R.A.F. was Vice-Admiral Sir Vyell Vyvyan. Dowding was serving under his command, and Vyvyan took it upon himself to intervene and to tell Trenchard, who was known to be exercising a close personal interest in all the appointments to permanent commissions, that he was making a mistake in allowing his antagonism towards Dowding to go so far.

'Vyvyan had had plenty of opportunity to sum me up during the time I served under his command,' Dowding recalled. 'He was quite capable of forming his own opinion. That led him to tackle Trenchard four or five times about my future. He went out of his way to do that.'

The position that Dowding was placed in through Trenchard's actions was an extremely difficult one. 'I had become very interested in aviation,' he has pointed out. 'I felt that there was a great future in the R.A.F. and I wanted to remain in it. After having been in the R.F.C. and then the R.A.F. for over four years, and having had a great deal of experience, with rapid promotion, flying had become my career. In terms of the Army, and having to return to it, I was in a very bad position.

There were plenty of those who had made their way up in the Army during the war, as I had in flying, who were well-equipped for careers in that Service. I was not. My qualifications were by then in flying.'

Dowding was up against a brick wall through not being wanted in either the Army or the Royal Air Force, or so it would seem, and of that he has said: 'It was certainly a very worrying time, and I could not help feeling that perhaps I deserved better than being kept waiting as I was for a decision that would affect the rest of my life. I could think of no particular reason why I was treated in that way.'

Eventually Admiral Vyvyan managed to convince Trenchard that it was quite wrong to keep Dowding in this state of suspension, and Dowding was granted a permanent commission, with the rank of Group Captain, in the R.A.F. 'It was a great relief,' Dowding has said. 'I felt then that I could at least look forward to doing something in which I had developed a very keen interest.'

The early months of the peace brought to Dowding responsibilities, both personal and professional, which were heavier than might have been expected. He had developed his intense interest in the air, but the uncertainty about his future when others around him were being granted permanent commissions had been very unsettling, and he had the unpleasant prospect of having to face that situation which dogs all Service careers: the possibility of being passed over in the ladder of promotion. He also had the responsibilities of his marriage and, with the birth of his son, a family. For all the relief that came with the granting of his permanent commission in the R.A.F., 1919 was a year, as it was for many others, of worry about the future.

The Royal Air Force went through the expected demobilization with enough trouble to start with, but it was then subjected to cuts that were so severe that they amounted almost to dismemberment. Dowding's brother Arthur was in a secure position as an officer enjoying the stability of a career in the Royal Navy, which he had joined before the war. His other brother Kenneth, who had won a Distinguished Flying Cross as a pilot in the R.F.C. during the war, elected to return to civilian life. But for those around Dowding who wanted to stay in the new Service it was a time of anxiety and frustration.

For all the enormous strides that had been made in aviation during the four years of the war, there was still no great public belief in its future. Incredible as it now sounds, that was also true of the position in the United States. Military leaders there who fought for their beliefs were even subjected, as the far-sighted Billy Mitchell was, to what almost amounted to persecution. Trenchard was subjected to enormous pressures in his struggle to maintain the independence of the R.A.F., but not treated as badly as Mitchell in the United States.

There were many in the infant Royal Air Force who came to feel that there was too little promise in its future to merit their staying in it; and two present Marshals of the Royal Air Force—Lord Douglas of Kirtleside and Sir John Slessor—left to go out into the cold world of private enterprise. Sholto Douglas was for a time a civil pilot, and then made a start in his father's field as an art historian. Slessor also spent a short time in civil flying.

In the close watch that he was keeping on the granting of permanent commissions in the R.A.F., Trenchard suddenly realized that altogether too many of the better men were leaving the Service, and he made a strong personal effort to stop the rot that threatened to sap the essential strength of all that he was trying to create. One of those whom he brought back into the Service was Sholto Douglas. 'My luck was in, and I knew it,' Douglas commented long afterwards.

Typical of a humour that is all his own, and which has endeared him to everybody who ever had the good fortune to come in contact with him, Jack Slessor described his early career as 'coming to a slightly premature but welcome end by a serious difference of opinion with a certain senior officer, who soon afterwards relapsed into the obscurity from which he should never have arisen.' Commenting in more detail on what happened, Slessor wrote:

I am ashamed to say that I was extremely insubordinate and indulged myself in the agreeable but very improper luxury of telling him in most intolerant terms exactly what I thought of him. It was then thought appropriate that I should, lest worse befall, avail myself of the opportunity of claiming demobilization.

So out of the Service went Jack Slessor. But after 'spending my war gratuity on riotous living and . . . four gay but not very profitable months', he returned to it; and thirty years later Slessor was to serve a term of particular distinction as a Chief of the Air Staff. 'He was one of the best of the young men brought back in time,' Dowding commented.

Under his immediate command in those early days, Dowding had both Sholto Douglas and Keith Park, who were then young Squadron Leaders. Douglas had good reason to be grateful that Dowding so persistently refused, even then, to be brow-beaten by anybody, and least of all by the Air Ministry. Threatened with a court martial over something that had happened that was not his fault, Douglas found himself in a position that could have been extremely difficult for him, and might even have ruined his whole career.

' . . . orders were received by him from the Air Ministry to proceed with my court martial,' Sholto Douglas recalled. 'As might be expected of Dowding, he felt very strongly about how unfair it all was, and he promptly . . . refused to take any action. It was a courageous as well as an honest stand for Dowding to take because there was still doubt about his own permanent commission being confirmed, and it could so easily have jeopardized his own chances of making a career for himself in the R.A.F.'

When he was questioned many years later about this incident, Dowding allowed himself the crisp comment: 'I remember it well. As usual, the Air Ministry were being stupid.'

That period immediately after the war was a time of turmoil for those at the top who were trying to lay the foundations for the new air Service. The Secretary of State for War and for Air— a double and inevitably divided responsibility—was Winston Churchill, and he led Trenchard a lively enough dance in the battles that the C.A.S. had with his opponents outside the Service. But there was a great fighting spirit engendered by Trenchard in all those around him. There were those even in the R.A.F. who at times disagreed with him; but there will never be any doubt that Trenchard achieved a very great deal. And for all the stress imposed on the new Service in its fight for survival—with both the Army and the Royal Navy trying to seize control of it—Dowding was at least able to try to settle down to the peace-time routine of a Service life with which he was already thoroughly familiar.

But almost immediately there came a personal blow which was to have a very great affect on his whole future. After only two years of marriage his wife died following a serious illness, leaving him alone with his infant son. Dowding returned to live in his father's home, and after that he became even more reserved in his manner, while at the same time starting out on the course of dedication to his work that was to lay the foundation for all that was ahead for him.

The first appointment for Dowding after the war had in it, in its physical location, a pointer towards the shape of things to come. He was given command of No. 1 Group, with Headquarters at Kenley and this entailed control of other airfields such as Biggin Hill, Manston and Hawkinge, all of which were to play such a big part in the Battle of Britain. While there he was active in the organisation of the first of the well-known Tournaments or Pageants—later known as Displays—at Hendon, as well as those of later years. It will surprise those who participated in these Displays, and enjoyed that participation with such care-free abandon, to know that for Dowding the work involved left him 'in a state of complete physical and mental collapse', as he has put it, adding: 'Nothing has ever induced in me a comparable state of prostration.'

This part of England, the south-east, that was Dowding's command was to be the setting for the beginning of the whole-hearted devotion that he was to give to his career as an Air Force officer, and during the next three years he was to come to know it very well. But that was only the beginning. There was further knowledge of it to come in other appointments. Eventually, no man could have had a longer or more intimate knowledge of that part of the country from the point of view of the airman, which was yet another feature about Dowding's great experience that was of such value in 1940. Today, at the age of eighty-seven, he lives at Tunbridge Wells, which could be described as being almost in the middle, geographically, of that part of England.

The first appointment that brought Dowding to Uxbridge—which was to become so well-known in the Battle of Britain as the Headquarters of his No. 11 Group—followed immediately after his time at Kenley. He was made Chief Staff Officer at the Headquarters of what was then known as Inland Area, and which was under the command of Air Vice-Marshal J. F. A. (later Sir John) Higgins. Another of the early individualists in the Royal Air Force, Josh Higgins was noted for his ability to read files backwards at high speed, and the nickname that he rejoiced in of 'Bum and Eyeglass'.

When Higgins went out to command Iraq two years later, with his Headquarters in Baghdad, he took Dowding with him as his Chief Staff Officer. The role of the R.A.F. was the policing of Iraq from the air in place of an army on the ground. 'During most of my time in Iraq a small war was flickering inter-mittently with the Kurdish tribes on the eastern frontier,' Dowding has recalled. 'Frontier troubles were more or less chronic, and were suppressed with the maximum of economy and the minimum of bloodshed by means of attack with small bombs.'

The earlier obstructions that had threatened Dowding's career seemed to be disappearing, and in the spring of 1926, after a shorter time in Iraq than might have been expected, he was brought home to England to the first of a long series of appointments at the Air Ministry in London. He became Director of Training, a post for which, in view of his earlier experience, he was particularly well suited.

Among the members of his Directorate in the old Adastral House in Kingsway, Dowding found his brother, Arthur, who was a Commander serving as the Naval Liaison Officer, as well as Sholto Douglas and Arthur Tedder, both then Wing Com-manders. Keith Park was just about to resume active flying as Commanding Officer of a fighter squadron after going through the Staff College and a tour of duty in the Middle East; and Trafford Leigh-Mallory was at the Staff College after further specialisation in Army co-operation.

'My brother shared a room with three R.A.F. Staff Officers, and it seemed to me that they spent a great deal of their time working up endless practical jokes,' Dowding commented with some approval. Any puncturing of pomposity met with his approval, and it was becoming appreciated by then that despite his nick-name, which still clung to him, Stuffy Dowding had a very alert sense of humour, and his quick expression of that, made in short, sharp bursts, was making itself felt.

Of more importance than that, however, was the distinct improvement in his relationship with the Chief of the Air Staff. 'I was under the direct control of Trenchard,' Dowding explained. 'To my surprise there was no friction between us.' There was an even better development than that, which Dowding has described as 'large-minded' on Trenchard's part.

'Dowding . . . I don't often make mistakes about people,' Trenchard admitted in a conversation between the two men one day. 'I made one about you.'

'On the whole, it was an uneventful three years that I spent as Director of Training,' Dowding has commented. At the end of that time, in September, 1929, he was given by Trenchard a very different and most difficult task which had in it a close association with all that is happening today in the clash of interests in the Middle East.

'The Arabs and the Jews in Palestine were making concerted attacks on each other,' Dowding said of the start of the trouble. There were reprisals, and the attacks that were made by both sides on each other led the High Commissioner in Palestine to ask for a large increase in the British troops out there. 'He feared a general Arab uprising and a massacre of Europeans,' Dowding has commented.

In Trenchard's view this was unnecessary because he believed that air control, as there was in Iraq, with some troops on the ground would be enough to keep the situation under control. 'He sent me out at forty-eight hours' notice, giving me a fortnight to write an "Appreciation of the Situation", ' Dowding said, 'and to advise on the minimum force which would suffice to maintain order in Palestine.'

By this time in 1929 Dowding was an Air Vice-Marshal. His formal instruction signed by Trenchard, which consisted of many pages, read: 'You have been appointed Air Officer Commanding the Forces in Transjordan and Palestine and

you are to assume command upon your arrival in Jerusalem
. . .' There followed a list of the Naval, Military and Air
Force units that would be under his command. 'The general
deduction to be made is that the country cannot be considered
as in rebellion against the Government,' the orders continued,
'but rather that the disorders are the result of inter-racial
feeling, between the Moslems and the Jews . . .'

In the voluminous file that exists in Dowding's private papers
there is to be found information of the greatest interest on the
task that he had to perform, and the way in which he went
about it. Not the least interesting in this file are the many
long letters marked 'personal and private' that Trenchard
addressed to Dowding. There are also long confidential reports
written, in longhand, by Dowding to the C.A.S. Trenchard's
interest in what was going on in the Middle East was acute,
and his comments, expressed privately in these letters, are
remarkable in their revelation of the nature of the man and
his way of expressing himself. They also clearly indicate that he
had complete faith in Dowding, and in one letter he stated:
'I would like to take this opportunity of saying how well you
are doing everything I want.'

The High Commissioner in Palestine during this difficult
time was Sir John Chancellor, and Dowding was made welcome
at Government House in Jerusalem, which he often visited for
moments of relaxation. He met there and enjoyed the company
of Rosemary Chancellor, the High Commissioner's daughter,
and a young Flight Lieutenant in the R.A.F. to whom she was
engaged to be married, who was working as a liaison officer
with the French in Syria. His name was William Elliot, and
eighteen years later, after the Second World War, he was to
become Air Officer Commanding-in-Chief, Fighter Command.
Today that young couple who gave Dowding reason to remember them for their kindness are known with general affection
and regard as Air Chief Marshal Sir William and Lady Elliot.

'I started my investigation with a completely open mind—
in other words in a state of complete ignorance of Jewish,
Arab and Palestinian problems and politics,' Dowding said.
What he discovered disturbed him greatly, and he soon came

to feel that the British were guilty, in their violation of agreements with the Arabs that had been reached during the Great War, of 'a dishonesty for which we have never ceased to suffer', as he put it many years later.

In an early letter, Trenchard warned Dowding that the problem was 'very nearly purely political'. Very soon after he got there Dowding found himself becoming deeply involved in trying to unravel and understand the intrigues that are endemic in that part of the world; and it was not long before he was told to stay in Palestine until the end of the year. The riots and the attacks were continuing, and causing the authorities a great deal of anxiety.

'I had no adventures, but a good many frights,' Dowding recalled, 'due mainly to the proclivity of my official car, an eighteen year old open Rolls, to backfire violently when running down hill. Passers-by took this to be the beginning of a new pogrom and pistols appeared by magic from the recesses of their clothing.'

In all that he was doing, Dowding was able to call on his earlier experiences while serving in Iraq. But now it was a clash between Jews and Arabs. At one time, in writing to him about his reports, Trenchard stated: 'Your letters certainly are very human and interesting.' That was in addition to the vast amount of detailed comment in letters and signals on the work in general. At another time Trenchard wrote: 'The atmosphere at home is that you are doing very well, and that you are the one cheerful spot.'

But when, eventually, Dowding found himself becoming involved in what amounted to a certain number of secret service activities, the situation was even more political than Trenchard had intimated that it might become. In the very lengthy appreciation that he prepared for Trenchard on the whole situation in the Middle East, Dowding finished with the comment:

I feel that we must not allow our sympathy to lead us into any condonation of murder and robbery by whomsoever they may be committed. If the Zionist Policy is to be imposed on the country, it can only be imposed by Force; for the Arab will never believe that it has any sanction in Equity. If this Force is applied half-heartedly, or with insufficient means, further outbreaks are to be apprehended; and a further outbreak must not be allowed to occur. If it does occur on a considerable scale in Palestine, it is my firm belief that it will not be confined to this country, and that its eventual consequences will be incalculable.

That was the situation as Dowding saw it in 1929.

On his return from Palestine at the end of that year, Dowding became the Air Officer Commanding the Inland Area (the Fighter Group) in the structure known then as the Air Defence of Great Britain. 'It was not equipped in such a way as to make it a very formidable defence against air attack,' Dowding has commented; but it was yet another step in the very comprehensive experience that he was to have in the work of the defence of the country.

Less than a year later there was another important change for Dowding when he was appointed to the Air Council as Air Member for Supply and Research. It was in work connected with all that this title implied that he was to continue for the next six years. And in that work he was to show the remarkable capacity that he had for understanding and dealing with technical matters although neither trained in scientific work nor of a particularly scientific bent. This was to be added during those years to the extensive knowledge that he had already acquired of fighters and their use.

After having been in his new appointment as Air Member for Supply and Research for only a month, Dowding became deeply involved in one of the major disasters in the history of British aviation. Through that he was to learn another hard lesson in the ways of politicians, and of the disregard that they can so easily display for expert advice when it comes to a matter of their political interests. The disaster was the crash of the airship R.101 that occurred in October, 1930.

As Air Member for Supply and Research, Dowding bore a large share of the responsibility for the decisions about the use that was to be made of this new airship, the largest in the world, and the others that were in use or being built. R.101 was the pride of British aviation, and it was hoped that giant airships like these would be of great use in the future of air transport. So keen was the interest of the politicians in furthering this use that the Secretary of State for Air, Lord Thomson, decided to fly to India in the R.101, for an important conference, taking with him a number of distinguished passengers.

'The venture seemed to me reasonably safe,' Dowding has said of his thoughts at the time. He was on board as a passenger on the last test flight of sixteen hours that the huge airship was put through before it set off for India. It was the first technical appointment that Dowding had held, apart from the work that he had done with wireless in 1915, and he has admitted that he was 'not sufficiently self-confident to set my individual opinion against that of the technical experts'.

The airship had had extensive work done on it in structural alterations, all executed in a hurry in order to meet the demand of the Secretary of State for Air that it should be ready for use on the day specified by him. By that date there was doubt in the minds of some about its fitness for service. 'But I must make it quite clear that no direct pressure was ever exercised on me to sanction the departure without extensive trials,' Dowding said. 'I knew, of course, that I would have been unpopular if I had vetoed a journey on which such important hearts were set.'

The one test flight made after the completion of the alterations, in which Dowding participated, was uneventful except for a minor defect in one of the engines. The distinguished passengers and crew embarked, and on the evening of Saturday, 4 October, the R.101 set off from Cardington, near Bedford, on its flight to India, via Egypt. At ten minutes to three the next morning, only a few hours later, the airship crashed near Beauvais, in northern France and burst into flames. Of the fifty-four passengers and crew on board, forty-seven, including the Secretary of State for Air, were killed.

The crash of the R.101 put an end to all further British planning for the use of airships, and all work in progress was abandoned. 'I think I was wrong not to insist on much more extensive trials and tests,' Dowding commented long afterwards. 'The construction of the ship was novel and previously untried, and the engines were of a new design which should have been subjected to flight tests of many hours.'

There has been a great deal of controversy down the years over this disaster, and the cause of it. In Dowding's opinion, it was the decision to start the journey in bad weather that was 'the greatest mistake.' The airship had to fly low in order to conserve the gas in its envelope, and in the gale conditions prevailing at the time, in which it should not have been flying, it went out of control and crashed.

One of the first of the important plans that Dowding had a direct hand in making as Air Member for Supply and Research was an outcome of Britain's winning in September 1931, for the third time, the famous international competition in the Schneider Trophy air races. The principal competitors had been Britain, America and Italy, and the trophy was won outright by the R.A.F. team. The races had been for seaplanes, and after finally winning the trophy for good, and so ending the competition, it was suggested at the Air Ministry that Britain should present another trophy for further international competition along the same lines as before.

'I was strongly opposed to this,' Dowding recalled, 'because the float-planes we had developed were perfectly useless for any military purpose. There was absolutely no value in them as a combat machine, and what value they did have was limited to flying from sheltered waters in light wind conditions. What I wanted was to invite private tenders from two firms to cash in on the experience that had been gained in aircraft construction and engine progress so that we could order two of the fastest machines which it was possible to build with no restriction except landing speed, and that had to be on grass airfields.'

This proposal of Dowding's was accepted by the Air Ministry. In his words: 'The result was the emergence of the Hurricane and the Spitfire which the Air Staff very sensibly pounced on. They were fitted with eight guns, and that put our own fighters on more equal terms with any potential enemy in performance and hitting power.' Dowding has pointed out that the famous Hurricane and Spitfire were not originally 'built to any military specification', and that they had no armament. 'They were purely experimental aircraft,' he has added.

Such was the worth of the aircraft that were produced, and

they were the outcome of Dowding's insistence in planning for the future in a realistic sense rather than as a matter of prestige, that it was possible to adapt them very rapidly to military purposes. Another aspect of their opportunity for development was his decision at an early stage back in the 'thirties that a high priority should be given to the elimination of wood and a substitution of metal in aircraft construction.

In August 1933, the first discussions were held at Hawkers, the well-known aircraft manufacturers, about what was called then the 'Fury Monoplane'. The first prototype was ordered by the Air Ministry in February 1935; and the first flight of this aircraft was on 6 November 1935. This was the Hurricane. The first order for 600 of them was placed in June 1936. It came into service with the R.A.F. in December 1937.

Out of the Supermarine racing seaplane that had won the Schneider Trophy in 1931, there was developed at the same time as the Hurricane the Supermarine single-seat fighter. The prototype first flew on 5 March 1936, and three months later the Air Ministry placed an initial order for 310 of this, the Spitfire. The first batch was delivered to the R.A.F. in June 1938, and the first squadron started receiving them just before the Munich crisis.

Today, when rocket propulsion is an established and highly successful source of power, its origins have become of historical rather than any practical interest. There is a note in Dowding's papers of an interest that he came to find in this well over thirty-five years ago; and of its fruitless pursuit. Two or three years after he had become Air Member for Supply and Research, some photographs were shown to him, from a private source, of German tests that were being conducted 'of rockets designed for use in aircraft against air or ground targets'. Dowding recorded that he was asked 'to be circumspect in my use of this information on account of the danger which could threaten' the source in Germany.

'I at once realised the immense importance of this information,' Dowding wrote some years later, 'and sought permission to initiate a development programme in my own Department.' But permission was refused on the grounds that it was up to the

Army to do such development work. 'From time to time I went down to see firing tests from the ground at Portland Bill,' Dowding has recalled, 'and used to see rockets turning end over end in the air, shedding their cordite propellant the while.' After two or three years, and despite Dowding's efforts to keep the work going, the whole programme was abandoned.

By January 1935 it was realised that all the work entailed in the development of new devices, and the explorations of research, was enough for one Member of the Air Council, without his being burdened with all the problems of supply as well. Dowding's office was split in two, and he became Air Member for Research and Development. The other half of the work that he had been doing was placed in the hands of what became known as the Air Member for Supply and Organisation. The officer appointed to that was Cyril Newall. Again the careers of the two subalterns of those far off days in India became linked: they were both by then knighted, and they were both Air Marshals.

The most important development in his work after Dowding became the Air Member for Research and Development was in what is today known as radar. That word itself is of American origin—one definition is that it stands for range and direction and resolution—and it was not coined until well on into the Second World War. The British used the name 'radio direction finding', and it was as R.D.F. that it came to play an honoured part in the Battle of Britain.

Efforts at finding some means of obtaining early warning for the defence of the country in the detection of approaching aircraft had been exercising everybody's minds for a very long time. It was not until 1935 that British scientists—who were only just ahead of other countries in their research—provided a practical answer. 'It was with lively satisfaction that I heard that a civilian scientist by the name of Robert (now Sir Robert) Watson-Watt, while conducting experiments in obtaining radio echoes from the Heaviside Layer, had demonstrated that similar echoes could also be obtained from aircraft and recorded on a cathode-ray tube,' Dowding once wrote.

On 25 February 1935, 'the most critically-watched aircraft in the history of British aviation'—as Peter Wykeham, who became a distinguished member of the Air Staff but who was then a youth, has described the occasion—provided for a demonstration by the scientists that R.D.F. was a fact, and that here was the source for an entirely new *and* very effective *and* long-range early warning system. As Air Member for Research and Development, Dowding saw it as 'a discovery of the highest importance', and he was one of the original band of enthusiasts that set to work to develop its use with all possible speed. It was this foresight as much as any other factor that was to contribute to the means whereby the R.A.F. was able to fight so successfully the great air battle of 1940.

CHAPTER THREE

THAT LONG PREPARATION

By the spring of 1936 it had become, in Dowding's words, 'obviously unsound to have one man responsible for both the bombing and fighting roles of the R.A.F. in the ponderous command known as Air Defence of Great Britain'. In expressing this view, which was held by everybody, he has added: 'There was far too much work for one thing, and the two branches were inevitably competitive for available resources. It was almost humanly impossible for any one man to be so detached as to hold the scales fairly between the competing interests.'

The operational commands of the Royal Air Force at home were divided into three new ones: Bomber Command, Fighter Command, and Coastal Command, each with their own distinct tasks to perform, as indicated in the names that were given to them. There was also a distinct competition between them for the equipment that their respective commanders believed they should have if they were to perform their assigned roles. In that alone Dowding was to step out of the non-partisan role that he had to fulfil as a Member of the Air Council, and to become so human in his interests that he was to make history in more ways than one. He became the first Commander-in-Chief of Fighter Command.

On 5 March 1936, the prototype of the Spitfire had made its first flight; and on 1 April Dowding had handed over his appointment as Air Member for Research and Development to Sir Wilfrid Freeman. The end was by then well in sight of that period of the 1930s of which Peter Wykeham has written: ' . . . German preparations were plain and German treaty violations obvious, even to the most uninformed, while at the same time the German leaders blandly assured onlookers that [these] rearmaments were an illusion.'

In an indignant comment about that period that must be considered a thoroughly fair appreciation of the state of affairs as viewed by those younger men who were to have to bear the brunt of the actual fighting when it came, Wykeham has added: 'The mind boggles at the credulity of the European politicians who believed this tale. It is so inconceivable that one is led inevitably to the conclusion that those who declared they believed, and they were many and distinguished, were either displaying obtuseness bordering on idiocy or wishful thinking close to treachery.'

That spring and summer of 1936 was to see the start of a new course being set, a more determined course, in the defence of the United Kingdom, and the news from abroad made apparent the necessity for that. On the morning of 14 July, Dowding arrived at Bentley Priory, an old and historic house standing in its own extensive grounds to the north-west of London, on a hill above Stanmore and looking out over Harrow Weald. He was to start setting up Headquarters of his new Command.

It has long been the custom in all countries for Commanders-in-Chief in the Services, on assuming command, to have to conduct themselves at the moment of taking up their new appointments with pomp and ceremony, and a ritual exchange of courtesies. There is something almost amusing, and most indicative of the nature of the man, that Dowding's arrival at his new Headquarters could not have been less demonstrative. He arrived quietly, alone and unheralded, and for a description of what happened then none is better than that supplied by Peter Wykeham who wrote:

True to character from the first, Dowding arrived at the gate sharp at nine o'clock in the morning. Equally true to character, he was both unexpected and unaccompanied, and the guard only let him in after that solemn inspection of a pass that goes by the name of Security. No staff had yet arrived, and there was only a holding party under the command of the Camp Commandant, but as he was away for the day on business, the honours were done by Sergeant Cornthwaite, the N.C.O. in charge of the Orderly Room. Cornthwaite was not the sort of man to get flustered over a sudden visitation of this kind, but he was relieved to learn that the lack of a formal greeting suited Dowding perfectly, and that the Air Marshal would be content to look quietly around the premises under his guidance. Together they explored the Priory and grounds. When the tour was over, the new Commander-in-Chief selected a room looking south that contained some office furniture, and told Cornthwaite to put his name on the door.

It was in that room that Dowding was to work for the next four and a half years, building from scratch in that short time the great machine of Fighter Command and directing from it the fighting of what was to become a unique battle. Thirty-two years later, in 1968, Dowding visited the film studios at Pinewood to watch some of the work being done on the making of the film 'Battle of Britain'. He was shown the reproduction that had been built of that room on one of the stages. It was exact down to the last detail. When it was suggested to Dowding that he might like to sit behind the desk, he did so; and in reply to a question about what he thought of it all, he looked around and without the slightest hesitation replied: 'It's like coming home.'

But it was right at that time back in 1936, when Dowding had barely settled down in his new home, that there developed in Europe a situation that was to give the Germans all too good a head start in the race for preparedness that was now under way. Three days after Dowding arrived at Bentley Priory, the Spanish Civil War started. General Francisco Franco returned from the Canary Islands to become Generalissimo of the Nationalist forces and eventually set up his own government in Spain.

One of the first moves that Franco made was to solicit help from Italy and Germany, and that help was quickly given to the insurgents. Both countries saw in the civil war outside their own territory opportunities to conduct experiments that would be of advantage to them. After the Second World War, when he was tried at Nuremberg, Hermann Goering stated:

When the Civil War broke out in Spain, Franco sent a call for help to Germany and asked for support, particularly in the air. Franco with his troops was stationed in Africa and . . . he could not get his troops across, as the fleet was in the hands of the Communists . . . the decisive factor was, first of all, to get his troops to Spain . . . the Fuehrer thought the matter over. I urged him to give support under all circumstances: firstly, to prevent the further spread of Communism; secondly, to test my young Luftwaffe in this or that technical respect.

Adolf Hitler was attending the Wagner Festival in Bayreuth. He agreed immediately to the use of aircraft of the Luftwaffe and their crews for the purpose of ferrying Spanish Foreign Legion and Moroccan troops from Tetuan to Seville. The first of these aircraft flew out from Berlin, and that was the start of the very great participation by the German Luftwaffe in the Spanish Civil War, and the testing of equipment and the training of their air crews under actual conditions of war. And it was all done at a time when the R.A.F. was only just getting into its stride as an air force of any consequence, with Dowding at Fighter Command beginning his long struggle to provide for the defence of the United Kingdom.

Early in 1936, towards the end of his time on the Air Staff as the Member of the Air Council for Research and Development, there was repeated to Dowding by both Edward Ellington, the Chief of the Air Staff, and the Air Member for Personnel, who was then the well-known Ginger Bowhill, something that he had been told much earlier by Sir John Salmond, a former C.A.S. It was that Dowding would be succeeding Ellington as Chief of the Air Staff when Ellington finished his time in that office in the coming year. It was with that knowledge at the back of his mind that Dowding had proceeded with his work as the first Air Officer Commanding-in-Chief of Fighter Command.

On 3 February 1937, Dowding received a handwritten letter from the Chief of the Air Staff in which Ellington stated: 'The S. of S. has asked me to let you know, in advance of the official announcement, that he has decided that Newall will succeed me as C.A.S. at the end of August next. Though the King and the P.M. have approved, this information is confidential at present.' The Secretary of State for Air at whose request Ellington was giving Dowding this information was Viscount Swinton.

It had been a long time since that early morning back in 1909, twenty-eight years before, when, in a mountain pass in India, the paths of the two young subalterns Newall and Dowding had first crossed. Now it looked as if the long trail was ending. Dowding was three months senior to Newall in the rank of Air Chief Marshal, having been promoted on

1 January 1937. While he was still a member of the Air Council he had come to see quite a lot of Newall, who had become the Air Member for Supply and Organisation in 1935.

In view of what Dowding had been told before he left the Air Ministry about his becoming C.A.S., he naturally felt a little surprised that a decision had now been made in favour of someone else; but he controlled any great expression of disappointment. 'No reason was given for this change in the selection,' he commented, 'and to this day I have no idea what lay behind it. Naturally it came as somewhat of a blow. It is always an attractive prospect to reach the top of the tree. But when I look back on this incident, in the light of later events, I see how fortunate this decision really was.'

In the reply that he wrote to Ellington two days later, Dowding stated: 'Thank you for letting me know your plans. I trust that I may be permitted to continue to serve until I have completed a year in my present rank. On November 2nd I wrote you a letter about the armouring of bombers and attack of armoured aircraft by fighters; and I gave you some further comments on the subject at an interview in December. I did this at a time when I had reason to believe that I should be your successor and should in due course find myself responsible for the equipment of the Air Force. In the altered circumstances I have no *locus standi* for pressing my views, and I would ask you to disregard my papers, except in so far as you may yourself be convinced of their soundness.'

The phrase that Dowding had used in speaking about 'your plans' was not intended as Ellington took it, and it caused the C.A.S., in a reply three days later, to sound slightly on the defensive. It was also more detailed than Dowding had expected, but it did contain information which was an assurance to Dowding about his own future.

In your letter . . . you write of my plans. The selection of the C.A.S. is a matter for the S. of S. who may not even consult the old C.A.S. and if he does, he need not take any notice of his advice. As regards yourself, it has been established as a practice that an officer of your rank will be employed as far as is possible up to the age of 60 so that there is no question of your not serving for a year unless, of course, you want to retire. I hope, however, that you will continue to serve at any rate for two or three years. I do not

see why you should not continue to put forward views on such
subjects as the armouring of bombers, and I feel sure my successor
would welcome your views on such subjects.

Although Dowding does not remember now the exact mood
in which he replied to this letter of Ellington's, there is nevertheless in his letter to the C.A.S. of 9 February an unmistakable
note of sprightliness. He wrote:

First of all let me say that I have always had rather a contemptuous pity for superseded officers who complain of their treatment
and produce long lists of their valuable services, and I have no
intention of joining their ranks. But, passing from the particular to
the general, it seems to me in the highest degree undesirable that
it should be possible for a civilian Minister to select the future head
of one of the fighting services without seeking the advice of its
existing Chief. His knowledge of the Service and its personalities
must necessarily be sketchy and his own position is ephemeral,
depending as it does on the favour of the Premier and other political
considerations. I should probably not be alone in thinking that the
Service Members of Council should go to considerable lengths in
order to prevent the acceptance of such a principle.

Turning now to my own plans, I am definitely anxious to complete at least a year's service in my present rank, because it will
make a big difference to my pension.

I am also keenly interested in my present work, particularly in
the organisation of my Operations Room, the introduction of R.D.F.,
and the transfer of the Observer Corps to a war footing.

But there is the attitude of the new C.A.S. to be considered. He
might find it embarrassing if anyone senior to himself should
wish to stay on in the Service for some years.

In the views that he held at the time and has held ever since
then, Dowding has stressed that although there was unquestionably an element of disappointment in his not becoming C.A.S.
he was able to accept it with some equanimity. 'In the first
place I didn't think I would make a very good C.A.S.,' he has
said, 'and in the second place I was quite sure that what I was
doing, the work I was doing, would be of supreme importance
and a real man's job. There was all the complicated organisation of the new Fighter Command that had to be worked out.
I dare say I was rather conceited, but I thought that I was in
a better position to do that, to devise and get it all into operation, than any probable successor at the time.'

That Dowding's attitude was a relief to the C.A.S. is indicated in Ellington's reply dated 11 February, in another handwritten letter:

I am afraid that the selection of S. of Ss of Chiefs of Staff is an evil, if it be an evil, of long standing. Henry Wilson told me fifteen years ago that he did not know who was to be his successor until he saw it in the paper, and was never consulted. The rule is that the S. of S. decides himself whether he will consult anyone, and having consulted or not, makes his own decision, and this was the position when you were a member of Air Council at the time Geoffrey Salmond was selected, and after his death when I was selected. I only mentioned this before and do so again because in your first letter you wrote of 'my plans' as if it was my decision who was to succeed me. As regards your staying in the Service, I know that Newall will wish it, and I hope you will decide to stay on.

For Dowding his future at Fighter Command was more than a matter of just staying on. His heart and soul were in the work that he was doing. He has remarked many times how often he came to feel glad that he had not become Chief of the Air Staff. As Commander-in-Chief of Fighter Command he could give his undivided attention to building up the increasingly complex system which was to provide for the defence of the country. The two main components in that system were the further development as rapidly as possible of the early warning radar screen, and of the new fighters, the Hurricane and the Spitfire, which were coming forward.

With the construction around the coasts of Britain of the R.D.F. stations, there came the ability to see with the help of radar far beyond what could be seen and heard with the human eye and ear; and with these new fighters there would be the means to offer at least an adequate resistance, if enough of them could be built in time, by a swift interception of any and every intrusion. The next step that Dowding took was to bring these two extremes together and to link the two entirely new elements in the overall machinery of defence.

There then came into existence the third component that was unique: the creation of an elaborate system of communications and control. The radar stations were all linked by direct land-lines with a focal point at Dowding's headquarters at Bentley Priory which was known as the Filter Room. In this room all the radar information that had been picked up by the stations around the coasts was plotted and sorted out, or filtered, and tracks were determined of all the movements of the aircraft that were being observed by the electronic screen. This alone was one of Britain's greatest and most carefully guarded secrets.

The moment that the tracks of these aircraft had been established, the information was automatically passed over more land-lines, and in a continuous stream, to the Operations Rooms of the Group Headquarters and of the Sector Stations—the airfields—of the Groups at which the fighters were based. All this in itself called for a most elaborate tie-up in exclusive telephone lines, and when the need came they were to be constantly manned by women of the W.A.A.F., whom Dowding gladly agreed to have right from the beginning even at the forward radar stations, as well as the men of the R.A.F., and they were kept open for the passing of all this vitally important and highly secret information.

This great machine, with which Dowding was thoroughly familiar down to the smallest detail, provided for the actual instructions for the fighting of any air battle against intruders to be issued by the Group Controllers, who were themselves under the immediate control of the Air Officers Commanding the Groups. Once the orders had been given by the Group Controllers—all of whom were themselves pilots with up-to-date experience—to the Sector Controllers immediate action followed, with the latter ordering off whatever fighters were needed and directing them towards making interceptions. From the moment that the fighters were airborne the communications were maintained through a highly developed system of radio contact and control, including mainly radio telephone. No executive action was taken at the Headquarters at Bentley Priory about the precise use that was to be made of the fighters, although provision was made for watch to be kept in the operations room on the overall situation so that Dowding could see at a glance and at any time of the day or night what was happening around the coasts of and over Great Britain.

With the evolution of this intricate but smoothly working system, Fighter Command then had ready a means whereby it took no more than a few moments for the information about aircraft approaching Britain that was seen on the cathode ray tubes at the radar stations to be passed to the airborne fighter pilots. It was a distinct technical achievement that was far ahead of any such system of defence that was even being thought about anywhere else in the world, and it restored to Britain what safety there was in its position as an island.

It was the speed and efficiency of this system under Dowding's control that was to mystify the Germans so much when they came to launch their attacks against Britain in 1940. They knew that the R.A.F. had something up their sleeve: they had no idea that it was this very efficient means of detecting incoming aircraft. It was by no means infallible, and there were shortcomings in devices that were so new and revolutionary in technique—particularly in the radar readings of heights— and these persisted even on into the Battle of Britain.

'But even with those shortcomings where would we have been without R.D.F. and all that went with it?' Dowding has asked. 'We could never have maintained the vast number of standing patrols that would have been necessary if we had not had that magic sight.'

One aspect of all this extraordinary and rapid development that Dowding has always hoped would be clearly understood is that he, as Commander-in-Chief of the Command that was standing on guard, had a very great deal of help and support from many different people. He has always thought of himself as one of a great team.

'For one thing, I was fortunate in having such a capable and far-seeing staff,' he has said of the men whom he had around him at Fighter Command during those years just before the war. 'They were an ingenious lot. But it must also be remembered that there were many first-rate scientists and civilian technicians who helped so much to build up, quite apart from planning, the whole system. I received a great deal of help from all sorts of different, and unexpected, sources.'

The years that Dowding had spent at the Air Ministry as the member of the Air Council responsible for research and development paid handsome dividends when it came to the application of that research and development to the needs of his Command in the field. He had been in at the birth of some very radical systems in the control of the air; and he was later, even before he had to use them in war, in the fortunate position of being able to foster their growth with an understanding that placed him in a unique category as a Commander-in-Chief in a highly technical Service.

When Dowding became Commander-in-Chief of the new Fighter Command, it also became necessary to provide for his use, in the customary fashion, an official C.-in-C.'s residence. A house was found for this purpose in Stanmore, at the bottom of the hill from Bentley Priory. It was a large, old-fashioned place named 'Montrose'; and Dowding's sister, Miss Hilda Dowding, came to live with him and took charge of running it. Although she was inexperienced in the social aspects of a senior officer's life in the Service, Hilda Dowding shared her brother's tastes, and she ran the house well for him in a quiet and effective manner, and Dowding was able to do the entertaining that was called for through long-established custom. Her brother was punctilious about that, and did his full share of it, both official and unofficial, and to a certain extent he enjoyed it.

On one occasion some time before the war, she has recalled, they entertained Winston Churchill at 'Montrose' along with several other guests. 'I remember that Mr Churchill did all the talking,' Miss Dowding said with a chuckle that is extraordinarily similar in its dryness to her brother's. 'He brought Mr Lindemann with him, and he distinguished himself by not uttering a word.'

Together, Dowding and his sister made 'Montrose' a home of their own. It was the first of his own that he had had for many years, and he looked forward, as much as his interests outside of his work would permit, to settling down there for a while. It was also to be a home for his son Derek. After going to school at Winchester, Derek Dowding went straight to the Royal Air Force College at Cranwell, in the autumn of 1937, and while his father was engrossed in creating Fighter Command he was trained as a pilot. From Cranwell he went to a squadron in Fighter Command in the spring of 1939, and he took part in the fighting before and during the Battle of Britain.

Not all Dowding's problems during the years of the development of Fighter Command were purely technical ones. As the Command expanded and the needs for the personal control of its physical structure became more urgent, Dowding had to give some consideration to the natures, or characters, of those officers of more senior rank who were serving and would continue to serve under him. Because of the rapidity of the expansion and the need for more and more experienced officers, there was always the grave risk of the round holes becoming jammed with square pegs. The selection of officers was largely an Air Ministry responsibility, but it was important to Dowding that he should try to know, and understand as much as possible, the senior officers who were most responsible to him. The two who were to play the most important roles in all that was to happen were Keith Park and Trafford Leigh-Mallory.

In the early summer of 1938, after a brief spell as the Commanding Officer of the fighter aerodrome at Tangmere, in Sussex, Keith Park became Dowding's Senior Air Staff Officer, working directly with him at the Headquarters of Fighter Command. Dowding could not possibly have had a more experienced expert in the use of fighters, most of Park's career having been devoted to them and their use. In their relationship these two men, one an Air Commodore and the other an Air Chief Marshal—with a difference of some ten years in their ages—were in complete harmony in their understanding of their task. They were together for two years, building the operational side of the Command, until just before the Battle of Britain; and then, in the spring of 1940, Park left to take over command of No. 11 Group, which covered south-east England and was in the front line in defence.

To the north of No. 11 Group stood No. 12 Group, which reached from the east coast of England across the heart of the precious industrial areas of the Midlands. Trafford Leigh-Mallory had become the Air Officer Commanding No. 12 Group at the end of 1937, with promotion a year later to the rank of Air Vice-Marshal. He was of approximately the same age as Park, but in comparison with Park he had had very little experience of fighters, his time having been spent mainly in army co-operation, in which he had specialized from the time of the First World War.

It was Dowding's belief during the time when he was building up his command and on into the Battle of Britain that he could place his complete faith and trust in both these men, his two most important subordinates. They held positions of great responsibility, and Dowding did not hesitate to delegate to them a great deal of authority as his two principal Group Commanders.

While still believing that he was right to follow the general course that he did, Dowding feels now that he might, perhaps, have kept a closer control over the freedom that went with that delegation of the responsibility for the tactical fighting of a battle under his strategic control. He was still ultimately responsible for everything that happened in his Command; but what he did not allow for, and could not provide for when he had no reason to suspect a misuse of that freedom, was the difference in the responses that came to his word of command. There was the utmost loyalty from one, Keith Park; but from the other—Leigh-Mallory—there was to come a reaction that caused Dowding the gravest difficulties without his being able to understand, for a very long time, why they should ever have developed as they did inside and outside his Command.

Having been left in peace about his appointment for some sixteen months, Dowding received a letter from the Chief of the Air Staff, in July, 1938, in which Newall told him that, in Dowding's words, 'my services would not be required after the end of June 1939.' On the 4 August the Air Ministry wrote to him officially, confirming that information. The letter read: 'I am commanded by the Air Council to inform you that they have recently had your case under review and have come with regret to the conclusion that they will be unable to offer you any further employment in the Royal Air Force after the end of June, 1939.'

When one reads now of Dowding's 'case under review', and the Air Council coming 'with regret to the conclusion' there is a note in it that suggests the findings of a court of appeal. But who was appealing, and against whom? The statement about being 'unable to offer you any further employment' was a clear enough indication that Dowding was to be retired from the Royal Air Force on that date. He would then be only fifty-seven years of age but, since this was clearly a firm decision, he went ahead with his own personal plans: at the end of June 1939, he would become a civilian.

After the C.A.S.'s notification to Dowding, and a few days before the writing to him of the official letter by the Air Ministry, Air Vice-Marshal C. L. (now Air Chief Marshal Sir Christopher) Courtney was advised by Newall that it was intended that he should take over Fighter Command from Dowding on 1 July 1939. Courtney was a distinguished airman who had come to the Royal Air Force from the Royal Naval Air Service. As a young naval officer he had learnt to fly in 1912, and in 1918 he had enjoyed, for a brief period, the unique position of being, at the age of only twenty-eight, the youngest Brigadier-General in the newly formed R.A.F. Now, when the time came, he was to relinquish his own Reserve Command and take up this appointment in Dowding's place. But scarcely were these notifications of changes in high command issued than there came a sudden speeding up in the rush towards the war that it is now seen was so inevitable.

In 1938, there came the Munich crisis. It was real enough in the threat that it posed, but there was much in it that was a political trial of strength. As such that might be considered to have been beyond the immediate sphere of Dowding's concern. But in the fact that he was responsible for the defence of the United Kingdom there existed a distinct line between what was of direct and what was of indirect responsibility. Dowding's only concern was the state of his Command, and he knew that defence in the air was still far from being anything near adequate.

For one thing, Fighter Command had only twenty-nine squadrons of fighters, which was a pitifully small force. No Spitfire squadrons were yet operational and the Hurricanes that Dowding had—only ninety-three of them all told—were of no use above fifteen thousand feet because provision had not yet been made for their guns to be of any use in the cold above that height even in the summer. The rest of Dowding's force of fighters was made up of out-dated biplanes. 'We had so very little,' he said.

From all that was known at the time, this strength of Fighter Command would never have been an adequate enough force to counter any German attack. That the Luftwaffe needed time as much as the R.A.F. to bring itself up to strength was not known until long afterwards. It was the situation as it existed at the time that had to be considered, and, for an understanding of Dowding's position, must always be considered. Dowding knew exactly what he had, and he knew that his forces were inadequate. The Air Ministry also knew that, and the politicians were fully informed about it.

The Munich Pact, messy though it was, gave the R.A.F. a year of grace which was desperately needed, and Dowding had to rely on the politicians to achieve that. That they did is recognised, and speaking on behalf of the Air Staff, Marshal of the R.A.F. Sir John Slessor has referred to 'my relief that we were not called upon to answer' an air attack on this country at the time of Munich. 'The climax of misjudgment which was the inevitable culmination of the policies of the preceding years,' Slessor has commented, 'and from which as inexorably followed the calamities of the years that came after, was the surrender at Munich in September, 1938.'

But to these views, Slessor added: 'There is a too common tendency to argue the matter in the light of what we know today . . . and not of what we knew—or thought we knew. . . .' In addition to uncertainty about, or lack of knowledge of, the plans being made by the French Army, there was the situation that Slessor has described as 'that political maladministration [which] had ravaged the French Air Force'.

The views that have been expressed by Slessor are representative of the views held by all of those in the Royal Air Force at that time. 'I find it impossible to convince myself that any British Government could have brought itself to face taking the country into war in our then shocking state of unpreparedness in the air,' he said. That state was made abundantly clear by the R.A.F. to the Prime Minister, and Neville Chamberlain acted as he did over Munich with the sobering knowledge at the back of his mind of our hopeless position in the air.

'It was a very good thing that he did act in that way,' Dowding commented.

In a reference to the period of rearmament after the Munich crisis, Viscount Templewood, who, as Sir Samuel Hoare, was then a member of the Government and a one-time Secretary of State for Air, wrote: 'None of the military experts either in London or Paris ever expressed a doubt as to the French ability to resist. Churchill, most experienced of observers, and close friend of General Georges, the most active of the French Generals, never questioned this joint opinion of the French and British Staffs, either before or after he joined the Government.'

But it was the shock of Munich that compelled the Government to make, as Templewood put it, 'one important change in the air programme'. It was in this that a more than important step was taken. Templewood then went on to say:

This change concerned the priority to be given to bombers over fighters. Hitherto, the emphasis in the programme had been on the bomber force. The threat of Prague had, however, made the danger of German raids much more formidable. When, therefore, Air Marshal Dowding pressed for a substantial increase of the fighter squadrons, the priority was changed in favour of fighter defence. I doubt whether we then realised the full importance of the new decision. Dowding saw dangers at hand that many thought to be still distant. It was due to his foresight that the programme was changed, and new fighter squadrons added to it over and above the existing plans.

Internally, the most crying need that Dowding had in his Command was for Operations Rooms at all levels. For too long, he commented, 'it will scarcely be believed that there was absolutely no establishment for the manning of any operations rooms.' Moreover, he added: 'There was no plan for bringing the Observer Corps to a war footing. They were all volunteers who trained for a few hours in the evenings after their day's work was done. There was no mobilization scheme and no authority for paying them.' That situation of over thirty years ago will sound a familiar note for the devoted Observer Corps workers of today.

One of the bitterest struggles that Dowding had with the Air

Staff was over the provision at the aerodromes of all-weather runways. At first there were none. 'During the winter of 1936/37,' Dowding recalled, 'there were three consecutive weeks during which not a single aircraft could take off from or land on Kenley.' This was one of his most important airfields; but, Dowding explained, 'The Air Staff fought against this vital need for all-weather runways because an imported Army Staff Officer had devised a system of camouflaging aerodromes, and he said that runways would spoil the camouflage.'

By 1938, Dowding began to feel, in his attendance at conferences at the Air Ministry, a steadily increasing irritation over what appeared to be an inability by many of those on the Air Staff to understand the need for realistic thinking. 'At one of these conferences I asked that bullet-proof glass should be provided for the windscreens of the Hurricane and Spitfire,' he recalled some years ago. To his astonishment those around the table dissolved into gusts of laughter, making his request sound as if he had asked, as he put it, 'for something grotesquely impossible'. Dowding's reply was the sharp retort: 'If Chicago gangsters can have bullet-proof glass in their cars I can't see any reason why my pilots should not have the same.'

With all the work that had to be done to secure the defence of the country, Dowding hoped that he was going to be left in peace until the time for his retirement at the end of June 1939. But that peace in which to complete his work was not to be granted him. In his handwritten notes there is a long comment that he prepared late in February of that year which states the whole position as he saw it at that time. The reason for this attempt to make such a summary of his position is contained in the first paragraph which reads: 'Last Friday evening (24th Feb) I was rung up by the C.A.S. who told me that a paragraph concerning my retirement and my successor had appeared in the *Evening Standard*. The Air Ministry proposed to reply to enquiries that "no change would be made during the present year." '

This was the first indication that was given Dowding that he might now be required to continue to serve beyond the end of June 1939. 'I thanked C.A.S. for letting me know,' Dowding wrote. He was told by Newall that a letter would be sent to him confirming that.

'I have received very cavalier treatment at the hands of the Air Ministry during the past two years,' Dowding continued in his notes. He spoke about the way in which the understanding that he would become C.A.S. in 1937 had been handled, and of his own 'contemptuous pity for the "disgruntled" senior officer' and his efforts to accept the situation 'without rancour or argument'.

'I thought that the new C.A.S. might find it awkward to have an officer senior to himself serving under his command,' he commented, 'and I only asked that I might be allowed to serve for the further six months then necessary for pension purposes.' Dowding then spoke of the statement that had been made that 'it was not the intention of the Air Council to dispense with the services of the most senior officers until they had reached the age of sixty.' He noted that he was now fifty-six years of age.

'I have no grievance over these decisions, except as regards the discourtesy with which they were effected,' Dowding recorded. 'There was no need to inform me that I was next in succession as C.A.S., nor that I might expect to be retained up to the age of sixty; but the reversal of these intentions was boldly conveyed to me without any form of explanation.'

So clear had Dowding's understanding been of what was expected of him that, he wrote, 'I have made my preparations for leaving the Service in June, and have withdrawn my house from the hands of the agents.' He recorded that before he could consider altering his plans he felt that he was entitled to place on record 'something of the history of the past events'.

When it came to an examination of the present, Dowding wrote, 'I can say without fear of contradiction that since I have held my present post I have dealt with or am in process of dealing with a number of vital matters which generations of Air Staff have neglected for the past fifteen years.' He offered as instances the placing of the Observer Corps on a war footing, the manning of Operations Rooms, the problems of the identification of friendly aircraft, the unserviceability of aerodromes, and no adequate Air Raid Warning System. 'This work has had to be carried out against the inertia of the Air Staff,' he commented, 'a statement which I can abundantly prove if necessary.'

But that was not all. 'I have continually had to complain that the Air Staff take decisions vitally affecting my Command without the slightest consultation with me or my Staff,' he continued. 'I was prepared to agree that many of these omissions were due to oversights on the part of busy people, and I wrote a letter to D.C.A.S. telling him what was happening and begging him to ensure a proper liaison and consultation in matters affecting my Command.'

These were not idle accusations that Dowding was making, and he recorded two incidents that had occurred only recently 'which proved beyond question that my exclusion is deliberate and not inadvertent'. The first of these had to do with a paper that he had submitted to the Air Ministry which dealt with 'Inland R.D.F.' It was about a system of radar stations that would be additional to that of the main radar chain around the south and east coasts, and it would enable track to be kept by additional radar coverage of incoming formations across sparsely populated areas after coming in across the coast, in areas which could not be effectively covered by the Observer Corps.

'A number of these stations, vital to my plans, were struck out and the mutilated remainder was forwarded to the Committee of Imperial Defence,' Dowding commented. 'The Air Ministry did not even write and tell me what they had done.'

Believing that his retirement was so near, Dowding had made no protest, he pointed out, at this extraordinarily off-hand treatment by officialdom. He ventured the hope that 'my successor would be "persona grata" and would not have to work under such difficulties'.

The far-ranging and far-seeing interests that were Dowding's are indicated in the last paragraph of these notes; but there is added to it a note of deep regret. 'In spite of my intense interest in the fighter problems of the immediate future,' he recorded: 'air to air R.D.F., night fighting tactics, the cannon gun, the rocket, etc., there is little in my past or present treatment at the hands of the Air Ministry to encourage me to undertake a further period of service.'

A few days after committing his thoughts to paper in these notes, Dowding was able to express his views fully to the Secretary of State for Air—who was at that time Kingsley Wood—in the presence of Cyril Newall when an opportunity was given him at a meeting between them at the Air Ministry. He covered the whole of the ground that he had recorded in his notes, offering the points that he had wanted to make as support of what he regarded as a thoroughly unsatisfactory position.

Shortly after that, on 17 March, Dowding wrote by hand to Kingsley Wood reminding him of the talk that they had had. 'I told you that I was not anxious to remain in the Service after the end of June, for reasons which I explained to you,' he stated, pointing out that he had also made it clear that 'if it was desired to extend my period of Command, I felt that I should have a letter from you asking me to stay on and telling me that I had the confidence, and should have the support, of the Air Council.' He reminded the Secretary of State that he himself had said that 'this seemed to be a reasonable request.'

'I know that you are very busy,' Dowding added, 'but it is now three weeks since the subject was first mentioned to me, and I should be very much obliged if you could let me know what course you have decided to adopt.'

The answer to Dowding's letter came not from the Secretary of State, but from the Chief of the Air Staff. On 20 March, Newall wrote referring to his letter to Dowding 'dated 1st July, 1938, conveying to you the decision that you should relinquish command of the Fighter Command at the end of June, 1939'. There was a conflict of decisions there for Dowding because he had been notified officially by the Air Ministry that there would not be 'any further employment' for him, which meant retirement, and not merely the relinquishing of his command to which Newall was now referring.

In his letter Newall spoke of 'our conversation on the telephone a short time ago in connection with the statement regarding your retirement which had appeared in the *Evening Standard*'. Newall repeated the information that 'the Press Section were instructed that, should they receive any enquiries in connection with this statement in the Press, they should reply to the effect that no change in command of the Fighter Command was likely during 1939.'

There was then the clear statement by Newall: 'In view of the importance of the efficiency of the Fighter Command and the desire to avoid the coincidence of crises and changes in the higher appointments in operational commands, it has been decided to ask you to defer your retirement until the end of March 1940. I hope this will be agreeable to you.'

Knowing in his heart that, despite all the frustrations and the doubts that still remained about whether he was to be retired or merely to relinquish his command, he was too deeply concerned with what he was doing to cast it all aside, Dowding agreed to stay on, and he accepted this second postponement of all his plans. At the end of the month he received an official letter from the Air Ministry concerning this latest arrangement. Dated 31 May 1939, and in cold, factual detail that, in view of what was to happen in the course of the next eighteen months, only added to its brusqueness it read:

With reference to this department's letter of the 4th August last, intimating that it would not be possible to employ you in the Royal Air Force after the end of June, 1939, I am commanded by the Air Council to inform you that, after further consideration, they have decided to continue your employment until the end of March, 1940.

So, for a second time, Dowding had to re-adjust all his plans about looking forward to the time when he would be among the unemployed.

On 5 June 1939, Christopher Courtney, who was still at Reserve Command and who had been promoted to the rank of Air Marshal, was informed by the Air Ministry that Dowding was to stay at Fighter Command until 31 March 1940, but that it was still planned that he would succeed Dowding on that date. Three weeks later Courtney was in a bad crash in an aircraft, and received severe injuries to one leg. This led to his being out of action for some time; but on 25 August, only a matter of days before the outbreak of the Second World War, he was assured again by the Air Ministry that he was still to take over Fighter Command as arranged at the end of March 1940.

These Air Marshals of the Royal Air Force had become a race apart from the usual run of Service chiefs. While in some respects there was a blending of their Army and Navy backgrounds, the air had given them something more than just a Service background. The outstanding quality in that was that it made of them men who were nearly all pronounced individualists. It was that which caused Dowding, for one, to rebel so strenuously against conformity merely for conformity's sake, and against authority which could not accept a fair measure of responsibility for looking ahead.

'I've always been against all governments,' Dowding once commented in a light-hearted but nevertheless quite determined way. Taxed with that, he added: 'Wherever I've been, and in whatever I have tried to do, it seemed that there was always somebody in the Government who was hampering my efforts. I do not mean, of course, that I am against Government as such. I am against people whose minds have got into a groove about existing practices. In my own experience, for instance, there were the Army Council and the Air Council, and before that the Staff College. I have always been against those whose first inclination, because of those grooves, is to resist any suggestion about modification or change in the existing state of affairs, and to go on causing further obstruction merely because of existing practice.'

It was this freedom in his own thinking, a trait for which he has always been noted, that made Dowding fight so hard against the inflexible, established, or accepted, role of the Royal Air Force in war. Dominated by Trenchard's views about always being on the offensive, a doctrine which had evolved under his guidance, or on his insistence, in the First World War, Air Staff thinking was directed for too long to the wholly offensive role. But what of defence?

'No subject during the expansion of the Royal Air Force received, or repaid, closer study than this problem of air defence,' the historian Denis Richards has written. 'It was a problem easy to pose, infinitely difficult to answer. From this central dilemma of air defence . . . had arisen the conviction of the Air Staff that the whole defensive apparatus . . . could be only a part—and not the major part—of our protection against the enemy. The real solution, the Air Staff held, must lie in offence, in reducing the scale of the enemy's attack by crippling his air force on and over his own soil. The essence of well-directed air warfare clearly lay in attack, not defence. On the doctrine of the offensive, tirelessly preached by Lord Trenchard—a great man whose vision saw first things steadily and saw them whole—the Royal Air Force was thus built; and until the last declining year of peace at least two new bomber squadrons were formed for every new squadron of fighters.'

This was the doctrine against which Dowding was so strongly opposed, that opposition being rooted in the belief that before anything else there must be considered the security of the base. And since that actual security was also his responsibility he fought that much harder against what he believed was only a 'half truth', as he called it, in the Air Staff thinking. That the long struggle which Dowding made at Fighter Command to prove his view about the need for the security of the base did eventually prevail is supported by Peter Wykeham in his statement: 'In three years the whole basic idea of air defence had been revolutionized, and with it the complete Air Force doctrine. No longer could it be said that the only defence was counter-attack . . .'

With a man as hard-headed and as realistic as Dowding, and those qualities were of a strength that was at times almost scaring to some of those who opposed him, it was not a matter of merely forming views and then talking about them. Not given to talking, he established his views through actions, and it was the actions that he took while he was at Fighter Command during those troublesome months just before the outbreak of the Second World War that proved his point and brought about this revolution in Air Force doctrine. Trenchard played his part, as Denis Richards has pointed out, in the evolution of the Service as a whole; and Dowding played his part in defining more exactly and correctly those aspects of that evolution which were inclined to be of questionable value.

Dowding had to think of and build a whole complex Command, basing it all on his view about the needs for effective defence. But he has never tried to claim that he achieved all that alone. He guided his own views almost alone along what proved to be the right channels; but he was provided with ample support from those under his command which enabled him to argue effectively in the higher councils.

'I got very valuable help from all sorts of people, and more particularly in connection with communications,' Dowding added to his earlier statement about that. 'Radio was making advances all the time, and radar was a tremendous leap forward. All these things were coming on at the right time, and many people and their good work were made immediately available for putting into effect, in the system we were devising, some quite revolutionary things.'

CHAPTER FOUR

...FOR WAR

When the Second World War finally came, as it had to, on
1 September 1939, with Great Britain becoming involved
two days later, it was the start, for Dowding, of the testing time.
By then everybody, civilian and service alike, the unknowing
and the expert, had very strongly in mind the expectation of
devastating attacks from the air. That had been the mounting
general thinking, leading to an almost universal belief, ever
since the First World War of twenty years before, and all the
plans were made on the assumption that there would be
all-out air attacks from the moment of the outbreak of any
war.

So far as Britain was concerned, the first air raid warning
came within minutes of the formal broadcast declaration by
the Prime Minister that there existed a state of war. It origina-
ted at the Headquarters of Fighter Command. The officer on
watch at the time in that secret Filter Room into which all the
R.D.F. information was fed from the radar stations around the
south and east coast of Britain was Squadron Leader Walter
(now Air Marshal Sir Walter) Pretty, who was both a pilot and
an electronics specialist. He watched the appearance of the
track of an aircraft on the table below him as the information
was filtered, and it was clearly on its way across the Channel
from France. The Filter Room staff were on their toes, and this
information was automatically fed through to the Operations
Room, and from there Pretty received orders to concentrate on
supplying all available radar information on this incoming
aircraft.

Nothing was on record in the Operations Room about the
customary and required notice having been given of the move-
ment of such an aircraft from France. Immediate action had
to be taken by the staff in the Operations Room, and there was
no time to spare for any guess-work. The air raid alarm was
sounded from there. The people of Britain had an immediate
taste, within those first few minutes of the realisation that they

were again at war with Germany, of the dreaded threat of war from the air. Everybody took cover.

On the sounding of the alarm Dowding went down from his office, where he had been working, to the Filter and Operations Rooms. He discovered within a few minutes that it had been found that the aircraft was a French one bound for Croydon, bringing to England some French officers on official business. No filing in the approved manner of a flight plan had been made by the French, so the incoming aircraft had had to be treated as potentially hostile.

By the time that the 'All Clear' was sounded there had been a wide-spread disruption of the day's activities at all levels, right up to the top in an already overheated Whitehall. An immediate enquiry was ordered, and that occupied the rest of the day, the first of the war, for those most closely concerned with the matter. The radar watch was on the alert, but there was nothing more untoward to report, and by late afternoon Walter Pretty and his staff in the Filter Room were looking at a blank table.

Dowding was also looking at it. He had appeared again, later in the day, in the Filter Room, and he was sitting beside Walter Pretty, gazing down at the table. Everybody was on the alert, and expectant, but there was complete silence with no activity of any nature whatsoever. All aircraft of the R.A.F., fighter, bomber, and coastal, as well as foreign, were at rest. A daddy-longlegs appeared from nowhere and settled on the table in the area of the Channel, and then made its way slowly along the south coast of England. Everybody watched, amused, but not a word was said. It was left to Dowding, who was resting his chin on his arm on the railing as he looked down at the table, to break the silence.

'A Coastal Command sweep, I presume,' he said in an aside to Walter Pretty.

Following the air exercises that had been held during the early part of August, less than a month before the outbreak of war, it was arranged by the Air Ministry that Dowding should speak on the B.B.C. about what had been achieved. The note that Dowding sounded was to give the country, in the words of C. G. Grey, one of aviation's acutest observers, 'a feeling of quiet confidence in our defence organisation, while not neglecting wise precautions to minimise the effects of such attacks as did get through.'

In referring to the 33,000 men, 1300 aeroplanes, 110 guns, 700 searchlights, and 100 barrage balloons which had taken part in the exercises, Dowding stated that they did not at all represent all the resources available in the country. 'It only remains for us to see that our technical equipment keeps ahead of that of our potential enemies,' he stated. 'What we have been doing is to work towards the hundred per cent which is our goal. I am satisfied with our progress, and I confidently believe that serious air attacks on these islands would be brought to a standstill in a short time.'

In what Grey described as 'an admirably foresighted view,' Dowding also stated: 'The rapidity with which Air Ministry scientists produce one invention on top of another is almost embarrassing at times, because the Air Staff can never standardize any arm of defensive detail but must keep their methods fluid so as to incorporate each new device as it materialises.'

But for all that, there was one immediate problem about what would happen when they went to war that had greatly worried Dowding even before the war started. He was having to face what he has described as 'the competing demands for fighters from the Army and from Home Defence'. His first concern was with home defence, but it became clear to him right at the outset that there would be 'heavy demands from overseas for fighters both to satisfy initial requirements and to replace casualties, and these demands would conflict with the even more vital demands of the air defence of the Home Country'.

In trying to find a solution to this problem, Dowding had asked, before the war started, for a principle to be laid down then and there rather than 'leave matters in a hopeful haze and possibly have a bitter dispute at some critical period of the war'. He received from the Air Ministry two answers. 'One was that attack was the best form of defence,' he has recalled, 'and the other was that in no circumstances would any Expeditionary Force leave our country until the safety of our Homeland was assured.'

With distinct perplexity, Dowding has since commented: 'I still can't make up my mind which of these answers was the sillier.'

In his broadcast Dowding had spoken about the guns, the searchlights and the balloons that had taken part in the August exercise, linking them in with the aircraft of Fighter Command. He was able to refer in that way to all the other aspects of defence because, apart from the role that they all played, with the fighters, in the defence of the country, he also had under his control for operations the resources of the Army's Anti-Aircraft Command and Balloon Command of the R.A.F. Dowding was the overall operational commander of all the means that were available for the defence of the country in the air.

Anti-aircraft defence through the use of guns and search-lights had a history going back to the First World War, but as with all other matters of military preparedness it had been woefully neglected and starved through the political trends between the wars. With the awakening to the threat that was posed, it was finally decided, in June, 1938, to do something about it. The inquiries after the Munich crisis later in that year revealed that precious little had been done; and it was not until 1 April 1939, that the Army got around to forming Anti-Aircraft Command.

With Headquarters in a large house named Glenthorn in the same grounds as the Headquarters of Fighter Command, and only a few hundred yards from Bentley Priory, the first General Officer Commanding-in-Chief of Anti-Aircraft Command was General Sir Alan Brooke (later Field-Marshal Viscount Alanbrooke). But within only a very short time, on 28 July 1939, his place was taken by General Sir Frederick Pile. He was to serve as the man in charge of the anti-aircraft defence of the country for the uniquely long period of the rest of the war.

General Pile was an Irishman who was small in stature but large in heart and mind, of a pleasant and genial nature, known to his intimates as Tim. He was at 'the Shop' at Wool-wich only a couple of years after Dowding, and his career in the army had been a sound one all the way through. 'Dowding discovered that he had gained . . . in Sir Frederick Pile a wise and sympathetic confidant and friend,' Peter Wykeham commented quite correctly about the relationship between these two men of which he could not have had any first-hand knowledge. He added, 'The command arrangement was not straightforward for either of them, and could have led to disastrous disagreements.'

It was General Pile's conduct and his genial temperament which went such a long way towards winning the respect of Dowding, who still had an aversion to 'soldiers with a capital S'. Pile was a soldier of the very best type, and Dowding realised that, and it was on that sound basis that there developed this warm relationship between these two men, both important commanders, who were so different from each other in almost every way. Together they presented a decidely united front.

For operational purposes Dowding had three prongs in the defence of the country: his own fighters, the anti-aircraft guns and search-lights, and the balloons. He was also responsible for the work of the Observer Corps, and for the system for Air Raid Warnings. All these had been built up under his watchful eye and at his urgent prodding of authority.

In addition to being a very capable commander, General Pile was also a shrewd judge of men, and he knew from the beginning that Dowding had played an important part for quite some time in the creation of the defences of the country; and it was of further help to both men when they found that there was much that they shared in their relationships with their respective masters. Quite early in his own experiences of Anti-Aircraft Command, Pile encountered just the same difficulties in his relationship with the War Office that Dowding was having to put up with in his troubled relationships with the Air Ministry, and he later spoke about that with feeling and understanding for Dowding's position. It was a position that in its personal aspects was becoming all the time increasingly difficult.

There are many of those who adopt the profession of arms as a career who do not find their opportunity—or cannot make the opportunity—to further the normal course of their careers under the conditions of peace. They need the goad of actual war to bring them forward. That, it could be said, is what they are intended for, and in many cases it is all that they are equipped for. Such was never the case with Dowding.

A thorough-going professional in his chosen field, he had devoted himself unsparingly to preparing in war and in peace for what he might be able to do, and through that his ability to be of value and service to his country no matter what might happen. In peace he did not think of it as a time of merely waiting for war. He thought in terms of his profession, and, as with all intelligent professionals in his field, there was as much in his thoughts that had to do with the deterrent against war as there was with the active preparation for the waging of war. He was the last man who could ever be accused—not that he ever was—of being a war opportunist.

By that summer of 1939, Dowding was the most senior officer in rank on active service with the Royal Air Force, and among the most senior in all the three fighting services. He was also carrying on his shoulders the enormous responsibility of the defence of the United Kingdom. His authority was very great, and that and his seniority combined to make the load that he was carrying a very heavy burden. But it was not a burden to Dowding because he would not let it become one. He gave no thought to any burdens.

There was a responsibility that Dowding had accepted and he was fully conscious of that, and being the realist that he was he knew that it was his duty to discharge it. His high office was by force of circumstance, both private and professional, a very lonely one. That was generally understood and appreciated. Only he knew how extraordinarily uncertain, even with war now a reality, it was in tenure. It was fortunate for everybody that Dowding's self-discipline precluded any unnecessary worry about that at the time. Even prescience can have its disadvantages.

Only a few days after the outbreak of war there came for Dowding a strong reminder that there was still a firm limitation on his time as Commander-in-Chief of Fighter Command. On 11 September a notification was sent to Christopher Courtney by the Air Ministry telling him that he should hold himself in readiness to give Dowding some assistance before the time came for him to take over Fighter Command. Reference was made to the strain now being imposed on the C.-in-C., Fighter

Command, who, it was said, appeared to be working twenty-three and a half hours a day.

It was considered that Dowding was having to carry at Fighter Command a responsibility in work alone that was too great, and that he could not share it adequately with a somewhat junior staff. The same, it was felt, was true of all the very high and responsible posts, and consideration was being given to the need for a general double-banking, with several changes in the appointments of the more senior officers.

Accepting this position, Christopher Courtney went to the Headquarters of Fighter Command as a deputy to the Commander-in-Chief. But it was to be for only a very short time. Dowding, he found, seemed to be quite capable of handling everything himself. Courtney then asked to be allowed to fill some other post until the time came for him to take over Fighter Command. This was agreed to, and he was sent to Canada to help in the organisation of the vast Empire Training Scheme for pilots and other air crews. Dowding was left to carry on in his own fashion.

Instead of the fierce onslaught of bombing from the air that was expected by everybody when war broke out, the people of Britain found themselves facing long months of exactly the opposite. There seemed to be nothing but the tedium of what has been so wretchedly called the phoney war, when, it seemed, everything was more or less at a standstill. The fate of Poland at the hands of the German army, and the war in Finland, actions at sea and the limited air operations became items of propaganda, and it was the way that this propaganda treated the war, bleating away with all its old clichés, that was phoney.

But Dowding had no time to think about that. He was too concerned with the twin problems of preserving his command and at the same time making provision for the fighters which had to be sent to France. 'The first major problem arose during the discussion of the question of sending Fighter Squadrons to France,' he wrote some years later. 'The decisive factor was that of Supply.' He pointed out that during those early months of the war England was safely beyond the range of any German fighters, and that he had reason to believe that unescorted bomber raids on the country could be met and defeated with only very small losses to his own fighters. 'But there could be no illusions concerning the wastage which would occur if we came up against the German fighters in France,' he added.

In the threat of that very realistic 'wastage' there was the nightmare that came to haunt Dowding, and he spoke of how he 'regarded with some apprehension the general policy of sending Home Defence Fighter Units to France'. But he knew that the political considerations were such that fighters had to be sent. He had to accept that. And out of that came the long and lonely struggle that he was to have to wage during those first eight months of the war to maintain, let alone build up, what he felt must be sufficient forces for the air defence of the country.

'There was still so much to be done,' he said, 'and I was being asked to give up too much for despatch overseas.' The strength that Fighter Command needed for the defence of the country, it had been agreed, was 53 squadrons, but such was the position that even by the outbreak of war Dowding only had, he pointed out, 'the equivalent of 34 . . .'

It was a one-sided enough struggle, as is revealed in Dowding's official despatch alone, with constant appeals from him to the Air Ministry, and repeated delays in decisions and replies to him about those decisions which were of such vital importance to the safety of Britain. The over-riding consideration appeared to be the support that had to be given to the British Expeditionary Force in France. In the political view, that was where the obligation had to be met; but that was not Dowding's view. Home defence came first.

Of those delays in completing the structure of his Command that Dowding was asking for so urgently he has said that they were 'presumably unavoidable', but he has gone on to point out that 'the result was that the organisation and development of the defences of the south and west of England were very incomplete . . .' In commenting on the position that Dowding was in, Denis Richards has written: 'Allied to his inherent singleness of purpose, this inevitably prompted him to a rigid regard for priorities.'

But such was the general attitude towards the war during

those early months of 1940 that it was at times almost as if the twenty years of peace since the ending of the Great War had scarcely existed. The mood of the British people, prompted by the general propaganda to which they were subjected in the press and over the radio, was one of cheerful optimism, if not of a certain arrogance, about what they were going to do to the Germans. It was a sad hang-over from the earlier days when it was felt seemly to express belligerence. There was a blind eagerness to get to France, where, it was felt, a show-down with the Germans would soon produce results. The phoney war was the result of a great deal of phoney thinking.

One of the men closest to Dowding without being on intimate terms with him during the months before the Battle of Britain and for a time during the battle itself was Francis Wilkinson, his Personal Assistant. Since Wilkinson is another of those strong individualists in which the Royal Air Force abounds, and has always been as outspoken as he is shrewd in his judgement of men, his assessments of Dowding and his actions during that time have in them a strong tinge of realism.

After joining the Royal Air Force with a short service commission in 1924, Francis Wilkinson had a great deal of experience in fighter squadrons. He became an instructor at the Central Flying School, which gave him the highest rating as a pilot that it was possible to get. But when he found that there was no possibility of his gaining a permanent commission he left the R.A.F. and joined the Colonial Service, and went out to Nigeria.

When war broke out, Wilkinson returned to England with the hope of re-joining the R.A.F. and of getting back to flying. He was welcomed back, but he was told at the Air Ministry that he was to report immediately to the Headquarters of Fighter Command for duty as Personal Assistant to the Commander-in-Chief. When he started to complain, saying that he had not come back merely to sit behind a desk, he was stopped short with the explanation: 'We want somebody who isn't likely to be afraid of Dowding.' He was warned that the C.-in-C. was a tartar.

Forty-eight hours after landing back in England, and while

still in civilian clothes, Wilkinson reported to Dowding at Bentley Priory. Dowding did not seem to take it in that Wilkinson was a pilot with a great deal of experience, and he agreed to try him out, telling him that he wanted him there in forty-eight hours' time.

'I managed to get uniforms in time and of course I was sporting my wings, and I turned up on time at Bentley Priory,' Wilkinson has recalled. 'Dowding took one look at me and exclaimed, "But you're a pilot!" '

'I hope so, sir,' Wilkinson replied. 'I was a pilot for nine years and I suppose I've done about three thousand hours of flying here and there. I'd like to get back to flying.'

'Isn't that just like the Air Ministry!' Dowding then explained. 'I've just let the P.A. I had go because he was a pilot and wanted to get back to flying. And now they send me another pilot!'

But in the next moment Dowding won over Wilkinson with the statement: 'Oh, well . . . let's see how we get on. I'll see what I can do later about getting you back to flying.'

'And he did, as you know,' Wilkinson has reminded me. 'Right slap in the middle of the Battle of Britain, with everything bearing down on him, he could still be thoughtful enough to help me arrange to get back to flying and to hand over the job to you.'

In handing over what is described in the Air Force List as a 'Personal Appointment,' although Wilkinson has cheerfully described it as being 'just a dogsbody', he also handed over a warning. 'You'll hear an awful lot,' he said at the time, 'and you'll find out an awful lot. The way those boys at the top go after each other, sniping at each other with telescopic sights, is staggering.' They were the words of an experienced man of the world, and he had good reason, from the time that he spent working in Dowding's office, to express himself in that way.

When he was reminded many years later of what he had said, Wilkinson replied: 'And it was true, as you came to know. But it never applied to Stuffy. There was none of that with him, which is perhaps why he got into so much trouble. The one man above all the others, he was of the highest integrity . . . the very highest. Perhaps that was why he was so lonely.'

As with Dowding, General Pile was also having his difficulties over the provision of sufficient equipment for his own Command with which he could support Dowding. Pile was also discovering from Dowding, as he later admitted, more of what it meant to have to face squarely up to the obtuseness of officialdom, and he expressed his own delight in learning a little from Dowding about how to try to deal with that.

Referring to the state of the amount of the equipment available—and speaking of the limited demands made upon it during the first winter of the war as 'a merciful respite'—Pile said in a humorous aside: 'And Stanmore, the point on which hinged the whole fighter defence and air raid warning system of the country, had to be content with 4 heavy A.A. guns.' Those in the field who held strong views about the value of Headquarters staffs might say that that was four too many. They could be forgiven; but there was more at stake then than the questionable value of some staff officers.

Together Pile and Dowding had this pressing matter of shortages for ever on their minds. 'This whole question of the country's resources, as I told the War Office, clearly needed revision,' Pile wrote. 'Dowding had already pointed out the quandary that he was in.' Pile recorded that at one time Dowding was informed that a certain important committee having to do with defence, of which both he and Dowding had been members, no longer existed. But they were also told that the work of the committee was being done by other people at the War Office and the Air Ministry with no reference to either of them. And then they were told that Dowding was responsible and should make the decisions himself. Pile remarked: 'It was all rather confusing.'

With his own particular brand of humour, Pile was learning quickly, as he freely acknowledged. In a situation that developed over the very unsatisfactory accommodation for the anti-aircraft defenders of the R.A.F.'s radar stations, he wrote: 'Eventually, after consulting Dowding, I sent a telegram to the War Office asking them to inform the Air Ministry that I proposed to remove my troops from all sites where accommodation had not been provided. This led to a most satisfactory burst of energy . . .' There is now a humorous aspect to the thought of officialdom having to face from both these resolute commanders this decisive method of attack, and, as Pile has recorded, it was to continue.

On the relationship that existed between the Army and the R.A.F., Pile has said that his own Command 'was sometimes called a private army—it was certainly an army.' And to that he added: 'It was an army controlled by the R.A.F., and the organisation was working admirably.' Pile once offered the view of one of his own senior officers, who stated: 'For once we have a unified command. "Stuffy" Dowding is solely responsible for A.D.G.B. My Chief goes to see him practically every day, and the wheels go round like oiled clockwork.'

In a general assessment that Pile once made of Dowding, he wrote: 'Of the great Service leaders, Dowding was the outstanding airman I met in the war. A difficult man, a self-opinionated man, a most determined man, and a man who knew more than anybody about all aspects of aerial warfare. He was a good friend to me on many occasions, and history will undoubtedly record his great contribution to the Allied victory.'

The daily meetings between Dowding and Pile were held in Dowding's office in Bentley Priory. Pile would walk across from his own Headquarters and present himself with his usual quiet cheerfulness, always immaculately turned out, and it became a moment in the day for Dowding that he looked forward to because, different though the two men were, he had come to feel that Pile was the one man he could talk to. Not even Pile fully realised the necessity for Dowding to unburden himself, which was why he spoke about that as if Dowding was inclined to do it to everybody. He did not, and Pile was one of the very few to whom Dowding did speak so freely.

'Dowding loved to walk about the room and talk to people as if he were delivering a lecture,' Pile recorded. 'Every morning, punctually at ten, I used to arrive in his office, and for an hour he would walk about lecturing me on every conceivable subject. I wish I could have recorded his views, as they were full of interest, and he only spoke about things that he had already thought deeply over.'

In all that was developing, despite the apparent quietness

of the war, Dowding has always stressed that there was an unremitting struggle to bring his defences to the state which would be effective in the face of what he believed was going to happen. The lull after the conquest of Poland and the gestures that were made by the enemy towards, and their talk about, peace moves left him unmoved. That was for the politicians to deal with. Many years before Trenchard had referred to him as a 'dismal Jimmy', and had been wrong. There is a vast difference between being dismal and being able to face facts. For Dowding it was always a case of hard facts; and the fact that worried him now was the deficiency in the security of the base. He was not dismal, but he was apprehensive, and he had reason enough to be in that state, as Pile was also, in the face of what he regarded as too much dithering at the top.

'There's only one thing about that,' Francis Wilkinson once said, 'and it is that Stuffy was not the only commander who had to fight for what he thought was right. All through military history they were having these battles to get their own way. That's what they're there for. But Stuffy fought a dam' sight harder than most.'

Working as closely as he did in handling the affairs of Dowding's office, Wilkinson also came to see other aspects of his master's problems. 'There were smaller things about his dislikes, but wasn't that only to be expected?' he commented. 'For instance, he seemed to be absolutely incapable of understanding the Navy, even though his brother was a naval officer. I did hear him go as far once as to say that he thought that the Battle of the River Plate was a good show. That's about as far as he got. He had to fight them, as we know he had to fight everybody else, and it was that which made him feel so angry about their lack of understanding of the air.'

There was also the accumulation of all the internal problems of his rapidly expanding Command. As the Air Ministry had rightly advised Christopher Courtney, that was an added load of responsibility for Dowding. But at this early stage that did not worry him unduly, and he went about this side of his work with his usual quiet thoroughness. He had serious enough problems, but they were not cause for alarm. Even the shortage of pilots was not, then, as grave as it was to become later.

'When I first joined him at Bentley Priory, in the beginning of the year, it seemed that the youngsters were crashing more Spitfires and Hurricanes than were coming out of the factories,' Francis Wilkinson has recalled. 'Then it was shortage of aircraft that was worrying Dowding.'

In the concern expressed by the Air Ministry about the burden of responsibility and work that, with the outbreak of war, was now bearing down on Dowding's shoulders there was understanding enough of his position; but there were lighter moments provided, albeit unintentionally, by those dwelling in the spheres of higher authority. One letter that he received from on high contained a request for his views about the advisibility of the wearing of an aiguillette by Personal Assistants.

'I understand that this expensive bauble has something to do with the tethering of horses,' Dowding replied. 'I do not understand what that can possibly have to do with the Royal Air Force.'

The position in which Dowding's Personal Assistant was placed—he worked in an inner office which separated those of the Commander-in-Chief and his Senior Air Staff Officer— gave the P.A. ample opportunity to become familiar with the manners, the styles of both men, and the relationship that existed between them. Francis Wilkinson had met Keith Park years before, when he had first been in the R.A.F.

'Park was awfully good,' he once recalled of the time just before Park left the Headquarters to take over command of No. 11 Group. 'He had Stuffy's complete confidence. And he worked the most awful hours. He was always in his office before even the cleaners showed up. I had the most enormous respect for him.'

On one occasion when Dowding was away from Headquarters, Park had to make a quick decision about a matter having to do with a silly disagreement that was going on with one of the other services. He asked Wilkinson if he knew what the Commander-in-Chief's views were in the matter, and Wilkinson gave them to him. But in the still of the night, after he had gone to bed, Wilkinson woke up in a panic. 'I realised that I'd dropped an awful clanger,' he has said. But he had to wait until dawn before he could tell Park that he had got things the wrong way round. 'I could scarcely wait to get into the office in the morning, and even then Park was there before me.'

Wilkinson explained to Park where he had gone wrong, and to his relief Park 'merely smiled in that easy way of his, told me not to worry, and commented that in any case the people who were causing the trouble were far too stupid to be able to spot the mistake I'd made'.

There was no doubt whatsoever about Keith Park's loyalty to Dowding, and he has made public statements about that. He has also spoken about the severe test to which it was put in a disagreement that he had with Leigh-Mallory, the Air Officer Commanding No. 12 Group, only a short time before Dowding was due to relinquish his command at the end of March 1940.

'I had been Dowding's Senior Air Staff Officer for nearly two years by then,' Park stated. 'Leigh-Mallory came striding into my office at Headquarters one day after an interview with the C.-in-C. He was very angry and he made a rude comment about what he called Dowding's obstinacy. He said that he would move heaven and earth to get Dowding sacked from his job. I was very annoyed at this, and I told Leigh-Mallory so. Although at that time I was only an Air Commodore and he was an Air Vice-Marshal, I told him just what I thought of such a remark and his obvious disloyalty.'

Dowding did not hear about this incident until the summer of 1968, when Park made the statement about it that was widely reported in the press in New Zealand and which was brought to Dowding's attention. 'I should have been grateful for earlier information about it,' Dowding commented. 'It was an awful thing for Park to have to experience. Leigh-Mallory couldn't have complained if Park had reported the incident to me immediately. I had no idea at that time that there was such a feeling of enmity towards me on Leigh-Mallory's part. What a very foolish thing for him to say, and what a wretched position for him to place Park in.'

It was less than two months after this incident, by which time he had become Air Officer Commanding No. 11 Group, that Park came to know that he was also going to have to endure this curious enmity of Leigh-Mallory's. In commenting on that many years later, Park said: 'As regards my personal relations with Leigh-Mallory, from the time of the Dunkirk evacuation, when I was in charge of fighter operations, Leigh-Mallory made it quite clear to me that he was very jealous of my Group, which was in the front line.'

Another of those who came to know well both Dowding and Park, and to understand the relationship that existed between them, was Lord Willoughby de Broke, who is so well-known in racing circles. He first met Dowding shortly after the outbreak of war. At that time he was, as he has put it, 'a somewhat elderly squadron commander' stationed at Tangmere. He was, in fact, doing very well in commanding at his age a Hurricane squadron of the Auxiliary Air Force. 'I got to know him better when I became a Controller at No. 11 Group Headquarters,' he recalled; and of his time on Park's staff, he added, 'I don't think that I could have had a more exciting, interesting and rewarding job.'

As a Controller in such a responsible post, Willoughby de Broke saw and heard a great deal of what happened in the actual working relationship and exchanges between Dowding and Park. 'Make no mistake about it, we all knew that Dowding had a brain, and that he used it,' he has said. 'He was exceptionally well-informed in all technical matters, and our whole system of operating, which was highly scientific and most technical, was mainly due to his planning. Everybody had a tremendous admiration for him for that alone. And we weren't fooled by that nickname. He wasn't stuffy. It was his own particular kind of shyness.'

Despite all that had been happening in the rapid expansion of the Royal Air Force, and the cataclysm that had overtaken the world with its immediate threat to this country, Dowding was still under notice, which he fully understood and accepted, that he was to relinquish his command and retire from the Royal Air Force on 31 March. He had made his plans with that firmly in mind. But at the very last moment, only the day before he was due to go, he received a long letter from the Chief of the Air Staff that threw everything, yet again, into the melting pot.

'On the 20th March last year I wrote to ask you if you would defer your retirement until the end of March, 1940,' Newall wrote. He made no mention of that date being the very next day. 'Even at that time of disturbed and uneasy peace your Command was of the very greatest importance, and since then war has intervened with a consequent increase in your responsibilities. In the circumstances it has been decided to ask you to continue in your present position until July 14th of this year, on which date you will have completed four years as Air Officer Commanding-in-Chief.'

With all that was staring the country in the face, this was a postponement of only three and a half months, and in its own way it illustrated the unreality of the thinking of that time when it came to planning for even the immediate future. Newall continued: 'I shall personally be very glad if you are willing to accept this extension, as I feel it would be undesirable for a change to take place at Fighter Command at this stage when we may be on the verge of intensified air activity. Whether that be so or not, I am well aware how high the efficiency of Fighter Command stands today and I fully realise how much we owe to your personal leadership in preparing the command and bringing it so successfully into action.'

Despite the upheaval that this latest notice meant for him at the very last moment, Dowding felt that all that Newall was saying was pleasant enough, and obviously well-intentioned, and that after the objection that he had raised a year ago it would not be advisable to go over all that again. But there was nevertheless something of a sting in the tail of Newall's letter, which read:

As I mentioned to you previously, I have the uncongenial task of informing the more senior officers in the Service when it becomes necessary to call upon them to make way for others in order to keep up a sufficient flow of promotions. I must now confirm the information that, so far as can at present be seen, it will be necessary for you to retire when you relinquish your Command on July 14th next. An official letter to this effect will be sent to you in due course. I know you will appreciate the difficulties involved in this decision, and believe me when I say that the Royal Air Force as a whole will greatly regret the conclusion of your active duties in the Service.

There was no lack of decision in this final notice. Dowding was to relinquish his Command and retire. That was stated categorically, and there was nothing that he could do but accept it and make his plans with this new date in mind.

In his reply, the next day, Dowding merely stated: 'I shall be glad to continue in my present Command until July 14th of this year.' He added only one other sentence: 'Can you tell me who my successor will be?'

There was no reply to this request. Nor was there any official letter which Newall had said would 'be sent to you in due course': the customary official letter confirming the extension of Dowding's last few weeks of service in the Royal Air Force until 14 July.

In terms of the battle that must surely take place before long, and as was hinted at by Newall, time was drawing short. For that reason, talk about Dowding having to relinquish his Command and retire was beginning to smack to him very much of changing horses in mid-stream. So far as the proposal that Christopher Courtney should become Commander-in-Chief of Fighter Command was concerned, that seemed to have fallen by the wayside. On 15 January 1940, he had become the Air Member for Supply and Organization, and he was to continue to fill that appointment for the rest of the war.

When the Germans made their long-awaited attack in the west, and fighting broke out in France in May, bringing everybody to a very sudden and very sharp realisation of the gravity of what was happening, Dowding was one of the few who, if he did not actually shake his head, at least stood firm. He saw happening just what he had thought all along would happen, and he would not, perhaps even could not, be panicked by it. He had thought about all that might happen, and he had examined everything in such careful detail, and he would not allow himself to be misled.

In the fighting that started on 10 May, the severe losses of aircraft, including fighters, suffered by the R.A.F. caused an alarm in high quarters that was so sudden that to Dowding it approached imbecility. He was told by a senior officer on the Air Staff of the Air Ministry, who had come to report to him, about the grave losses of Hurricanes that were being reported from France, as though such losses were a complete surprise.

'What do you expect?' Dowding snapped, finding it hard to contain himself. 'When you get into a war you have to lose things, including precious aircraft. That's exactly what I've been warning you about.'

In what to Dowding was the Air Staff's grave lack of realism there was one of the main reasons for the differences of opinions which were steadily developing between him and the Air Ministry. 'The fundamental stupidity of too many people on the Air Staff was almost unbelievable,' Francis Wilkinson has commented. When he was challenged on the reasons for his feeling that way, he snapped: 'I didn't just feel it! I knew it from what Dowding was having to put up with. What used to beat me completely was how those people could sit up there in their ignorance and have the audacity to set themselves up to pass judgement on matters that they simply didn't seem to be able to understand.'

The vehemence of that statement was to find some support in my own experience in serving under Dowding later in the year, and an even stronger support when, over the years since then, a closer examination was made of the treatment that was accorded Dowding. At the time of the fighting in France, even though he was disturbed, Dowding sounded a more restrained note when he said, '. . . my fears about the incidence of wastage in this type of fighting began to be realised.'

CHAPTER FIVE

AT READINESS

If it is true that war is a stage in the development of national policy by means other than political, is it not also true that in failing to maintain peace the political leaders also fail in their purpose? And if they fail in that purpose, to what extent are they to be trusted in the conduct of the war that then takes place? 'I have always distrusted all politicians,' Dowding once said, 'if only because, being what they are, they cannot be relied upon.' That statement was made out of many years of bitter experience.

It is the rule that military leaders are, by their training and uninterrupted experience, qualified professionals. They can be wrong, and they can make mistakes, and they can also be stupid. But they are qualified practitioners, and not, as the politicians cannot help being, will-o'-the-wisps. And yet they must always be subject, even in war, to political control, even when the political leaders have themselves failed and have had to call on the same military leaders to bring about a solution of their problems.

When both politicians and military leaders jointly make a hash of their responsibilities, there has to come an inevitable reckoning. Such a state was reached in Britain's affairs early in May 1940. The politicians had been running around Westminster, torturing their minds over a state of affairs which Anthony Eden, the Secretary of State for War, noted on 9 May as 'Parliamentary position too difficult' when it came to a firm decision about who was to lead the country. In the early hours of the morning of the next day the Germans let loose their blitzkrieg in the west, raging into neutral Holland, Belgium and Luxembourg. This was no great surprise for Dowding. There was so much in that move that resembled what had happened at the start of the First World War that one could only wonder why there should be any surprise, and in any case the planning, or all of what planning there had been, was directed towards such a move being made. 'It was win or lose,' Eden wrote.

But the British managed to pull themselves together and to call upon the one man who, for all his curious habits and unpredictable ways, for all his arrogance and contempt for the military leaders, was the only one who could sound the clarion call that was to rally the country in a fashion that inspired the free world's respect. On the other hand, much as the country at large welcomed Winston Churchill when he became Prime Minister in the evening of 10 May, there were reservations among those who were to have to work with him.

'. . . the mere thought of Winston Churchill as Prime Minister sent a cold chill down the spines of the staff at 10 Downing Street,' John Colville wrote of that moment. He was then Assistant Private Secretary to the Prime Minister. He added that their feelings were widely shared throughout White-hall. But, he added, 'within a fortnight all was changed'.

The fact alone that Churchill came to power, however, did not prevent many who were in high office, particularly in France, from whirling around in a state of unrelieved confusion and vacillation. Not all, it must be admitted, were in that curious state; but those who were not were a mere handful. Of that select group, one who stood firmest of all while those about him were losing their heads was unquestionably Dowding.

'He was agitated over the news that was coming from France,' Francis Wilkinson has recalled, 'but he never for a moment showed the slightest sign of panic.'

'It would have been a pretty dreadful state of affairs if I had,' Dowding remarked when that comment was reported to him. 'I was far too busy to be in such a state as that.'

On 13 May, Anthony Eden received from Gort a personal telegram stating: 'We have to support in the air not only the B.E.F. but also our Allies who have suffered heavy air attacks . . . our main defence in the air is fighters . . . I earnestly hope War Cabinet will decide to give additional air assistance . . . for Allied success in the coming battle.'

While fully aware of the position that Gort was in out in France, Dowding had to consider a different battle. The thought of having to continue to send more of his precious fighters and air crews to France appalled him. He had already lost over two hundred Hurricanes—an alarming figure in view of the onslaught that Dowding anticipated—and on 13 May he had been forced to send thirty-two more. It was then that he took a step which, in his own words, 'must have been most unusual in military history'. Faced with the possibility of having to give up more of his fighters for what he felt, in his own mind, must become a losing battle, and knowing what the position would then be, he asked to be allowed to appear before and to state his case to the Cabinet.

'I had to do it because I believed that the Air Ministry would not support me firmly enough against the Prime Minister in his strong wish to send more fighter squadrons and parts of squadrons to France in response to the frantic appeals coming from across the Channel,' Dowding stated.

The application had to go through the normal Air Ministry channels. 'It would have been confounded impertinence on my part if I had made the request direct to the War Cabinet or the Prime Minister,' Dowding said. But he knew what he was up against. 'The Air Ministry themselves ought to have been fighting tooth and nail,' he added. 'Perhaps some of them were, but I could not be sure of that. I felt that everybody was too frightened of Winston Churchill.'

To his surprise, and it was a surprise, Dowding was asked to attend a Cabinet meeting. 'I say I was surprised because I very much doubt if either the C.A.S. or the Secretary of State realised just what I wanted to say,' he commented. 'What I was so greatly concerned about was that this was a job that the Air Ministry should have been doing, and I felt that if they weren't prepared to do that then I would, only the less I said about that to them on the way up the better.'

Armed with the understanding and foresight which were so uniquely his, Dowding drove from Bentley Priory to No. 10 Downing Street. He was shown into the Cabinet Room, which was also the Prime Minister's office. Most of the room was filled by the large table in the centre, with chairs all around it. The Prime Minister's place was in the middle. The entrance to the room was behind where he sat, in the corner to his right. Other chairs were placed around the walls, away from the table at which various people sat.

On the Service side there were present, in addition to the Chiefs of Staff, the Service members of the Secretariat, one of whom was William Elliot, who was by then a Group Captain. He noticed a marked difference between the very senior Air Chief Marshal now presenting himself before the Cabinet and the man whom he had first met in Palestine ten years before. The strain of the years of responsibility were showing through even the iron control of Dowding's self-discipline.

At first, Elliot felt that a distinct discourtesy was shown Dowding in view of the very senior officer that he was, when he was asked to take a place, while other business was discussed, on one of the chairs against the wall. When it came to the matter that was the reason for his being there, Dowding was asked to take a chair at the table, a few places to the right of the Prime Minister. The meeting then discussed the most important item on the agenda, which was an urgent request from the French Government for more help in the air.

It has been stressed that the situation that had developed was particularly acute for Churchill. His feeling for France, and the depth of his emotional response to the cries for help, made demands upon him that were possibly just as heavy as those made upon Dowding in his emotional feeling about the need to provide for the defence of the United Kingdom.

'. . . it was already clear that the continuance of fighting on this scale would soon completely consume the British Air Force in spite of its individual ascendancy,' Churchill wrote later. 'The hard question of how much we could send from Britain without leaving ourselves defenceless and thus losing the power to continue the war pressed itself henceforward upon us. Our own natural promptings and many weighty military arguments lent force to the incessant, vehement French appeals. On the other hand, there was a limit, and that limit if transgressed would cost us our life.'

That was an admirable enough summary of the position when viewed in hindsight, several years after the event. It was understandable that Churchill was in a state of tension. He had been Prime Minister for only five days. The situation in France was disastrous. Only that morning the French Premier had been on the phone to him declaring: 'We have been defeated We are beaten; we have lost the battle.' With that on his mind—of which Dowding could not have any knowledge—and the collapse of the resistance in Holland during the course of the morning, Churchill had to face what he described as 'a general impression of defeat' which he also had to overcome.

Many years later William Elliot said of that Cabinet meeting that it was one of the most highly charged that he had ever attended. Churchill did most of the talking, and it was an occassion for him to express himself with deep feeling and in his own style. There has remained in Elliot's mind, though, a vivid impression of the great contrast between the way that Dowding spoke and the style of the other speakers. He was factual and to the point, the professional airman stating expertly and concisely a case that had to be made. There was no room for rhetoric.

'I felt from the outset that I was making little impression,' Dowding said later, 'and it was so urgent that I should make clear the effects that sending so many of our fighters to France were having on the efficiency of my Command and on the possibility of our surviving the assault which I was sure would be made on this country.'

To Dowding it seemed that the Prime Minister was going to have his own way with little or no opposition from those who should have been taking a more realistic stand. Both the Secretary of State for Air, Sir Archibald Sinclair, and the Chief of the Air Staff, Cyril Newall, were present at the meeting. Sinclair had been in office only four days. What Dowding did not know was that Churchill and Sinclair were personal friends of many years' standing. In 1915, in the First World War, Winston Churchill had commanded, as a Lieutenant-Colonel, the 6th Royal Scots Fusiliers in the front line on the Western Front, and his second-in-command had been Archibald Sinclair. Afterwards they had come to see and know a great deal of each other as Members of Parliament.

However, that could not have had any particular bearing

on what happened around the table at that Cabinet meeting. Of more importance, because of the lack of his experience, was the fact that the Secretary of State for Air was so new to his appointment. In the urgency of what he was trying to impress upon Churchill, Dowding needed desperately all the help that he could possibly get, particularly from the Air Ministry representatives.

'I should have been able to count on them for support in what I was saying,' Dowding stated later of the position that he found himself in. 'But I got none. Newall had been rebuffed a little earlier by Churchill over something inconsequential, and he was silent. Sinclair was sitting forward with his arms on the table eagerly trying to guess what Churchill was going to say next.'

As the meeting progressed, with Churchill emotionally influenced by what he felt was a paramount need to help the French, Dowding began to feel something akin to despair, and with that the need for some firm action. 'I was desperately occupied with the vital necessity of convincing the P.M. of the urgency of the situation,' he has said.

That morning, in a very agitated state of mind over the details of the heavy losses in France, Dowding had taken his own counsel in preparation for the meeting that he was to attend. With only his Personal Assistant to help him, and working in the quiet of his office at Bentley Priory, he had prepared a graph. He now made use of it, and he recollects: 'I got to my feet, and taking my graph with me I walked around to the seat occupied by the Prime Minister. I leant forward and laid the graph on the table in front of him, and I said: "If the present rate of wastage continues for another fortnight we shall not have a single Hurricane left in France or in this country." I laid a particular emphasis on "or in this country".'

During the time that it took Dowding to turn away after making his statement and walk back to his place at the table, there was complete silence, with Churchill glaring down at the graph in front of him. For the moment there was nothing more that anybody could say.

'It must not be imagined that this was an attempt at a prophecy on my part of what losses I should have,' Dowding has explained. 'It was actually the statement of the losses that I had already suffered which had led me to prepare the graph showing that with losses going on as they had been, we would soon be down to nothing.'

The desperate need that he felt that this vital point should be clearly understood was made all the more urgent, in Dowding's eyes, by the silence of those who, he believed, should have been supporting him. 'The Air Ministry representatives took no part in this discussion,' Dowding wrote in his notes, 'despite all that has been said to the contrary.'

Describing these events in his *English History, 1914-1945,* A. J. P. Taylor wrote: 'Dowding resisted successfully, though only after appearing in person at the war cabinet and threatening to resign. When argument failed, Dowding laid down his pencil on the cabinet table. This gentle gesture was a warning of immeasurable significance. The war cabinet cringed, and Dowding's pencil won the battle of Britain.'

When that statement was called to Dowding's attention, he commented: 'That remark about the Cabinet cringing is really very absurd. I may have thrown down the pencil in exasperation, although I have no recollection of doing so. But of one thing I am absolutely sure. I should never have dreamed of resigning in such circumstances and the thought never for a moment entered my mind.

'High as my regard was, and still is, for Lord Beaverbrook, and he was a very good friend of mine, he was particularly wrong in holding the view that I was threatening to resign. I know that he regarded it as a magnificent gesture on my part, but that was, I am afraid, his imagination becoming a little too heated.

'To look at it another way, I should have been very wrong if I had threatened to resign in a case like that because it was at a most critical time in the early days of the war. I don't think, and the record proves it, that there was anybody else who, at that time and in those circumstances, could have replaced me with advantage. There were plenty of people who would have done as well as I could have, or even better, perhaps, if they had been at it as long as I had and knew all about the working of the whole system. But suddenly swopping horses at that critical time would have defeated all that I was trying to achieve, and no matter what Churchill said or did, I would not have resigned.'

That Dowding was right in that view is supported by the actions of the Air Ministry in asking him to go on postponing the date of his relinquishment of his Command. There was no one else who could take his place. Dowding had work to do and he meant to do it, and resigning was no way of achieving that.

In a comment that he later made about the meeting, General Sir Ian Jacob, who was Military Assistant Secretary, wrote: 'The decision was one of the hardest to make in the whole war, and opinion swayed back and forth. Dowding, an austere man, spoke up clearly and well, and his case for retaining the whole of Fighter Command for home defence was very strong. The Prime Minister was torn in two.'

'I felt that I was doing a lot of talking,' Dowding once admitted. When he read many years later this comment made by Ian Jacob, he added: 'I'm glad to hear that. I was speaking from the heart about the terrible results that I was sure would occur from sending more fighters overseas.'

The strength of Dowding's presentation of his case was enough to make it decisive. There was little left that could be said by anyone after such a convincing argument. While that was a relief for Dowding, it had to be qualified, and for two reasons. He knew, in the first place, that in crossing Churchill as he did—and there could be no doubt about his having done that—he was placing himself, in certain respects, in a very awkward position. Secondly, there was at the back of his mind the knowledge that the decision reached had been a political one, and he could not help wondering how much reliance he could place upon that.

Long afterwards, I once asked Dowding just what it was that had compelled him to take the step that he did in going right to the top. He replied: 'It was very simple, I think. It was an intense desire to prevent this country from being over-run by the Germans and thereafter becoming a third-class power. That was what made me go and beard Churchill in his den. I wouldn't have done that for any less or any smaller motive.'

When the question was raised about the curious distortion of the decisions reached about the fighters that is found recorded by Churchill in his own account of those times, Dowding commented: 'You couldn't very well expect him to admit that he came within a hair's breadth of wrecking Fighter Command before the Battle ever started.'

In the garden of No. 10 Downing Street immediately after the meeting in the Cabinet Room, and even while Dowding was still on his way back to Bentley Priory, the Prime Minister and a few others stood talking. Among them was Ian Jacob, and of what then happened he has written: '. . . second thoughts prevailed. The decision was reversed. The scene is clearly stamped on my memory, more so than the actual decision . . . I believe it was the only occasion in the whole war on which, a firm decision having been reached, the Prime Minister changed his mind.'

Orders were then given that four more fighter squadrons should be sent to France immediately. Churchill's own account of that reads: '. . . the Cabinet had given me authority to move four more squadrons to France.' He made no mention of the appearance of Dowding before the Cabinet, of Dowding's statement, or of the decision reached that he, himself, reversed immediately after the meeting.

In the description that he gave of Winston Churchill's ability in sizing up men—in this instance Wavell—John Colville wrote: 'He was, of course, subjective in his assessment of people, and the main reason for his failure to establish a close relationship with Wavell was because Wavell was so unforthcoming.'

That is not altogether true of Wavell, but, in the face of political hectoring, it was in Dowding's character to be as 'unforthcoming' as his old school-friend. When, some months after this Cabinet meeting, Dowding told Wavell about what had happened, Wavell warned him that from that moment of crossing Churchill his days were numbered. Neither Wavell nor Dowding ever had any illusions about Churchill's opinions of military leaders. 'Churchill's sentiments about generals were ambivalent from his earliest youth onwards,' Wavell's biographer, John Connell, has written, 'He distrusted and despised them, yet he yearned to be himself a super-general. . . .'

There was never any doubt in Dowding's mind about his own distrust of politicians, and he has recalled that immediately after that Cabinet meeting he returned to his Headquarters 'fully expecting to receive a letter telling me that I was through'. That might well have come had not Churchill been too greatly pre-occupied with second thoughts about the decision that had only just been made in favour of Dowding's plea.

'I did not know Winston Churchill, although I had met him, and I was certainly never friendly with him,' Dowding once explained. 'After the meeting of 15 May there was no chance of our ever becoming friendly. I had opposed him, and he had had to change his very stubborn mind in front of a large gathering of senior officers and officials over a very important issue. I've always felt that he didn't like it.'

In a further comment on what happened, A. J. P. Taylor has gone even further than that in his assessment of Winston Churchill's reaction. Speaking of what might have happened, he wrote: 'If he had had his way, British fighter squadrons would have been sent unavailingly to France, and victory in the Battle of Britain would have been jeopardized.' Taylor then continued: 'Dowding, the head of Fighter Command, resisted this generous impulse—a resistance which Churchill did not forgive.'

Keith Park has spoken of what he has called 'the personal conflict' between Dowding and the Air Ministry. He has described it as beginning 'long before the war started in 1939 when the Air Ministry failed to supply the C.-in-C. of Fighter Command with the squadrons, the radar and other equipment which he had been promised for the effective air defence of Great Britain.'

'I agree broadly with Park's statement,' Dowding commented on that; and in an attempt to strike a fair balance, he added: 'But I should be surprised if it could be shown that at any time I allowed fair comment to become personal recrimination.'

In writing about his own experiences at that time, General Pile recalled with vigour his understanding of Dowding's position, and what he said is of particular value in that it comes from an Army officer of such seniority venturing to express an opinion from a source outside the Royal Air Force. 'Daily he became more anxious as his squadrons were removed from him; he used to tell me that it was like pouring water into the sands of the desert,' Pile wrote. 'Within two or three days of their arrival in France the squadrons had been so decimated as barely to exist.'

In his own thoughts, Pile admitted, 'the rest of us were so engrossed in the drama of the retreating British Army, of the heroic defence of Calais, and of the slender hope there seemed to be of getting anyone back, that the future in which an invasion of this country was likely hardly worried us.' But, he added, 'Dowding had only one thought: how he could retain sufficient fighter squadrons and anti-aircraft guns to fight the battle which he so clearly foresaw was inevitable.'

This was a time—in May, 1940—when those who were the leaders, or who were to become leaders, were all necessarily larger than life. And yet there was a pattern; there had to be a pattern. They could not all be great individualists, or eccentrics, flaring off in all directions.

On the other hand, as John Colville has said of the views expressed by Lord Moran on Winston Churchill, 'the subject had to be made to fit into the accepted framework.' And 'fitting him into an accepted framework' could not be done with Churchill. It was also impossible to do with Dowding. Churchill was conditioned, as far as it was possible to condition him, by what Colville has described as 'the rancour and asperity of party politics', but he was a great individualist before that. Dowding was also an individualist, conditioned by a lifetime of military discipline; but he shared with Churchill that quality of always being himself before any other influence could be brought to bear on him. The other great quality that Dowding shared with Churchill was that of fearlessness. It was that which led him to take his next step.

Dowding's distrust of any decisions that politicians might make was such that he was compelled to take further action to drive home to authority the seriousness of the position as he saw it. As soon as he got back to his Headquarters, and while the little group was still talking in the garden of No. 10 Downing Street, he set to work committing to paper his thoughts about all that was happening and was likely to happen.

'He didn't say anything to me or, so far as I know, to anybody else about what had happened at the meeting,' Francis Wilkinson recalled, 'but immediately afterwards I talked with somebody who was there, and from what I was told I got the strong impression that Stuffy had won the day.'

'There was a very great deal on my mind when I came to prepare that statement,' Dowding later admitted. 'They had been nibbling away at my Command, and I was already down to thirty-six squadrons against the fifty-two that I was supposed to have. There had already been serious enough casualties in France, and they alone were worrying me a very great deal. I had to know how much longer the drain was going on, and I had to ask for a figure at which they would shut the stable door and say no more squadrons would be sent to France.'

Of what effect he expected that any further statement that he made might have, Dowding said: 'I didn't really expect to get a direct answer. I meant that this letter should be shown to the Prime Minister, so that he himself would stop making these demands. I couldn't ask for an interview with the War Cabinet every time a new demand was made. It had to be a strong statement of the case, made once and for all. That was why I wrote it.'

In the last resort, there was another card that Dowding had up his sleeve about which nothing has ever been said and about which, as it happened, nothing was done because there was no need for it. 'I'm sure, from what he said, that Stuffy at one time seriously thought about trying to stop them by using the broadcast that he had had to make just before the war,' Francis Wilkinson has commented. 'Churchill was trying in every way possible to get more fighters for France, and Stuffy knew that he would go on trying to get them because the French were crying out for more and more fighter squadrons. And it was more than Stuffy could stand. He had to put his foot down.'

When Dowding had been asked to reassure the British people in his broadcast in 1939 that with the fighter strength that he had he could protect the country, 'he did it on the understanding that he was to have a minimum of fifty-two squadrons,' Wilkinson has pointed out. 'He could so easily have made it known that if he had to go on doing what they were asking for and keep on sending more and more squadrons to France then he would have to say publicly, in some way or other, that all his plans for the defence of the country were being wrecked, and so tell the British people, "I'm not now in a position to guarantee your safety." It would have shaken everybody to the core, and it would have meant an awful lot of trouble for Stuffy. But I am sure he would have done it, regardless of the trouble that it would have caused him, if he had been forced that far.'

On one occasion, in discussing the mood that he was in when he came to prepare that letter, Dowding admitted that it was one almost of despair. But there is no sign of that in what he wrote.

Immaculately typed on two sheets of official foolscap bearing the heading of the Headquarters of Fighter Command, and addressed formally to the Under Secretary of State at the Air Ministry, it speaks for itself with a clear, ringing call to reason and to arms. Dowding wrote:

I have the honour to refer to the very serious calls which have recently been made upon the Home Defence Fighter Units in an attempt to stem the German invasion on the Continent.

I hope and believe that our Armies may yet be victorious in France and Belgium, but we have to face the possibility that they may be defeated.

In this case I presume that there is no-one who will deny that England should fight on, even though the remainder of the Continent of Europe is dominated by the Germans.

For this purpose it is necessary to retain some minimum fighter strength in this country and I must request that the Air Council will inform me what they consider this minimum strength to be, in order that I may make my dispositions accordingly.

I would remind the Air Council that the last estimate which they made as to the force necessary to defend this country was 52 Squadrons, and my strength has now been reduced to the equivalent of 36 Squadrons.

Once a decision has been reached as to the limit on which the Air Council and the Cabinet are prepared to stake the existence of the country, it should be made clear to the Allied Commanders on the Continent that not a single aeroplane from Fighter Command beyond the limit will be sent across the Channel, no matter how desperate the situation may become.

It will, of course, be remembered that the estimate of 52 Squadrons was based on the assumption that the attack would come from the eastwards except in so far as the defences might be outflanked in flight. We have now to face the possibility that attacks may come from Spain or even from the North coast of France. The result is that our line is very much extended at the same time as our resources are reduced.

I must point out that within the last few days the equivalent of 10 Squadrons have been sent to France, that the Hurricane Squadrons remaining in this country are seriously depleted, and that the more Squadrons which are sent to France the higher will be the wastage and the more insistent the demands for reinforcements.

I must therefore request that as a matter of paramount urgency the Air Ministry will consider and decide what level of strength is to be left to the Fighter Command for the defences of this country, and will assure me that when this level has been reached, not one fighter will be sent across the Channel however urgent and insistent the appeals for help may be.

I believe that, if an adequate fighter force is kept in this country, if the fleet remains in being, and if Home Forces are suitably organized to resist invasion, we should be able to carry on the war single handed for some time, if not indefinitely. But, if the Home Defence Force is drained away in desperate attempts to remedy the situation in France, defeat in France will involve the final, complete and irremediable defeat of this country.

This letter is now looked upon as one of the important documents of the early stages of the Second World War. The original is framed and hangs in a place of honour in the Royal Air Force College at Cranwell.

CHAPTER SIX

TIME FOR RESOLUTION

Even while Dowding was starting work on his urgent and eloquent plea to the Air Ministry for a clear statement of what it was that they expected of him, and what resources were to be provided, the decision that had only just been reached at the Cabinet meeting was reversed, and the necessary steps were taken immediately to put into effect the new one. Orders that four more squadrons should go to France were passed to the Air Staff at the Air Ministry. It was the duty of the Deputy Chief of the Air Staff, Air Vice-Marshal W. S. (now Marshal of the R.A.F. Lord) Douglas to implement these orders, and it was his suggestion that instead of sending four complete squadrons there should be sent eight half squadrons.

The way in which this was handled has been explained by Sholto Douglas in the statement: 'The actual Cabinet instruction to us had been for four squadrons; but I managed to get an interpretation of that approved in the form of the eight flights. By doing it in that way I felt that we would at least preserve in this country the nucleus of the eight squadrons, and the draining away of the strength of Fighter Command would not be so severe.'

Despite Douglas's claim that 'it was part of my work to know what Dowding was thinking, and to be thoroughly familiar with the plans that he was making,' his suggestion about making use of half squadrons was of no appeal whatsoever to Dowding. In his official despatch he commented: 'This was done under the impression that the loss of eight Half-Squadrons would affect me less than that of four entire Squadrons, because it was supposed that I should be able to rebuild on the nuclei left behind. But this assumption was incorrect because I had neither the time nor the personnel available for purposes of reconstruction, and the remaining half-squadrons had to be amalgamated into Composite Units with a resulting disorganisation and loss of efficiency.' In addition to that, Dowding pointed out, he was 'ordered to

withdraw trained pilots from squadrons and to send them overseas as reinforcements.'

The impression that was made in Whitehall by Dowding's
letter of 16 May was immediate, and the strength of that is
reflected in the action that the Chief of the Air Staff took as
soon as he received it. He prepared a paper under the heading
'The Air Defence of Great Britain' for his fellow Chiefs of
Staff. To it Newall attached a copy of Dowding's letter,
referring to it as raising 'the final issue of a problem which
must have been in the forefront of all our minds in the last
few days, and which is of such vital importance to the security
of this country and the empire . . .' He asked the other Chiefs
of Staff to support him in putting forward to the War Cabinet
the expression of these views.

In referring to what Dowding had had to say, Newall pointed
out that the Air Council had come to the conclusion before
the war that theoretically the minimum strength of Fighter
Command should be 53 squadrons, with the necessary reserves.
'Even that was on the assumption that the bases for the enemy
attacks would be confined to Germany,' he added to what
Dowding had said, going on from that to say that there had
obviously been an increase in the requirements with the occupation of Norway and still more the occupation of Holland.

'Our strength in this country has now been reduced to 37
squadrons,' Newall stated; and even these squadrons, he pointed
out, had already suffered in operations on the Continent.
'Our reserves of fully equipped fighters . . . are totally inadequate
to meet the very high rate of wastage now being incurred in
the battle in France,' he warned.

In a reference to Dowding's comment about England possibly
having to fight on alone, Newall added the view: 'If this
situation should arise we shall . . . be faced with a very powerful
enemy bomber force, that can be escorted by fighters, with
bases stretching over 1,000 miles from Norway to the western
point of Europe.'

With these considerations firmly in mind, Newall stated that
he could come to no conclusion 'other than that we have
already reached the absolute limit of the air assistance that we

can afford to France, if we are to have any chance of protecting the United Kingdom, the Fleet, our sea-borne trade, our aircraft industry, and all the vital centres throughout the country on which we must depend for our ability to continue the war.'

The issue, Newall pointed out, was 'grave to the last degree'. He pointed out that if it were decided not to send any further fighters to France, or to give fighter support from squadrons based in England, the French army might give up. On the other hand, the constant drain on the vital defences of this country in order to sustain the French could lead to the disappearance of our own ability to defend our own country.

'I do not believe that to throw in a few more squadrons whose loss might vitally weaken the fighter line at home, would make the difference between victory and defeat in France,' Newall stated. He added to Dowding's final comment the words: 'It can, however, be said with absolute certainty that while the collapse of France would not necessarily mean the ultimate victory of Germany, the collapse of Great Britain would inevitably do so.'

The day before, at the Cabinet meeting, Dowding had found Newall lacking in the support that he felt that he had the right to expect from the Chief of the Air Staff. There could be no doubt about Newall's support now in the great effort that he made to win approval for a united backing of the view held by Dowding and the Royal Air Force on the needs for the defence of the country.

During that night the situation in France deteriorated still further, and the next day Winston Churchill flew to Paris to see the French Premier. He has left an ample record of his dismay over what he discovered. That dismay can be understood, but only up to a point. As Ian Jacob has put it: 'In his military thinking Churchill was a curious blend of old and new.' At this time there can be little doubt that he was out-of-date in that thinking. To that there was added the fact that, for all his contacts, he had been out of touch for a long time with first-hand developments. 'He tended to think in terms of "sabres and bayonets",' Jacob has commented. Churchill was also unquestionably deeply influenced at the Paris meetings by his own emotional response to the appalling position that the French were in.

The French Premier made a fervent plea for more R.A.F. fighters, and, despite all that Dowding had said only the day before, Churchill was won over. He sent an urgent request to the Cabinet in London for six more fighter squadrons to be sent to France. 'I again emphasised the mortal gravity of the hour,' he stated. Lord Ismay was with Churchill in Paris, and he handled the details of the actual transmission of the message and the reply; and Commander C. R. Thompson, Churchill's Personal Assistant, was also there. All three have recorded in published books that the cabinet replied immediately to Churchill's request with a firm agreement that these squadrons would be sent. This information was passed on by Churchill to the French, and he records in a markedly florid fashion the general jubilation and expressions of relief that were expressed that there should be forthcoming such wonderful support.

But for all that has been recorded by the principals in this affair, there was no such blanket agreement to Churchill's request, and these accounts are lacking in their telling of the full story. At the Cabinet meeting which was held in London late that night to consider the Churchill request there was naturally very serious consideration given to what was being asked for. Everybody present was acutely conscious of the situation as it had been made clear to them by Dowding in person only the day before. Now Cyril Newall and others had Dowding's letter, which, in its broad scope, left no room for any doubts about the gravity of the overall situation so far as these precious fighters were concerned.

Newall also had at hand all the information that he needed about the airfields that were still available for use in France in the face of the rapid advance by the German army. From that, as he pointed out to the meeting, it was obvious that there was not sufficient room to accommodate six more squadrons, even if it had been possible to send them to France. He argued strongly in support of Dowding's case for a consideration now of the position of Fighter Command.

From the strong view that Cyril Newall was able to present at the meeting it was obvious that the request from Paris for the six squadrons would have to be treated in some different way from that of merely sending them off to France. It was impossible to agree to the request in full, and it was not agreed to in the way in which it has been reported. Instead it was agreed that six squadrons for use in France should be based at forward airfields in the south of England. From these bases they would operate out over France, merely landing there for refuelling and rearming, but returning to their bases in England at the end of the day's work. This was a compromise won by Newall, and it was in Dowding's favour.

'I was glad to hear that Newall had the guts to fight for that,' Dowding commented long afterwards.

It is curious that Winston Churchill and the others who have written so authoritatively about this vitally important affair should have seen fit to record with such firmness this decision without offering the qualification that accompanied it. It could be argued that at the moment in Paris the message received by Ismay and immediately passed on to Churchill, and by him to the French, was a confirmation of the request for the six squadrons. The personal arrangement made by Ismay was for one word to be passed to him if there was agreement: the Hindustani for 'yes'. It came in that form. But out of that one word too much was made, and it led to incorrect information being given to the French. It also led later, to these incorrect versions being recorded of what was actually decided upon that night in London.

'At the time,' Dowding has recalled, 'I knew that Churchill was under tremendous pressure from the French to supply them with reinforcements. What I was so afraid of was that it would go beyond even that, and that what the French really wanted Churchill to do was to give them our whole fighter force, and for it all to be commanded by their generals in France. That would have meant the end of the war, because the French were already beaten.'

The demands from France for help came in all shapes and forms and sizes, and from various sources, often finishing up in the ears of recipients least able to do anything about them. One such demand at this time found its way to the Headquarters of No. 11 Group at Uxbridge.

'Through being able to speak French fairly fluently, I was called to the phone to cope with a call from General Georges,'

John Willoughby de Broke has recalled. 'It was nothing to do with me, but I did know that he was one of the senior French commanders, and here he was on the line from the other side of the Channel. Heaven knows how he got put through to us at 11 Group, but there he was on the phone and I had to listen to him, and he didn't half tell me what he thought about the lack of fighter support from us.'

Of what was happening at that time in France as well as elsewhere, one critic wrote recently: 'Thirty years afterwards it seems strange that the inevitability of what happened was not foreseen.' Stranger still were the extraordinary lengths to which so many responsible authorities saw fit to go, or were induced to go, in voicing opinions that were so contrary to what was actually happening. Propaganda was one thing: sheer blind stupidity was something else altogether.

An instance of that has been offered by Alistair Horne, without making any comment, in a quotation from the influential French newspaper *Le Temps*. In its issue of 16 May there was published the statement: 'If our tanks are distinctly superior to those of the enemy, our fighters dominate perhaps even more the enemy air force.' That was said at the very moment when the French Premier was imploring Winston Churchill to send more R.A.F. fighters to France to save the French from disaster.

In his own account of the events of those hectic hours in Paris which he later published in his own massive story on the Second World War, Winston Churchill made a statement which has given cause for Dowding to feel, ever since it was published, perplexity, some little anger, and no little embarrassment. Churchill wrote:

Air Chief Marshal Dowding, at the head of our metropolitan Fighter Command, had declared to me that with twenty-five squadrons of fighters he could defend the Island against the whole might of the German Air Force, but that with less he would be overpowered.

Some years ago, in commenting on that, Dowding said: 'How Mr Churchill, as he was then, ever came to put such an absurd statement into my mouth I simply do not know. I had just been waging a desperate battle in the Cabinet to be allowed to retain the equivalent of 36 squadrons against the 52 squadrons which was the Air Staff estimate of my requirements. Is it reasonable to suppose that I then told Mr Churchill personally that 25 would suffice? The suggestion is ridiculous. Furthermore, there was no opportunity for me to have given any personal estimate of my requirements to Mr Churchill before the Cabinet meeting and his departure for France. I had no contact with him at all. It is not for me to speculate on the origin of this mistake; I can only repeat categorically that I did not make, and in fact could not have made, such an absurd underestimate of the requirements of my Command.'

This assessment credited to Dowding by Winston Churchill has become accepted by historians, because of the authority of Churchill's name, as a true evaluation of the needs of Fighter Command, even though, in fact, it is quite erroneous. That acceptance has caused Dowding embarrassment because, as he has pointed out, it so grossly misrepresents, and has been allowed to go on misrepresenting, his views on the needs of those desperate times. One very well known Air Marshal, a contemporary of Dowding's, even published in a book a few years ago the comment: 'If this statement was truthful, and there is no reason to suppose that it was not, then Air Chief Marshal Dowding was at fault.'

Faced with repeated misrepresentations even after making his first statement, Dowding has asked: 'What can one say about Churchill's statement other than that it was totally untrue? I repeat that I never discussed such a point with him. I'd never had any opportunity to discuss with him anything about any such matter until the Cabinet meeting of 15 May, and then the point I made was only about the Hurricane wastage in the squadrons that were being sent to France. We had no other meeting at that time, and the subject that he claimed we'd discussed never came up.'

One perplexing aspect of this statement of Winston Churchill's is the revelation that, for all the briefing given him and for all his examination of the facts, he could not have understood the requirements that had been agreed upon for the strength of Fighter Command. Churchill once said of his own knowledge at this time about the fighting on the land that 'not having access to official information for so many years, I did not comprehend the violence of the revolution effected since the last war by the incursion of a mass of fast-moving heavy armour.'

From what Churchill credited Dowding with saying it would also appear that he did not comprehend at any time the hard facts of the needs, which had been agreed to, of Fighter Command; and this presents a quite remarkable state of affairs in relation to the important cabinet meeting of 15 May. For all that was said, Churchill must have been thinking then, only a few hours before, and unknown to everybody else, in terms of a minimum strength for Fighter Command of twenty-five squadrons. The only alternative to that is that there was some other reason in Churchill's mind for passing the responsibility to Dowding by alleging that he made a statement that it would have been impossible for him to make.

Why did Winston Churchill make this statement? And what led him to go on believing that Dowding had made such a very wrong assessment of his needs, and go on repeating that? Was it that assessment which led Churchill to make his further demand from Paris for another six squadrons for France, believing that there was still a safe margin? If that is true, and if his request had been agreed to in the manner which Churchill records, again incorrectly, in his book, the Battle of Britain would have been lost before it was even fought.

One of the more tiresome clichés bandied about by those who offer pretences to being knowledgeable is the comment that it is easy to be wise after the event. This has even gone so far as to cause reference to be made to a so-called view of the past that can be 'unclouded by hindsight'. That sounds as if it is considered that having the acumen to be able to evaluate what is past is some sort of mistake, whereas the mistake lies in allowing oneself to be so misled by such a cliché—or being so reluctant to face facts—that one is afraid of trying to be wise after the event. The question that must be posed is that surely one should be prepared to make the most of what one can learn from hindsight? Loose talk about being wise after the event is merely a glib excuse to avoid trying to exercise wisdom, and even possibly having to come to conclusions that are unpalatable.

It can be seen now that it was a good thing for Dowding's peace of mind that he did not know at the time about either this request of Winston Churchill's from Paris or the figures about Fighter Command strength that Churchill appeared to be harbouring in his mind. He had not been greatly surprised—although he strongly disapproved of the way in which it was done—when he was told to give up the eight half squadrons. It was with some measure of relief that he had to allow another six squadrons to operate from bases in the south of England instead of losing them through being based in France.

On the morning of that day, 17 May, when Dowding received that order for the last of his Hurricanes, Winston Churchill, who had arrived back in London, presided over a meeting of the War Cabinet and 'gave them an account' of his visit to Paris. 'I said I had told the French that unless they made a supreme effort we should not be justified in accepting the grave risk to the safety of our country that we were incurring by the dispatch of the additional fighter squadrons to France,' he wrote. To that he added: 'I felt that the question of air reinforcements was one of the gravest that a British Cabinet had ever had to face.'

Time was running out for the Allied cause in France. On 19 May, 'that fateful Sunday', as Denis Richards has described it, when the War Office and Admiralty had to face the possibility of the evacuation from France 'of a very large force in hazardous circumstances', more detailed consideration was given by the Cabinet to Dowding's letter of 16 May and Newall's appreciation of it. Richards referred further to 'the good sense of Newall and the obduracy of Dowding' which led to the Cabinet making a vitally important decision. The Prime Minister recorded that decision in a minute stating: 'No more squadrons of fighters will leave the country whatever the need of France.'

For Dowding this meant that, while there was still much to do in covering the evacuation from France, he could at least start to mend some fences.

During the latter part of May and on into June of that year of 1940, the slide into a state of chaos in the affairs of the Allies seemed to be heading straight for a major disaster. The anxiety felt by Dowding in his own grave concern is revealed in a comment that he made at the time to General Pile. Dowding's sole concern was with the dire need that had now developed to bring the defences of the country to the highest possible state of readiness; in his view that was the first consideration that should be taken into account.

There is also a touching compliment paid to Dowding's sincerity by Pile in his recording of that comment. At this time everybody's thoughts were on getting the Army back after the collapse in France. 'He even went so far as to say to me (a somewhat heroic thing to say to a soldier),' Pile wrote, 'that the best service the British Army could now render to its country was to lay down its arms and let such of the Air Force as could be salved return to this country for the ensuing battle.'

That must have been an unpalatable enough suggestion for Pile to have to digest. And yet he could still say of Dowding: 'He was continually on the telephone to the Air Ministry, to the Government, and always his back was against the wall— the one man who stood out firmly for the fact that, provided an adequate fighter force could be maintained in this country, even if the Army was lost, all was not necessarily lost.'

With the collapse in France, and the defence against the Germans in such shattering disarray, there came the need for yet further reassessments of the position in which Britain found herself. Commenting on our relationship with France at the time of Munich, twenty-one months before, Sir John Slessor wrote: '. . . it is horrifying to recall the extent of our ignorance about the military policy and the forces of the nation to whom by 1938 we were morally and practically, though not yet formally, committed . . .' By June, 1940, we had learnt, to our cost, that our partner had no military policy, and that her armed forces had fallen on very evil days.

It was no surprise for Dowding, saddened though he was at the fall of an old ally, but there was much in the past that gave him cause to be a realist about that. He was now a man of years—fifty-eight of them—and of a military understanding that was more comprehensive than that of many of those with whom he was working. His military career had started forty years before, during that far off era of the Boer War. There might have been some excuse for those who did not know him when they ventured to think that because of age alone he was becoming too old for the job: but anybody who felt that way obviously did not know him.

Age had made of Dowding more than a man of wisdom. It had produced a mind that was exceptionally alert, and it was an undeniable fact that his vision, and his skill in creating Fighter Command as he did, put him ahead of most of our leaders, and in a category where he stood head and shoulders above everybody in his understanding of the acute problems that were attached to his particular field. The fact that he was under notice to quit and would shortly have to relinquish his Command had been pushed into the back of his mind, and he thought only of how that Command of his was best to serve the purpose for which it had been created.

Fortunately for Britain—and through that for all the rest of the free world as well—this one far-seeing and experienced expert in the use of fighters was there resolutely in command of the defence of the country. He was fully prepared to fight against any influence that might threaten the strength of his Command, and his disagreements with the Air Ministry alone were by then becoming well known.

'I have been asked if I could not have settled those disagreements by more frequent personal visits,' Dowding once commented, 'and it may be that a just criticism lies behind that question.' Describing it as 'probably a defect in my character,' he has said that his experience has led him to believe that 'a stage in personal relations can be reached where more harm than good is done by verbal discussion'.

The matter of Dowding's seniority in rank also made it additionally difficult for him and the other senior officers with whom he had to work to come to terms with an easy give-and-take. 'I was senior to everyone at the Air Ministry with whom there could be anything to discuss,' he has pointed out; and without any wish to be at all pompous he has added: 'It was neither pleasant nor easy to have one's recommendations turned down by somebody who had quite recently been one's direct subordinate.'

That it would have been easy enough to have remained on good terms with the Air Staff, Dowding has admitted quite readily. 'But it would have meant that I would have had to be content to accept too many rulings without question,' he said. 'And since, in my view, the defence of the country had been allowed for too long to exist in a state of grave inefficiency, I was continually having to fight that situation while there was yet time.'

The relief for Dowding when the final decision was made that no more fighters should go to France was very great, but he could not spare it anything more than passing attention. 'The withdrawal of seven squadrons from France has converted a desperate into a serious situation,' he commented at the time. During the ten days between 8 and 18 May some two hundred and fifty Hurricanes had been lost by the ten squadrons that had been operating in France. As Dowding had pointed out at the meeting on 15 May, at this rate the entire Hurricane force of the R.A.F. would soon have been wiped out.

'Now the rate of loss in this country,' he wrote towards the end of May, 'has been reduced to about eight aircraft per diem.' He estimated that, after allowing for exaggerated claims, it was possible that three or four enemy aircraft were being brought down to every one lost by the R.A.F. 'This is a great, but insufficient, improvement,' he commented; but 'if we continue to exchange casualties on this scale we shall eventually be worn down by the weight of superior numbers.'

On the distinct advantages of actually fighting over England rather than France, Dowding offered the view that 'when a fighter is shot down, the pilot is seldom killed, and in many instances the damage to the aircraft is quite trivial and can be repaired quickly, provided that the machine descends in our own territory.' When that happens, he pointed out, the pilot and the aircraft could be flying again in a matter of days. 'Even when an aircraft is irreparably damaged in air combat, the pilot may descend by parachute and be immediately available again.'

The immediate worry for Dowding was that the present fighting out over the Channel and France during those last stages of the evacuation from Dunkirk was uneconomical because his home defence fighters were really being used in an overseas fighting role. 'I have hitherto made it almost an article of faith to preserve the Spitfire squadrons for Home Defence fighting,' he commented. But the various roles that Dowding had been ordered to undertake had made that quite impossible, and in addition to the hard-pressed Hurricane squadrons the Spitfire squadrons in No. 11 Group were now also in the fight and heavily committed, 'and are doing two or three sorties a day'.

That Fighter Command had its hands full even before the Battle of Britain started can be seen in the list—'the variety of tasks', as he called it—of Dowding's responsibilities. It covered a wide field of staggering variety, and included among other things, general protection of the Channel ports by continuous standing patrols, specific protection of individual ports during a particular operation, providing fighter escorts for bomber formations operating by day, continuous sweeps throughout daylight hours of areas in which fighting was taking place, continuous night patrols over Boulogne, specified tasks of relieving troops from the attentions of enemy observation aircraft and dive bombers, escorting convoys of food for the Field Force, carrying distinguished personages under escort to various destinations by air, dispatching secret documents to the Expeditionary Force Headquarters, and convoying of block-ships to Ostend and Zeebrugge.

'Each special requirement comes through at short notice and is more urgent and immediate than the last,' Dowding commented a little ruefully at the time.

While the British Expeditionary Force was still in some sort of existence—even if being evacuated from France—Dowding fully realised that it was, in his words, 'impossible to ignore their requirements for air protection.' But he felt compelled to sound the warning: 'All such fighting militates against the maintenance of a force adequate to protect this country in the event of our having to carry on the war single-handed against a Power possessed of all the resources of Europe.'

Going beyond that warning, Dowding voiced to the Air

Ministry yet another plea. 'I earnestly beg,' he wrote, 'that my commitments may be limited as far as possible unless it is the intention of the Government to surrender the country in the event of a decisive defeat in France.'

When he came to consider that plea many years later, Dowding chuckled and made the somewhat wry comment: 'That was rather cheeky.'

But Dowding was finding, even at that early stage, that his squadrons in the south of England were already beginning to show signs of tiredness, and he realised that he would have to relieve them by a system of rotation with squadrons from the midlands and the north. Moreover, if the forces across the Channel did manage to re-establish some sort of line, and the battle continued in France, he could see fighters being lost at the same rate as before. That would lead, in turn, to 'wrecking the Home Defence Units'.

Since, as Dowding put it in casting his thoughts ahead, 'air superiority must be maintained in this country if an invasion is to be prevented,' and 'the combined efforts of the Navy and Army alone will not suffice,' he made one of his more far-reaching suggestions, and went beyond the affairs of his own Command. He asked the Air Ministry if Bomber Command could be assigned to attacks 'mainly or exclusively on objectives which will slow up the impetus of the German air attack'. As he saw it, 'damage done to crossroads or railway sidings is very quickly repaired, but damage done to enemy aerodromes and aircraft on the ground will have an immediate effect, while the destruction of industrial plant and oil stocks will have an effect which, though slower, may prove to be decisive.'

In all that he placed on record in his appreciation of Dowding, General Pile is another of those who has spoken with authority of Dowding's great technical understanding of his needs and his shrewd ability to evaluate them. 'It is hard to exaggerate his influence on the new aircraft and new weapons that were almost daily being brought into production,' Pile wrote. 'When Lord Beaverbrook was Minister for Aircraft Production (a Minister who, I think, must be unequalled in the way he regarded us all as customers to be satisfied) he used to ring Dowding and myself up each day and ask what more he could do for us. On many occasions I was in Dowding's room when the call came through, and always there was a string of requests, and sometimes even of grouses. Dowding's cry was always for more and more speed . . .'

After the fall of France and the evacuation from that unhappy country, Dowding finally had a real opportunity of learning something at first hand about just what had gone on out there. In place of Keith Park as his Senior Air Staff Officer he received Air Vice-Marshal D. C. S. (now Air Chief Marshal Sir Douglas) Evill. Through his own experiences, Evill was particularly well-qualified to speak about what had happened to the Air Force in its attempts to support the French.

Another of the young naval officers who had learnt to fly before the First World War, Strath Evill, as he is known, had gone from the Royal Naval Air Service to the Royal Air Force when it was first formed in 1918. Over the years between the wars he established his reputation—he finished his career in the R.A.F. as Vice Chief of the Air Staff—as a staff officer of exceptional ability. Evill quickly became known at the Headquarters of Fighter Command as a man of a particularly pleasant and sincere nature; and, being of the quiet type to which it genuinely meant so much, he shared with Dowding the ideal of Manners.

When the Second World War broke out, Evill had gone out as Senior Air Staff Officer to the Air Officer Commanding-in-Chief of the British Air Forces in France. The operations in the final withdrawal of the R.A.F. from France were under his direct control, and his experiences in that task alone had been hectic. Now he was to be Dowding's S.A.S.O., and he was to continue in that office throughout the Battle of Britain and the Blitz that was to follow it. Evill was as aware as anybody of the heavy losses that were suffered by the R.A.F. in France. In May and June the total had been 959 aircraft, all, in Denis Richards' words, 'to little apparent avail'. Of that total, to Dowding's great distress, 477 were his precious fighters.

'When the Dunkerque evacuation was complete I had only 3 Day-Fighting Squadrons which had not been engaged in Continental fighting,' Dowding wrote in his despatch, 'and

12 Squadrons were in the line for the second time after having been withdrawn to rest and re-form.'

By July, Strath Evill was well settled into his work as Dowding's Senior Air Staff Officer, which meant dealing with the mass of detail having to do with operations that it was the S.A.S.O's task to handle for the Commander-in-Chief. The service that he was to render during the Battle of Britain has been rather overlooked. 'I could not have had a sounder or more reliable man supporting me during that time,' Dowding once commented. 'He was always there, always on the job, and always so pleasant in that quiet way of his.'

But for all that, and as with so many others, even Evill did not know very much about what was happening in Dowding's affairs having to do with his appointment, or about Dowding's strictly personal views on those affairs. But there was an understanding which enabled them to work well together, and there were rare exchanges between them which revealed a warm underlying humour in their relationship. An illustration of that occurred in my own experience later in the year, after the Germans had started their bombing at night.

Both Dowding and Evill were at work in their offices, and it was approaching midnight. The Personal Assistant's office was between those occupied by the C.-in-C. and the S.A.S.O., with doors which enabled them to go to and from each other's offices, through the P.A.'s, without having to go outside. The sound of aircraft and anti-aircraft fire could be heard, but it was a sound that, in its familiarity, attracted no attention until suddenly there was the reverberating crash of a bomb not far away, and apparently in the grounds of Bentley Priory. That immediately attracted attention.

There was the sound of Dowding moving out of his chair at his desk. He came out of his office, walked across in front of my desk with only a quick glance, and went into the S.A.S.O.'s office.

'Did you hear that, Evill,' I heard Dowding ask.

'I did, sir,' Evill answered.

Dowding was in one of his lighter moods. 'Well . . . what are you going to do about it?' he asked.

'There's only one thing I think can be done, sir,' Evill replied. 'I'll write a letter to Fighter Command about it.'

But that was a rare example of the more informal exchanges that occurred between these two men, both of whom were by nature so reticent. It was not until two years later, after he had left Fighter Command, that Evill came to learn of an incident which, to him, illustrated the full depth of Dowding's feeling about the position that Britain was placed in when France capitulated. He heard about it during the time when he was serving in the United States. The British ambassador in Washington was then Lord Halifax, and at the embassy there, Halifax described one day to Evill a visit that he had made, while he was Foreign Secretary, to Dowding's Headquarters in June, 1940.

During the talk that Halifax had with Dowding that day, he told Evill, they discussed what had just happened in the fall of France. After a while Dowding got up from his desk and went to one of the windows. He stood there in silence for a moment, looking out towards Harrow Weald. Then he turned back and faced Halifax.

'Thank God we're now alone,' Dowding said.

CHAPTER SEVEN

ON GUARD

After the fall of France, and with Britain finding herself standing alone, additional pressure was exerted to round out the structure of Fighter Command. In addition to the two principal Groups—Nos. 11 and 12—there were No. 10 Group covering the western part of Britain, and No. 13 the northern part of England and Scotland. No. 10 Group was under the command of Air Vice-Marshal Sir Quintin Brand, a South African who, like Park the New Zealander, had made his career in the R.A.F., and who was a pioneer in night fighting and in long-distance flying. No. 13 Group was commanded by Air Vice-Marshal R. E. Saul.

It is in a comparison between the men who were in high command in the Royal Air Force and those in the Luftwaffe that there is to be found an intensely interesting and revealing difference between the two air forces. The senior commanders in the R.A.F. were all men whose whole lives had been devoted entirely to military aviation, and whose careers had been a matter of steady progress up the ladder of promotion in training, experience and command. Dowding himself was an example of that, and his four Group Commanders—Park, Leigh-Mallory, Brand and Saul—had all progressed in the same fashion of unbroken continuity from the time when, after joining the Royal Flying Corps as youngsters in the First World War, they had served together as squadron commanders in the last year of the war.

The commanders in the Luftwaffe had not been so fortunate, and in comparison with the careers of their opponents their own experience had been shorter and much more haphazard, and totally at the mercy of violent political manoeuvering. Also, they were a more integrated part of a great military machine, in which the Luftwaffe played a role that was essentially a tactical one in support of the German army.

'I wouldn't like to differentiate between the material and the aircrews of the Luftwaffe and the Royal Air Force,'

Dowding once said about the actual flying side of the air forces that were lining themselves up for the coming contest. 'In technical skill and in courage we could claim no superiority over the Germans, although there was, of course, a very great difference in spirit. I don't think that any higher degree of skill and courage could possibly have been expected.'

A comparison between the actual structures of command of the opposing air powers—the German on the one side of the Channel and the British on the other all the way from the organisation of flights of aircraft right up to the high command —also reveals an extraordinary dissimilarity. 'I don't think there can be any doubt about our greater efficiency there,' Dowding said. 'We had evolved a system continuously over a long period of time. Their structure was the result of a rapid and entirely different development, although they did have more fighting experience than we did under modern conditions, in the Spanish Civil War and the campaign in Poland. And they also had to contend with the awkward fact that there was one man—one man's brain, if one may call Hitler's that, and a thoroughly uneducated one so far as the air was concerned—at the head of all their affairs.'

By the first week of July the indications of increasing enemy activity in the air were sufficient for Dowding to make certain that he was in very close touch with the Chiefs of Staff Committee—through the Air Ministry—and the Army and Navy commanders in the south of England. He called in all his Group Commanders for discussions about various points having to do with the possibility of invasion which had arisen out of an Air Ministry conference held at that time on this subject.

'I received my general instructions, and a priority of targets to be engaged when a choice presented itself, from the Air Council,' he recorded of the orders that had been given in case the enemy invaded. It was his understanding that he would go on receiving guidance from that source.

In presenting at this time his own personal views about what was likely to happen, Dowding commented: 'It is difficult to prophesy the exact sequence of events in an attempted invasion;

but it appears at least possible that the enemy might not launch any seaborne attack in heavy ships or barges until he had established a *pied-à-terre* somewhere on the coast by means of troops, guns, and even tanks, transported by air.' He did not think that the Royal Navy might have much to do 'in the opening phase of the battle'.

Well to the fore in Dowding's thoughts was the possible use by the enemy of parachute troops and gliders or troop-carriers which, he thought, might lead to an attempt being made to capture one of the aerodromes close to the sea. Hawkinge and Manston were foremost in his mind. If that were to be successful, he imagined that the enemy would 'continue pouring in troops and material by means of more carriers, combined with a beach landing in the vicinity.' He saw 'the eventual aim' of that initial operation as 'the capture of a harbour at which heavy equipment could be disembarked'.

Bearing in mind what had happened in Holland in May, Dowding believed that if such an attempt were made by air it 'would be made with the utmost fury and disregard of casualties', and he saw the possibility of the enemy using 'an umbrella of standing fighter patrols designed to protect the comparatively defenceless troop-carriers and the bombers operating in support'.

Of his own duty in the event of such an attempt at an airborne landing, Dowding saw it as a matter of delivering 'continuous and unremitting attacks on the aircraft carrying troops and equipment so as to prevent any considerable body of troops being landed and putting themselves in a state of defence'. He drew on the experiences of what had happened during the German occupation of Norway as an example of how difficult it was 'to dislodge German troops once they have gained a foothold'.

If the Royal Navy were to become involved in any way, Dowding realised, as he had told them, that it would 'come under the protection of the fighter squadrons which would be continuously engaged at maximum strength in attacking every German aircraft in sight'. He spoke of the German dive bombers—the Stukas—as being 'a conspicuous and attractive target', and commented that they would 'receive at least their full share of the fighters' energies'. There was something of a prophecy in that of what was to happen, in the battle that lay ahead, to the unfortunate Stukas.

'One might estimate that every R.A.F. fighter squadron within 100 miles of the main battle would be fully engaged,' Dowding wrote at the time of what would happen if the enemy were to attempt to invade. But there was one other consideration that, he stressed, should not be overlooked. '. . . so far as I am concerned,' he wrote, 'I have no desire other than to afford every possible assistance and protection to the Navy because I realise that, invasion or no invasion, we lose the war if we lose the command of the sea.'

In his speech in June, Winston Churchill also made detailed reference to what might soon be expected, and that Fighter Command and its air crews bore a fearful responsibility was made abundantly clear. His statement is very well-known, but it is worth recalling as a summary of what Dowding and his Command were about to face.

Upon this battle depends the survival of Christian civilization. Upon it depends our own British life, and the long continuity of our institutions and our Empire. The whole fury and might of the enemy must very soon be turned on us. Hitler knows that he will have to break us in this Island or lose the war. If we can stand up to him, all Europe may be free and the life of the world may move forward into broad, sunlit uplands. But if we fail, then the whole world, including the United States, including all that we have known and cared for, will sink into the abyss of a new Dark Age, made more sinister, and perhaps more protracted, by the lights of perverted science. Let us therefore brace ourselves to our duties, and so bear ourselves that, if the British Empire and its Commonwealth last for a thousand years, men will still say: 'This was their finest hour.'

On the personal level of Dowding's involvement, Francis Wilkinson said: 'It was entirely his foresight in being able to see where the strain was going to come, and to be able to take the measure of that strain, which allowed Fighter Command to bear the enormous, almost unbearable load that it had when the fighting came. Stuffy had foreseen that our fighter squadrons were going to be depleted in strength. He had foreseen that Sector Operations Rooms would be bombed. And he'd made plans for the rapid interchange of squadrons between Scotland and northern England and the south. If it hadn't been for his colossal foresight and meticulous planning right from the very beginning, we'd have had it.'

The ringing words of the Prime Minister's warning and the stimulation that Dowding and those who were under his command were made aware of on the eve of the onslaught were accepted in a way that was typical of them. Denis Richards referred to that, with a feeling that has been deeply appreciated, when he wrote:

. . . it was this very slenderness of the fighting force, allied to the greatness of the issue, that has given to the Battle of Britain the quality of an epic. But 'epic' is a word which would certainly have drawn disrespectful comments from Dowding's pilots. For one of the supreme qualities of those young men—few of them were older than 25—was their light-hearted refusal to take either their dangers or their achievements seriously. They had that natural buoyancy of spirit which comes from robust youth, perfect health, and an adventurous disposition; they demanded of existence not that it should be long or leisured, but that it should be lively. In the main gloriously extrovert . . . they drank cheerfully of life with few questions as to the quality of the beverage; and if death struck the cup from their hands long before the dregs were reached, there were worse ends than one which was sudden, swift, and encountered in the service of what they held dear.

But for all the fine appreciation that is shown in that statement of the spirit of those who went to meet sudden death, attention must be called to the fate of those for whom death was not the end. Wounds, not the least of which was the striking of the hazard of fire which was so ever-present for the airman, caused for many, in addition to those of 'the few' who were afflicted, a lingering wonderment. But even that could not detract from what is, perhaps, the most touching comment made by Denis Richards on those who fought in the air during the summer of 1940. 'The Battle of Britain was fought by the gayest company who ever fired their guns in anger,' he wrote. '. . . Dowding's pilots had something more than courage.'

There is a strong echo in that of the words of Walter Raleigh, the illustrious predecessor of Denis Richards in the ranks of the air historians. In 1922 there was published the first volume of the great history *The War in the Air*, which bore the sub-title 'The story of the part played in the Great War by the Royal Air Force'. Writing so soon after the ending of that war, Raleigh provided in his introduction to that first volume the most moving tribute to the new Air Force, and to the men who created it. In doing that he reminded the Service of something that it was never likely to forget; and it is worth noting what Raleigh had to say in 1922, and its bearing on the spirit of the R.A.F. on the eve of the great battle in 1940. He wrote:

The air service still flourishes; its health depends on a secret elixir of immortality, which enables a body to repair its severest losses. The name of this elixir is tradition, and the greatest of all the achievements of the air service is that in a very few years, under the hammer of war, it has fashioned and welded its tradition, and has made it sure. Critics who speak of what they have not felt and do not know have sometimes blamed the air service because, being young, it has not the decorum of age. The Latin poet said that it is decorous to die for one's country; in that decorum the service is perfectly instructed. But those who meet the members of a squadron in their hours of ease, among gramophones and pictorial works of art suggestive of luxury, forget that an actor in a tragedy, though he play his part nobly on the stage, is not commonly tragic in the green-room. If they desire intensity and gravity, let them follow the pilot out on to the aerodrome, and watch his face in its hood, when the chocks are pulled away, and he opens the throttle of the engine. No Greek sculpture is finer in its tendering of life and purpose. To see him at his best they would have to accompany him, through the storm of anti-aircraft guns, into those fields of air where every moment brings some new trial of the quickness of his brain and the steadiness of his nerve. He is now in the workshop where tradition is made, to be handed down as an heirloom to the coming genera-tions. It will not fail to reach them. The Royal Air Force is strong in the kind of virtue that propagates itself and attains to a life beyond a life. The tradition is safe.

The preserving of that tradition had been in the hands during the inter-war years of a small group of men of which Dowding was one. He had been among those who had laid the foundations for it in the first place, and now he was to be so much a part of the time of its severest testing. But at that time, on the eve of the start of the battle which he had long foreseen, all that Dowding knew for sure about his own position was that he would not be a part of it.

The date for Dowding's retirement from the Royal Air Force was still 14 July, and up until the beginning of that month he knew nothing more than that there was no future for him in the R.A.F. after that date. Of all the perplexing changes of course that were forced upon Dowding by the Air Ministry in his personal affairs, it was the one early in July that caused him to come closest to an actual outburst of anger.

'It was the desperate one,' Francis Wilkinson has recalled, 'because it came right at the beginning of the battle, when we were on a knife-edge. I honestly don't think that people realized, as Dowding did, what a knife-edge it was. It was the shortness of that notice to him of yet another postponement in his affairs that was so indefensible. He had understood firmly and for quite some time that he was going to retire on 14 July— four days after the date now set for the start of the battle. But only five days before that he got yet another change hurled at him. Is it any wonder he was angry?'

By the beginning of July it had become only too clear to Dowding that there was to be a heavy German onslaught on Britain from the air, and that his worst fears for the security of the country, and all that losing superiority in the air would do to that, were on the verge of being put to the test. And yet, for all the grimness of the situation, and even a certain element of desperation, it was a fact that there was at this most critical time still no word from the Air Ministry about who, it was proposed, would be taking over from him and so have to face the battle that must be fairly close at hand.

In his reply to the letter from Cyril Newall of 31 March—in which he had agreed to continue at Fighter Command until 14 July—Dowding had asked if Newall would let him know who was to take his place. There had been no reply, and now, with only a few days left before he was due to go, Dowding felt that, for the sake of the defence of the country as well as his own peace of mind, he must get the Air Ministry to reach a firm decision. The immediate command of the defence of the United Kingdom was at stake, and, in particular, the affairs of

Fighter Command, which was so obviously going to have to bear the brunt of the attack.

In a telephone conversation with the C.A.S., Dowding brought up this matter of his relinquishment of his Command, pointing out that it was due to take place in only a few days' time. 'I cannot say that Newall was at all apologetic,' Dowding commented, 'but the tone of what he said was an admission that somebody was making a mistake, or was being rather foolish.'

There was a somewhat strained exchange of views between the C.A.S. and Dowding in this talk, and it ended with Dowding saying: 'If you want to get rid of me, then get rid of me, but don't do it in this way.'

A few days later, on 5 July, Newall wrote a 'Personal and Confidential' letter to Dowding, in which he said:

> I am writing to ask if you will again defer your retirement beyond the date which I last gave you of July 14th. Under present conditions I should be more than loathe (*sic*) for you to leave Fighter Command on that date, and I would be very glad if you would continue in your appointment as Air Officer Commanding-in-Chief until the end of October. If, as I sincerely hope you will be, you are willing to accept the extension, an official letter to this effect will be sent to you in due course, and I will also write to you regarding your successor.

This latest postponement, which was yet another bowler hat being placed in readiness on the long shelf that already contained so many, drew from Dowding a firm protest at the way in which this important decision was being handled. Two days later, on 7 July, he wrote a long reply to Newall's letter.

'Referring to your letter of July 5th, I should like you to cast your eye down the following record,' he stated. He then listed the occasions, since February 1937, when the matter of his retirement and the relinquishment of his command had been discussed.

Pointing out that on that first date he had been told that he might continue for another 'two or three years', Dowding went on to list the other occasions. In August 1938, he had been told that he would relinquish his Command in June 1939. In

February 1939, he had been told that there would be no change that year. In March 1939, he was asked to defer his retirement until March 1940. One day before that last named date he was asked to defer his retirement until 14 July. Now, on 5 July, he was being asked, for the fifth time, to defer his retirement yet again, this time until October. He wrote:

Apart from the question of discourtesy, which I do not wish to stress, I must point out the lack of consideration involved in delaying a proposal of this nature until ten days before the date of my retirement. I have had four retiring dates given to me and now you are proposing a fifth. Before the war, as I told the S. of S., I should have been glad enough to retire; now I am anxious to stay, because I feel that there is no one else who will fight as I do when proposals are made which would reduce the Defence Forces of the Country below the extreme danger point.

Taking matters into his own hands in the belief that the time had come for a firm stand, Dowding concluded his letter with the comment: 'I would therefore suggest that I should not be called upon to retire otherwise than at my own request before the first retiring date given to me, viz. April 24th 1942 or at the end of the war, whichever is the earlier.'

So that there should be no misunderstanding about how strongly he had come to feel, Dowding also sent a copy of this letter that he had written to the C.A.S. to the Secretary of State for Air. That his outspoken comment in his letter to the Chief of the Air Staff must have shaken the Air Ministry into a realisation that there was something in what he claimed is revealed in three letters that Dowding then received. The first to arrive was one from Sir Archibald Sinclair, the Secretary of State for Air. It was dated 10 July, and in it Sinclair thanked Dowding for having sent him a copy of the letter which he had written to Newall. He stated:

I can only say that the Chief of the Air Staff consulted me before asking you to retain your Command until October, and that it was my wish that you should remain in command of our Fighter Squadrons, upon whose success in defeating the German attack upon our munition factories during the next three months will almost certainly depend the issue of this war.

In a conciliatory last paragraph, Sinclair added: 'I could

give you no higher proof of my confidence in you and, although perhaps it seems superfluous, let me add the assurance of my full support.'

With still no word from the Chief of the Air Staff, Dowding replied on 12 July to this letter from the Secretary of State. There was now an unqualified expression of support for him, in a political sense, but he felt compelled, because of past experience, to write in a manner that was still firm in trying to determine exactly what the Air Ministry had in mind about his retirement, or whether they were only talking about the relinquishment of his Command.

'I gratefully acknowledge that I have never received anything but courtesy and consideration at your hands,' Dowding wrote. 'My letter was addressed to Newall, but I was anxious that you should be acquainted with circumstances which occurred before you assumed your present office.' So many Secretaries of State had come and gone during his years in the Service that he had almost lost count of them. 'Since you have replied to my letter,' he added, 'I must assume that you take the view that there is nothing in the facts which I have tabulated which calls for explanation or apology, and that I am to be placed on the Retired List at the end of October 1940.'

The only comment that Dowding can make now on this situation is to point to the facts of the fighting that was going on, all of which have been amply recorded and to comment: 'So far as my personal position was concerned those letters speak for themselves.' But the view expressed many years later by the man who was closest to Dowding in the handling of his affairs leaves no doubt about the extraordinary way the Air Ministry dealt with this situation.

'To my mind,' Francis Wilkinson has recalled, 'it was fantastic that a Commander-in-Chief with all the burdens of the world on his shoulders and fighting one of the major battles of the world, should not know if he was going to be kept on and have to haggle about whether he was to relinquish his Command or to retire altogether from the Service. It was absolutely incredible. And remember that it didn't happen only once. He was being nagged about it time and time again.'

On 13 July, the Chief of the Air Staff wrote to Dowding at

length about his letter of the 7th. He explained that no one was more fully aware than he was of the inconvenience to which Dowding must have been put by the various changes in the date proposed for his retirement, and he said that he fully appreciated the view which Dowding had expressed. 'I can understand that you feel that you have not been treated with the consideration you would wish,' Newall stated, 'but I must ask you to put this down to the stress of events in recent years, of which we are both only too well aware. May I ask you to accept my sincere apologies.'

A fact that he was always having to face, Newall explained, was the consideration of the retirement of the more senior officers in order to maintain an adequate flow of promotions into the higher positions in the Service. He said that it was always his desire to give the officers concerned as much notice as possible. In the case of the highest commands in the Royal Air Force, the rapidly changing events of the last two years had forced new decisions upon the Air Ministry at short notice.

'You will recall that on two earlier occasions when you have been asked to defer your retirement, in March 1939 and March 1940, the country was, as it is today, faced with a critical threat,' Newall explained. 'The reasons which applied then do so now and compel me to try to avoid a change at Fighter Command.'

When it came to a consideration of Dowding's reason for suggesting that he should not be called upon to retire before 24 April 1942, or at the end of the war, whichever was the earlier, Newall stated that he was 'unable to agree that there is no one else who could resist as you do proposals to reduce the Defence Forces of this country below the extreme danger point'. He pointed out that from time to time, as they both well knew, there had been pressure on the political and other sides to divert the air defence of Great Britain in one way or another.

'While, only last month, I was glad to have your support at the Cabinet when the question of sending fighter squadrons to France was under consideration,' Newall stated, 'I must point out that the policy of the Air Staff has consistently been directed towards conserving our Air Defence Forces in the face of the various conflicting claims that have rightly or wrongly been made upon them.' It was the duty of the Air Staff, no less than of the Commands, he added, to give effect to the vital decisions the government had taken, 'whatever our personal views may be'.

It was the comment in this paragraph which caused Dowding at the time, and has gone on causing him ever since then, to feel intense annoyance. In the first place, the meeting that Newall referred to was not 'last month': it had been on 15 May, nearly two months before. But that was only a minor point. What roused Dowding's ire was the claim by Newall that he was 'glad to have your support' when, so far as Dowding was concerned, he had had to stand alone at that meeting with no support at that moment from either Newall or Sinclair.

'That was really going too far,' Dowding has since commented. Furthermore, he has always felt that there was expressed by Newall then altogether too ready an inclination to comply with what he referred to as 'the decisions the government had taken', particularly in the issue that had been fought out in May.

In referring to the copy of the letter which the Secretary of State had just written to Dowding, Newall commented that he was glad to see that that letter contained an explicit expression of confidence in him. Bearing in mind, however, the factors which he had outlined, he continued, he said that he could only repeat that so far as could be seen at that time, he had to ask Dowding to make it convenient to defer his retirement until the end of October.

On the same day on which the C.A.S. had written, 13 July, the Secretary of State for Air replied to Dowding's letter to him of the day before. In what was to Dowding a perfectly reasonable fashion, Sinclair explained his own position. 'I did not answer your letter to the Chief of the Air Staff—a letter which he will no doubt answer himself and which deals with a number of matters for which I have no responsibility,' he stated. 'My letter dealt only with a decision for which I am personally responsible to Parliament—the decision to request you to remain in command of our Fighter Squadrons until the end of October. I do not look beyond this point in which I believe the issue of the war will probably be determined. I must tell you quite frankly that my only pre-occupation was to ensure that the best available Commander was now occupying this key position.'

From what Sinclair was saying, there could be no doubt left in Dowding's mind that his letter to Newall had made upon the Air Ministry just the impact that he had hoped for, and that Sinclair, for one, was well aware of how difficult the position was becoming for Dowding. 'That decision must stand, but I am grateful to you for writing to me so frankly,' Sinclair continued, and then, in a statement that, in view of all that was to happen, must be kept firmly in mind, he added: 'I understand your point of view, I will take it fully into account before making any further decisions about your Command, and I appreciate the importance and the fairness of communicating with you in good time.'

With these two letters there also came an official letter for Dowding from the Air Ministry that, in strong contrast to the brusque tone of the previous official letters, was this time positively polite. It read: 'I am commanded by the Air Council to refer to personal correspondence between yourself and the Chief of the Air Staff and to enquire whether you would be good enough to accept an extension of your employment with the Royal Air Force until 31st October 1940.'

'If that proved nothing else,' Dowding commented recently with one of his characteristic chuckles, 'it showed that there were ways of writing even official letters that could vary in tone.'

That Saturday night, 13 July, Dowding spent at Chequers, dining with the Prime Minister. The next day, he replied officially to the Air Ministry letter, merely stating: '. . . I shall be pleased to accept an extension of my employment with the Royal Air Force for so long as my services may be required.'

In his own hand Dowding then wrote a personal letter to the Secretary of State for Air about the discussions that he had had with the Prime Minister the night before. 'He was good enough to tell me that I had secured his confidence,' he reported, 'and that he wished me to remain on the Active List for the time being, without any date for my retirement being fixed. He told me that he had written to you on the subject.'

Wanting to make sure, yet again, that there could never be any misunderstanding about how the Prime Minister came to make this statement, Dowding added: 'In case you should think that his intervention was something more than a coincidence, I may tell you that neither he nor any other minister was made aware of my approaching retirement through any action or word of mine.' Dowding then spoke about the change of temperature in his relationship with the Chief of the Air Staff. 'I may add that I have received a letter from Newall containing an apology which I have written to accept,' he stated.

The third letter that Dowding dispatched that Sunday was the reply to the letter from Newall. 'Many thanks for your letter . . . and for your apology which I accept in the spirit in which it is offered,' he wrote. 'With regard to the remainder of your letter, when I spoke of fighting against the reduction of the defence forces I was thinking at least as much of the events in the first two months of the war as of the danger which threatened us in May of this year. I realise, however, that this is a matter upon which we cannot be expected to see eye to eye, and further discussion would be unprofitable.' He concluded: 'With renewed thanks for your letter.'

Officialdom was this time on tip-toes. In further contrast to some of the earlier letters, the Air Ministry wrote on 17 July another official letter to Dowding stating: 'I am commanded by the Air Council to acknowledge receipt of your letter of the 14th July, 1940, and to inform you that they have noted with pleasure your willingness to continue in your present appointment.'

For all that the Prime Minister had said about no time limit being placed on the period of Dowding's service, and his report on that to the Secretary of State for Air, Dowding heard nothing more about it at that time. He was left to proceed then in terms of his retirement becoming effective at the end of October, and to plan for that.

To find a threat to Britain from a Continental power that can be compared in its decisive nature with the situation that had developed by the early summer of 1940, a glance back at history has to take in only two events: the clash with the Armada, and the Battle of Trafalgar. In 1588 Drake handled his small fleet with a skill that disposed of the far superior Spanish forces. At Trafalgar in 1805 Nelson repeated his predecessor's victory at sea. But by 1940 control of the sea, for all that Britain was still an island, was no longer the immediate factor. Now the air was the key. And in the position that had been occupied in their time by the Admirals Drake and Nelson there now stood Hugh Dowding, an Air Marshal.

Legend has it that Drake took his time, when threatened, by finishing his game of bowls, and that Nelson was given to peering at what he did not want to see by lifting his telescope to his blind eye. Dowding can claim no such idiosyncratic touches that will mark his name in history. His claims were of a more modern temper. Foremost among them must be his unostentatious courtesy, which could nevertheless be governed by his quick and sharp rejection, in a surprisingly gruff manner, of what he did not believe to be a correct appreciation of the truth of any situation.

In his manner at this time, Dowding presented to everybody an outwardly calm, even austere, mien which hid the depths and the sincerity of the emotions that were his. Just under six feet tall, slim, impassive, his presence in his own Headquarters when he made the frequent visits that he did to the huge underground block containing the Filter and Operations Rooms was marked by only one distinguishing characteristic. He always wore his cap. He was the only one to do that in the confines of the Headquarters whenever he ventured out of his own office.

But when any remark or comment called for a rejoinder, Dowding could be equally effective in an entirely different way. Such an occasion presented itself, Francis Wilkinson recalled, during a visit made by the Prime Minister to Dowding's Headquarters at an early stage in the battle. The Defiants, which were the R.A.F.'s only two-seater, single-engined fighters, had had spectacular success in their initial encounters with the Luftwaffe. But the Germans soon discovered how to cope with them, and the Defiant losses immediately became disastrous.

While Winston Churchill was with Dowding at Bentley Priory the news was given to them that one of the Defiant squadrons had just suffered very heavy casualties, and had been almost destroyed. Churchill looked grave. He was no less sensitive than Dowding about casualties, but he seemed to be more inclined to accept the bad news as the fortunes of war in a serious loss of aircraft.

'That may be so,' Dowding replied, 'but what I am conscious of is that so many of my men have died.'

In the face of that there was nothing more that Churchill could say. He looked quickly at Dowding, nodded, and turned away.

CHAPTER EIGHT

THE UNKNOWN STRESS

In the way in which he had organised, and then went on to run, his Command, Dowding provided an almost classic example of how a Commander-in-Chief should work. Over a long period of time he had evolved a method of formulating his plans in a strategic sense and of giving his orders. He had a complete grasp on the necessity of keeping his own eye on the long term view, planning ahead for what he believed would be the most likely course that future action would take, and the call that would have to be made for counter action.

Behind all the planning there was always the role that Dowding believed it was primarily his Command's function to fulfil. He has spoken of that many times, in order to make it quite clearly understood, and when it came to defining that role in the actual battle he said: 'There was a distinct difference between the objectives of the opposing sides. The Germans were out to facilitate a transfer of ground troops across the Channel, to invade this country, and so to finish the war. Now I wasn't trying with Fighter Command to win the war. I was trying desperately to prevent the Germans from succeeding in their preparations for an invasion. Mine was the purely defensive role of trying to stop the possibility of an invasion, and thus give this country a breathing spell. We might win or we might lose the war, or we might agree on a draw— anything might happen in the future. But it was Germany's objective to win the war by invasion, and it was my job to prevent an invasion from taking place. I had to do that by denying them control of the air.'

With that view of his strategy always in mind, and, he took it for granted, always understood by everybody, Dowding delegated the authority for much of the tactical fighting of the battle to his Group Commanders. 'That is a point that must not be ignored,' he commented. 'I might have been right, or I might have been wrong in doing that, but I did not want to control completely the tactical work of the Groups. That was mainly because I appreciated that different situations arose in different Groups, and I was most reluctant to give any of the Group Commanders daily orders about the tactics that were to be employed. I gave them general directives, which I expected them to follow, and in some ways, I suppose, it could be said that I gave them too much rope.'

In delegating authority to his Group Commanders, Dowding did not intend that they should be left alone, each to get on with his own methods of fighting. There was a great deal more to it than that. 'Standardising tactics throughout a Command as large as mine would have meant cramping the style of the different Groups,' Dowding explained. 'They all had different problems to face, but I had to know how they were going to face them, and I had to issue general directives.'

On the other hand, there has been criticism of Dowding for not having delegated enough authority to others. Francis Wilkinson is one of those who reject that. 'He kept to himself,' he commented, 'but dammit . . . he delegated a great deal of the tactical fighting of the Battle of Britain to his Group Commanders.'

Much of the misunderstanding that arose later stemmed from this habit of keeping to himself. His own technical knowledge and experience were such that he was quite capable of handling many problems himself without reference to others. 'There was the way, for instance, he would go off by himself to find out how the night fighters were doing with their radar,' Wilkinson has pointed out. 'He would not feel that it was necessary to discuss that with anybody but the absolute experts because he had such a very good technical mind himself, with the most extraordinary grasp on technical matters.'

Commenting on this, Dowding once said, 'But I should not like it to be thought that I was so full of myself that I believed that I was always right. I was very conscious of the necessity to be on my guard against making mistakes.'

This reserve that is so much a part of Dowding's character was recognised by everybody, and it was fully understood that by inclination he preferred to help himself and keep to himself rather than to have to rely too much on other people in matters which were of his concern as the Commander-in-Chief. In a way this reserve of his, and the increasing habit that he had acquired of trying to cope with so much himself led him to a position of loneliness which only added to his burdens.

But for all that loneliness, he was aware enough of what was going on in his Command, and even to a degree that would have surprised some if they had known about it. That is one of the more subtle aspects in the life of any Commander-in-Chief, and the way in which he can come to know, one way or another, far more about what is going on in his Command, in addition to the routine work that is done, is a factor that contributes to his success. It is part of the grasp that a C.-in-C. has on his Command that he should be able to receive information, both official and unofficial; and a further mark of his success is to be found in the way in which he handles or makes use of that information.

Some Commanders-in-Chief obtained their information by moving freely among those who were under their command, talking with and listening to everybody. Dowding was too reserved by nature for that, and, although those young pilots under his command never realised it, he was too hesitant about possibly intruding upon them ever to be able to sit down and gossip easily and informally with them. He genuinely felt that that might be an intrusion in the lives of those for whom he had such a high regard and respect, those who did the actual flying and fighting. Despite this, however, he knew so well the structure of his command, the natures of the men who were serving under him, and their motives, that he could assess rapidly from any of the vast numbers of papers that were put up to him, for instance, a surprising amount of information, more by intuition than by direct statement.

The outstandingly successful youngster among those pilots was a Sergeant (now Squadron Leader) named James H. Lacey. He has always been known with affection by everybody as Ginger Lacey, and as far as is known while still a young Sergeant he shot down during the Battle of Britain more enemy aircraft than any other pilot; and he was shot down himself nine times in achieving that.

A long time afterwards, Ginger Lacey said: 'Even as a sergeant pilot, when Stuffy Dowding was as remote as God himself, I was acutely aware that he was having to do something which had never been done before, and for which there was no precedent. I always felt, in 1940, that he was insular and un-approachable. As a sergeant this did not worry me, and I was more than a little thankful that throughout the whole of the Battle we were never afflicted with a visit from the A.O.C.-in-C. But I believe now that any apparent aloofness was probably due to his shyness combined with the loneliness of his appoint-ment.'

In a fleet action involving the Royal Navy one has in mind a picture of the Commander-in-Chief on the bridge of his flagship going into action surrounded by all the grey and impressive might of a powerful machine, and tended by a staff of fighting officers and men. A Commander-in-Chief of the Army in the field is seen as working in a trailer or a tent, or mounted on a tank. All that, in both cases, is rugged and impressive action. Nothing could be further from the atmo-sphere that surrounded Dowding, the Commander-in-Chief of the Fighter Command which, as its name alone implies, was such a formidable fighting outfit.

In his personal life, Dowding was a man of very simple tastes; and in his official life it was a matter of coping with a vast amount of detail with unruffled precision and through long hours spent at his desk. He awoke at a normal time each morning unless he was disturbed by urgent telephone calls such as those from the Prime Minister, and it was only a call of that urgency which the main switchboard at Headquarters would ever put through to Montrose before the start of the day's work. Dowding has described himself as 'a good break-faster'; and immediately after breakfast he would be driven in his official car—he had had the same civilian Air Ministry driver for many years—from Montrose up the hill to Bentley Priory. He usually arrived there promptly at nine o'clock each morning.

At a further stage of the battle Dowding arrived one morning a little later than usual. I knew that he had been away the night before at one of the airfields which was specialising in the work of the night fighters, and that he had not got back to Montrose until the small hours of the morning, and that he must be tired. As I followed him into his office and he sat down behind his desk I suggested that I should go with him on these night excursions if only to relieve him of the burden of having to make notes. Dowding glanced up at me, smiled suddenly in the way that could become in a flash very understanding, and said: 'That's a kind thought, but somebody has got to be in this office first thing in the morning.'

There was nothing whatsoever about Bentley Priory to suggest that it was in fact the great working Headquarters of Fighter Command other than the drab colour that it had been painted, which only served to make it even duller in appearance than it must have been in the first place. There were people in uniform to be seen everywhere, including a surprising number of girls in the W.A.A.F., but one found it hard, at first, to associate with it the idea of an Air Force.

From the outset, Dowding had accepted with readiness the very valuable work that could be done by the officers and airwomen of the Women's Auxiliary Air Force. In addition to having them working at the forward radar stations and airfields —where they were to serve in the front line on equal terms with the men of the R.A.F.—he also had many of them at his Group and Command Headquarters. He accepted them all as members of Fighter Command, and in his mind the men and women were all part of the one Service.

The feeling that was engendered in the young girls of the W.A.A.F. by the remote figure of the Commander-in-Chief who was old enough to be the grandfather of many of them was reflected in some information that came to me many years later from a friend who was an officer in the W.A.A.F. at the Headquarters at Bentley Priory. She had just received a letter from one of the girls who had served with her in the underground block: 'the Hole', as it was known to its inhabitants.

In this letter mention was made of an occasion when the writer, then a young girl, had been one of those intensely busy plotting on the table the information being passed to them during a heavy enemy raid. She had not realised that Dowding, who was merely doing the rounds, was standing nearby until she happened to glance his way. Of what she considered was the 'great reward' for what she was doing, she wrote about

'. . . dear Stuffy, smiling encouragement, and saying "well done" as he walked past me.'

The entrance to the building was through a prosaic portico into a large and gloomy hall. This led straight to a door in a rather dim passage opposite the main entrance. It had tacked on it a cardboard sign with black lettering bearing the name of the Air Officer Commanding-in-Chief. Entrance through that door led into the somewhat dingy and rather cramped office in which the Personal Assistant worked. In addition to handling all the incoming and outgoing paper work, the P.A. stood guard over admission to the inner office of the Commander-in-Chief, the entrance to which was from this outer office, and controlled all the telephone calls through the one extension to the C.-in-C. There was no impressive display there of any batteries of telephones or intercommunicating systems.

The office in which Dowding worked was a large, high-ceilinged room badly in need of redecorating with two sets of french windows which looked out over the pleasantly wooded grounds towards Harrow Hill. The wall opposite the door leading into the room was largely occupied by an ornate marble fire-place with, over it, a huge old-fashioned mirror that was a relic from a bygone era. In front of the fire-place, with his back to it and facing the only door leading into the room, Dowding worked at a rather small and plain desk which had on it a green-shaded lamp, trays for files, and a telephone. Later in the course of the battle a second green-coloured telephone was added which had attached to it a security scrambler. Two large leather chairs flanked the desk, and there was a book-case filling the wall facing it.

Except for people being in uniform, the whole atmosphere of the Commander-in-Chief's office could have given a first impression of being that of a somewhat staid and old-fashioned family business office in a provincial town. There was no shining or highly-polished military atmosphere whatsoever, and even when the pressure was at its greatest, the tempo there was quiet and orderly. In addition to his Personal Assistant, the C.-in-C. had his own staff of four clerks—two R.A.F. and two W.A.A.F.—who handled all the dictation and typing and files and reports. They worked in the awkward placing of their own office across the other side of the passage. But such was the structure of Bentley Priory. It was never meant to be used for the purposes of war.

The working day for Dowding throughout the battle extended in the same fashion day after day with no breaks for any days off. It started with that nine o'clock arrival in his office, and it went on until all hours of the night, and often on into the early hours of the morning. His time would be taken up with a very great amount of paper work at his desk, with meetings, discussions and conferences, and with quick trips down to the Operations and Filter Rooms. All the time he was also having to make journeys to London for further conferences and meetings; and there were as many visits as he could make to the various Group Headquarters and the aerodromes.

The only breaks in the day were for lunch and dinner, and for these Dowding would return to Montrose. He seldom had anything to drink, and never if he was at lunch or dinner with only his sister in the house, and he would quickly return to Bentley Priory. The time after dinner was usually spent cleaning up the day's paper work. The last thing that he would do at night, no matter how late, would be to pay another visit to the Operations and Filter Rooms for a final check on what was going on.

For all the pressure and the mass of work that he had to deal with, and Dowding at his desk was just as forceful as he was around the conference table, there was never lacking when it was called for, that sharp humour of his. He could have placed in the 'In' tray on his desk a formidable stack of files, sorted out in their degrees of urgency, and he could be counted on to deal with all of them promptly, and with firm decisions.

There were two small features about Dowding at his desk which have remained firmly in my mind as well as Francis Wilkinson's. The first was the use that he made of his spectacles. How old they were nobody knew. It was said that they had been bought off the counter of one of the popular chain stores, but that was a joke of private standing among those of his personal staff. They happened to look so old, and they appeared to be, in fact, no more than magnifying glasses of some mild strength. They were horn-rimmed, and Dowding wore them half-way down the bridge of his nose, and whenever he looked up he peered over the top of them with an inevitable expression of slight surprise.

'And do you remember the pen!' Francis Wilkinson reminded me many years later. It was a fountain pen of an even greater age than the spectacles. Lack of running repairs had long since nullified its usefulness as a fountain pen, but the nib was to Dowding's liking and that was all that mattered. In Wilkinson's words: 'While the rest of us were sporting the most expensive fountain pens, Stuffy worked away with that wonderful old pen of his, dipping it in a simple ink pot.'

In comparison to the simplicity and quietness of Dowding's methods of working there was on the other side of the Channel the grotesque figure of Hermann Goering. When it came to be made known, through studies after the war, what the true state of affairs had been at the beginning of the Luftwaffe attacks on Britain, one of the aspects that has never ceased to give Dowding cause to comment was the outrageous boastfulness of Hermann Goering, and the assurances that were made by him to Adolf Hitler.

'Since the Navy was strategically almost nonexistent and the Army could not transport itself across the English Channel, the Luftwaffe was the crucial element of the immediate strategic problem,' the American historian Telford Taylor commented, adding: '. . . its Commander-in-Chief, Hermann Goering, vowed to Hitler that with it he could crush the British and nail down the final victory.'

The Royal Air Force would be destroyed in four weeks, Goering had promised. It was that bloated optimism which led him to be so sure that he was going to achieve a success in the air that might even rule out the necessity of a German invasion.

'The wretched man seemed to be unable to think of us as anything but a contemptible little force,' Dowding commented, and there was that delighted chuckle in his voice as he said it.

On 1 August 1940, Reichsmarschall Hermann Goering held a conference which was attended by all the senior commanders of the German air force. This meeting took place at the Hague.

After what was described as extravagant praise of the part played by the Luftwaffe in the defeat of France, Goering announced: 'And now, gentlemen, the Fuehrer has ordered me to crush Britain with my Luftwaffe. By means of hard blows I plan to have this enemy, who has already suffered a decisive moral defeat, down on his knees in the nearest future, so that an occupation of the island by our troops can proceed without any risk.'

Plans were discussed at this conference for this operation, and Goering spoke disparagingly of the number and quality of the fighters of the Royal Air Force, and gloatingly of the vast numbers of aircraft that he had at his disposal. 'Count how many bombers alone we can put into the sky for this campaign!' he exclaimed.

It was estimated by Theo Osterkamp, a senior officer in the Luftwaffe who was renowned for his exploits as a pilot in both wars, and for his realistic assessments of situations which he did not hesitate to express to Goering, that the number would be between fifteen hundred and two thousand. Goering had been talking about four thousand five hundred. The reports from the two Commanders-in-Chief of the Luftflotten concerned then revealed that there would be available under seven hundred bombers.

'I was completely staggered,' even Theo Osterkamp has recorded. It was this revelation that caused Goering—whose 'consternation seemed genuine'—to look around and ask the plaintive question: 'Is this my Luftwaffe?' But that was only the start of the turn that he was to make on his own people, those whom he at first professed to cherish.

In contrast to that plaintive question, there was the mood that Dowding was in, and the feeling that he came to have about his people. He spoke about it later in his official despatch with the words: '. . . the situation was critical in the extreme.' He then went on to explain: 'Pilots had to be withdrawn from the Bomber and Coastal Commands and from the Fleet Air Arm and flung into the Battle after hasty preparation. The majority of the squadrons had been reduced to the status of training units, and were fit only for operations against bombers. The remainder were battling daily against heavy odds.'

Long afterwards I talked with Francis Wilkinson about the reason for the ability of Fighter Command to adjust so quickly to the stresses of the air war. So far as he was concerned, there was only one reason.

'I think that it was an achievement of Dowding's which has never been fully realised,' Wilkinson said. 'He organised Fighter Command so that it could meet the pressures which were going to come. When the crunch came, the Command worked. It didn't simply disintegrate under the awful pressures that were imposed upon it. In some way or other Dowding had been able to see all the difficultes that were going to be faced. They were thought of by Dowding, and they were thought out by him, and the planning and the arrangements were made with foresight. If those arrangements hadn't been made, whatever the gallantry of the Few may have been, we wouldn't have won the battle. I don't think that people realise quite how important that is: that amazing organisation that had been thought out and worked up.'

The determination of an exact date on which the Battle of Britain started depends very largely on the nature of the involvement of those who were concerned in it. Various dates have been set, all the way from the late spring to the summer of 1940. In a speech in the House of Commons on 18 June, Winston Churchill stated: '. . . the Battle of France is over. I expect that the Battle of Britain is about to begin.'

'The Battle may be said to have started when the Germans had disposed of the French resistance in the Summer of 1940, and turned their attention to this country,' Dowding wrote in his despatch. 'Leaving out of account peace-time preparations and training, the Battle of Britain began for me in the Autumn of 1939.' In the eyes of British historians, the date that has come to be recognised for the opening of the battle is 10 July.

The Germans recognise a later date for the start of their 'Adlerangriff': Eagle Attack. The opening day for them, in what they call their 'Adlertag', is 13 August. In his Directive No. 17 issued on 1 August 'For the conduct of air and sea warfare against England', Adolf Hitler ordered: 'The German Air

Force is to overpower the English Air Force with all the forces
at its command, in the shortest possible time.' He further
ordered: '. . . the air war may begin on or after 5 August. The
exact time is to be decided by the Air Force after the completion of preparations and in the light of the weather.'

As the momentum of the enemy attack increased, so did the
strain for Dowding. But there was no relaxation of his tight
control over what was happening. At times it seemed that only
he and a few of his senior officers and those who were doing the
actual flying and the controlling of it knew how serious the
situation had become. It was not a matter of a straight fight—
that would have been all too easy to handle—and never for a
moment would Dowding drop his guard. It might have meant
running the risk of a possible blow from some quarter or other
which could damage his Command.

'I think it was that which led him to have at least some of
those awful rows with those people at the Air Ministry,'
Francis Wilkinson once remarked. 'Some of them up there
simply didn't seem to know what was happening, or understand
what it was all about. One day an Air Commodore from the
Air Ministry came to see Dowding. It was right at the time
when we were very low on pilots who really knew how to
fly. I listened to him in astonishment when he said to Dowding:
"But I don't understand what you're worrying about . . . you've
got plenty of aeroplanes and pilots." I thought poor old Stuffy
would have a fit.'

What with that attitude by some of the officials at the Air
Ministry, and still having at the back of his mind the matter
of his probable retirement not being so far off, it is true that
Dowding was in no mood for any further quibbling. He was
too fully occupied with the state of the battle to give anything
but the battle a great deal of his attention; but that doubt about
the tenure of his office was still there.

In his letter of 14 July to the Secretary of State for Air,
Dowding had reported quite clearly the views expressed to
him by the Prime Minister and the wish that Churchill had
that Dowding should 'remain on the Active List for the time
being, without any date for my retirement being fixed'. He

had added to that note that Churchill had told him that 'he had written to you on the subject.'

Despite that, a month was to pass before Dowding heard anything more about this wish expressed by the Prime Minister, even though Churchill had said at the time that he had already written to the Secretary of State for Air about the matter. It was not until 12 August—the day of the heavy German attack on the radar stations—that Cyril Newall wrote another 'personal and confidential' letter to Dowding. There was no mention in it of any views expressed by the Prime Minister.

'When I wrote to you on July 13th I could not see any alternative to indicating the end of October as the time for your retirement,' Newall wrote. 'In the present circumstances, however, I fully realise the disadvantages involved in this decision and I am now glad to be able to say that it has been decided to cancel the time limit to the period of your appointment as C.-in-C. Fighter Command. I sincerely hope that this information will be agreeable to you.' Dowding noted that Newall spoke in terms of both 'retirement' and his present appointment.

With the strongest warning before him from the raids being staged by the Luftwaffe that this was the opening stage of an all-out attack on Britain, Dowding could do no more than acknowledge, on 13 August, receipt of Newall's letter. He thanked him for it, and merely added ' . . . the contents of which I have noted with pleasure.'

This was now the sixth time that the relinquishment of Dowding's command and his retirement from the Service had been postponed, but now it at least left him free to devote all his attention to the heavy fighting which was now upon them. There was also removed from his mind the necessity to give any further thought to the matter of the man who was to take his place. Although Newall had assured him on 5 July, five weeks before, that he would 'write to you regarding your successor', there had not been a word from any source about that.

It is possible, if one looks at it in a charitable light, that the severity of the battle was having an effect on the paper work at the Air Ministry, causing it to pile up, because it was not until 22 August that Dowding received an official letter from the Air Ministry about the latest change in the plans for his future. It stated: 'I am commanded by the Air Council to refer to their letter dated 13th July 1940, reference 809403/38/ S7c and to inform you that they have decided to cancel the time limit to the period of your appointment as Air Officer Commanding-in-Chief, Fighter Command.'

This official notification spoke only of his appointment. There was no mention of retirement. It was not until long afterwards that Dowding came to realise fully that in all the various letters to him about his term of office there was this curious jumbling of expressions of intent: sometimes he was told that he would have to relinquish his command, and at other times there were references to his retirement, and there were occasions when both were mixed up together.

'I never quite knew exactly where I stood,' he once commented.

CHAPTER NINE

FIGHTERS

The battle that was fought in the air between the Royal Air Force and the Luftwaffe during the summer of 1940 was not just one big set encounter in which the opposing forces met head on, slugged it out, and then called it a day. It was a head on clash, but there was a great deal more to it than just that; and it all lasted so very much longer, for a battle, than one associates with such affairs when one thinks of encounters between armies on the ground and fleets at sea. In Dowding's view, what came to be called the Battle of Britain went on with a mounting fury for some twelve weeks, and from day to day he never knew what was going to happen next. He had to be constantly on the alert during the whole time for a variation in the tactics on the part of the enemy which would call for a necessary, and often very rapid, change in his own defence.

In an official report on his views, Dowding stated: 'The Battle may be said to have divided itself broadly into four Phases: first, the attack on convoys and Coastal objectives, such as Ports, Coastal Aerodromes and Radio Location Stations. Second, the attack on Inland Fighter Aerodromes. Third, the attack on London. And fourth, the Fighter-Bomber stage, where the target was of importance quite subsidiary to the main object of drawing our Fighters into the air and engaging them in circumstances as disadvantageous to us as possible. These phases indicated only general tendencies; they overlapped and were not mutually exclusive.'

The first phase was an anxious time only in that it was the opening stage of the battle. Although coastal convoys were repeatedly attacked, the result, in Dowding's words, was that 'the amount of physical damage done was not excessive.' He regarded with more alarm the attacks on his R.D.F. stations, where there were 'rather severe damage and casualties'; and it was that aspect of the early enemy strikes at our radar installations which led him to write: 'The operating personnel, and particularly the women, behaved with great courage under threat of attack and actual bombardment.'

A question that has been posed many times is why the buildings housing the radar stations on the coast—as well as many of the sector operations rooms at the airfields—were so flimsy in structure, being mainly of wood, and so exposed by being openly above ground. It does not seem to have been understood by those who have asked this question that it had been impossible to do everything in the time that was allotted for preparedness in those short years before the war. 'It would have been admirable if fine underground installations could have been built,' Dowding has explained, 'but there simply was not time for that. The system had to be brought into being as quickly as possible, and the best was done in the time available.'

Criticism has also been expressed of the creation of underground operations rooms for the Headquarters of Fighter Command and Group Headquarters while there were no such elaborate safety precautions for the radar stations and sector operations rooms. Again, Dowding has pointed out, it was a matter of time, and of doing what could be done in the race against time. 'It was considered that the nerve centre should be protected first,' he said, 'with the protection of the nerve ends to come as soon after that as possible.' In the meantime, the nerve ends were given what protective wrapping could be provided in the time available.

'There was rather sporadic and intermittent fighting in the air after Dunkirk,' Dowding commented. 'It hadn't settled down to the steady, grim business that it became very shortly afterwards, but I didn't really feel that we were having a respite. There was so much to do in preparation for what I felt sure was going to happen, and which began on 10 July.'

Part of this preparation was to make sure that everybody knew what was being thought and done about the tactics that were to be employed, and not just leave people to take these matters into their own hands. As early as 26 June 1940 instructions were issued from the Headquarters of Fighter Command, over Dowding's name, to the Headquarters of Nos. 10, 11, 12 and 13 Groups on the subject of 'Fighter Tactics'. It was stated that it was considered 'most essential' that there should be a careful co-ordination of all planning in order that there should be 'a common doctrine'.

By that, Dowding was not intending to exercise any greater control than he already had in mind over his Group Commanders. But he did want to have their views on tactics passed to him at his Headquarters before any direct planning was embarked upon. For one thing, the Air Fighting Development Unit, which was part of Dowding's Command, was examining all aspects of tactics. There was a great need for flexibility, Dowding felt, both in the exercising of his own command and in the actual fighting. Also, they were all feeling their way in the first great air battle ever to be fought under such a structure of command. The attacking forces appeared to be so very much stronger than the smaller, but more highly organised, forces of the defence.

Through their great experience in the use of fighters—as well as their close association in having worked together before the war, when Park was Senior Air Staff Officer at Fighter Command—there was a thorough understanding between Dowding and Park about what they thought would be the most effective tactical use that could be made of the Command. When Park left Dowding's Headquarters to take over command of No. 11 Group he had a complete grasp of all that Dowding believed in. He also fully appreciated what Dowding wanted in this matter of tactics. Both men believed implicitly that the unit in all fighting must be the squadron. This belief determined the structure of the Command and the use that was to be made of it in fighting defensively for the security of the base.

Speed and flexibility were the two essentials in any defensive stand that Fighter Command would have to adopt in the face of attack; and it was Dowding's firm conviction, and Park's full understanding of that, which led to the basic plan. Dowding took it for granted that it was clearly understood throughout his Command that from the moment that orders were given by Group Controllers to Sector Controllers, those orders were to be executed in terms of squadrons. In turn, when it came to orders being given to counter any incoming raids, the Sector Controllers would order the forces into the air in units of squadrons.

It could be that squadrons were ordered off singly, or in pairs, or, depending on the nature of the raids, in larger formations, from nearby stations. Once in the air the squadrons were still controlled from the ground—through direct contact with the Sector Controllers—and directed towards the incoming raids. Where squadrons were operating together from the same Sector they would be under the orders of the same controller, and would, therefore, work more or less as a team. But when they were from different Sectors they remained under the control of their own Sectors and fought independently. The moment the enemy was sighted, the Squadron Commanders took over the interceptions, and the fighting of the battle, and no further efforts were made to contact them from the ground until it was reported to the Sector Controller that the action had ended.

It was the need for flexibility and the urgency of the time element which dominated all the decisions that had to be made by the Group Controllers before they ever gave orders to the Sector Controllers to send off any squadrons. The need for flexibility rested in the Group Controllers having to determine how and where the enemy were going to attack. They had to be on guard against other raids suddenly being mounted from other quarters as well as keeping an eye on the main attack, which might increase or decrease as the enemy tried to lure them into some trap or other. The time element had to be kept urgently in mind because Fighter Command's whole planning was based on keeping the fighter forces at readiness for action, rather than aimlessly wandering around the sky on fuel-consuming, and pointless, patrols. This was one of the features about the defence offered by Fighter Command that astonished the Germans, and something that they never seemed to be able to understand fully, when R.A.F. fighter squadrons appeared so rapidly to bar their way.

One of the most important features of Dowding's planning for the use of his forces was the nature of the duties of the Group Controllers. Within moments of the appearance of incoming aircraft on the cathode ray tubes at the coastal radar stations, the Group Controllers would see displayed on the Operations Room tables all the filtered information coming through from the Headquarters of Fighter Command. It was the task of the

Group Controllers to decide from the information being displayed what action should be taken. They each knew the exact state of every squadron in their Group, and, on the basis of this essential information, they had then to choose the precise moment for ordering the squadrons into the air.

It was essential that the Group Controllers should not waste effort by getting the squadrons off too early, or in too large a number, but it was of equal importance that they should get them into the air in sufficient time to make interceptions possible before the enemy got anywhere near their targets. There was, therefore, a fine balance that had to be maintained, and most of the time was spent by the Controllers interpreting the information passed to them—which was all too often suspect because of the limitations of the early radar—and juggling the limited defence forces that they had available in order to make the most effective interceptions. There was always in their minds the great need to throw their punches quickly, efficiently, and in the right direction, and in sufficient strength to be effective while still retaining some reserve.

While Dowding and Keith Park shared a complete understanding of the tactics best suited to the needs of Fighter Command, the same cannot be said of the No. 12 Group Commander. Leigh-Mallory appeared to believe that he knew more even than Dowding about how the fighters should be used. But, in fact, he was not nearly as well versed in fighter tactics as Dowding and Park, or even Quintin Brand of No. 10 Group, and for all his belief in himself there was an underlying lack of self-assurance that forced him to look for support for his beliefs, and he had to look elsewhere. Serving under his command he had one of the most famous and highly regarded pilots of the Battle of Britain, Douglas Bader, and it was through him that Leigh-Mallory was to find that support.

That Douglas Bader was one of the foremost participants in the battle is acknowledged with readiness by everybody. The very well-known book *Reach for the Sky*, which Bader accepts as his 'relevant' biography, reveals important points which deal with the attitudes of Dowding and other senior officers, as well as those of pilots serving in the Command. On close examination of this book, a story emerges that forcibly weaves its way, in a manner that cannot be disregarded, through any account that may be given of Dowding's experiences.

The achievements of Douglas Bader in the face of tremendous handicaps had made a deep impression on everybody, including Dowding. Leigh-Mallory had watched with admiration the astonishing progress that Bader had made right from the time he first appeared in one of the squadrons in No. 12 Group in February of 1940. He had fostered Bader's progress recognising, perhaps, a compulsion that also bedevilled him: a driving force of which Bader's biographer wrote, '. . . like a tide in him rose the need to prove himself.'

Just as Dowding had in his nature qualities that are so typically English, so, in his own way, did Douglas Bader. It is something of which he is, and has a right to be, proud. After losing both legs in an appalling crash in an aircraft of which he was the pilot as far back as December 1931, Bader had had to give up flying and his career as a pilot in the Royal Air Force, and with that at an end he had to leave the Service.

Eight years later, when the war broke out, Bader set about rejoining the R.A.F. and getting back to flying, and to everybody's astonishment he achieved that, and more. Against all sorts of opposition he found his way into a squadron as a fighter pilot, and from that moment on there was no holding him in the intensity of his drive to come to grips with the enemy.

Right from the time of his return to flying Bader was warned, his biographer points out, that nobody could know at that stage just what tactics should be adopted in the use of fighters. 'The boys in the last war knew, and the basic idea is the same now,' Bader is credited with having retorted, referring to the early development of wing formations, and that anyone who 'tried the Fighter Command attacks . . . probably wouldn't get back to report it'. Of Bader even then it was said: 'When he got an idea into his head he wouldn't budge.'

'. . . he always thought that he had to go on proving himself,' Bader's biographer wrote. 'It was never conscious. The exterior was always masterful but underneath hid the little demon born in him, aggravated in his childhood and again when he lost his legs. He just had to be better than anyone to find the deepest and unconsidered assurance.'

Dowding could understand that, but he was saddened by it, and after a while he came to feel that 'the little demon' that possessed Bader was perhaps driving him too hard, and that it might even cause him to do something which would not be in his own interests. Even while still only a very junior officer, Bader did not seem to be able to contain his impatience and he went on expressing his criticisms in the most decided, but injudicious, fashion. While going about his flying as a member of the squadron, and performing his duties in a thoroughly commendable and correct fashion, he nevertheless continued to speak freely of his views on the methods of the current Fighter Command attacks which had been evolved for use against enemy formations. '. . . on the ground later he . . . scathingly condemned them,' his biographer commented.

In a very short time, Bader became a flight commander in a squadron stationed at Duxford, and his biographer wrote: 'He told the pilots in his flight that the Fighter Command attacks were no damn' good except as training for flying discipline.'

'I agree that at the beginning of the war we paid too much attention to close formation flying,' Dowding said about that. 'If that's what he means, I agree with Bader. There was tight wing-tip to wing-tip flying, with everybody looking around to keep his correct distance from his neighbour and that sort of thing, and nobody had any time to do anything else. Circumstances forced us to relax that, and it was found that a much looser formation was necessary, as well as simpler tactics.'

From his own great experience as a fighter pilot Johnnie (now Air Vice-Marshal J. E.) Johnson commented: 'Fighting tactics were still a long way behind those of the Luftwaffe.' It was realised that the Luftwaffe pilots were a great deal more experienced in actual warfare than ours. They had learnt about tactics at first hand in the Spanish Civil War, and in the war in Poland, and then in the blitzkrieg in the west. But that was understood, he added, and '. . . fighting tactics . . . were in the melting pot.'

It was not likely that Douglas Bader would be able to contain what appeared to be an urgent need to criticise. With the pride that he had, justifiably, in having found his way back to the life which meant so much to him, there developed a situation in which, his biographer has stated, 'once more with responsibility and leadership, he spoke with unmistakable authority . . . he ran his flight with an enveloping gusto.'

From that time Bader went on to training his pilots in 'his own style of fighting'. And 'on his own he tested his nerve and skill with illegal low aerobatics,' his biographer recorded of Bader's effort to bring himself to the highest pitch of efficiency.

'It was rather sad that he should have had to do that,' Dowding has commented. 'Sad that, after all he had endured, he should have to go to that extreme.'

'Long ago the theoreticians at Fighter Command had decided that modern aircraft, especially fighters, were too fast for the dog-fight tactics of World War I,' Bader's biographer has stated. 'Bader, his head full of McCudden, Bishop and Ball, thought that was all nonsense . . .'

'His choice of heroes from the First World War was a fairly good one,' Dowding remarked. But in fairness to those who had been trying to work out how the fighters should be used it must be pointed out that Bader had not had the advantage of continuous work and study in fighter tactics. He had been completely away from it all for many years, and he was not thoroughly familiar with the work that had been done by many very able pilots and theoreticians. They were only too ready to admit that despite all their work there was much that they did not know.

'Some of the other pilots ragged him about being pre-war vintage and old fashioned,' it was reported. But Bader was 'convinced for all time of the superior virtues of individual attacks and dog-fights, as against unwieldy processions'.

In view of what was to happen so soon afterwards, Dowding has found Bader's early conviction 'for all time' that 'unwieldy processions' were not suitable to be more than a little confusing.

By the middle of June, Bader had made such amazing progress in his flying that he was both proficient and very confident. He had been back on flying as a fully operational fighter pilot for nearly four months. Then there came, to his intense delight, the final step in catching up with those who had been his contemporaries while he was a cadet at the R.A.F. College at Cranwell. He was given command of a Hurricane squadron, stationed at Coltishall, in Norfolk. In his account of how that came about, Bader's biographer states that it was Leigh-Mallory's doing.

In his official despatch, Dowding spoke about one aspect of the way in which the Luftwaffe was used that deeply impressed him. He wrote: 'I must emphasise, throughout, the extreme versatility of the German methods both in the timing and direction of their attacks, and in the tactical formations and methods employed.'

It was Park's actions in meeting this versatility that gave Dowding cause to add to the comment in his despatch: 'I must pay a very sincere tribute to the Air Officer Commanding No. 11 Group, Air Vice-Marshal K. R. Park, C.B., M.C., D.F.C. for the way in which he adjusted his tactics and inter-ception methods to meet each new development as it occurred.'

Many years later, when he was reminded of what he said then, Dowding added the comment: 'I have always been happy about having placed that on record. I meant every word of it.'

But the views held by Dowding in his appreciation of Park's tactical handling of the battle were not shared with him by everybody, and one of those in opposition was Leigh-Mallory, the A.O.C. of No. 12 Group. It seemed that he could not give this unqualified support to the way the fighting was being handled, even though it met with the approval of his own Commander-in-Chief.

For a development of the opinions that were held by Leigh-Mallory, it is necessary to turn again to the views that were held by Douglas Bader. Johnnie Johnson has commented that they 'were supported by his A.O.C., Leigh-Mallory'. Having found in those views what he considered was the practical idea that he was looking for, Leigh-Mallory had proceeded to give Bader very full support. In Dowding's eyes, that was going too far.

After delegating to his Group Commanders so much author-ity to develop their own tactics in the fighting of the battle,

Dowding was hesitant about making too hasty an interference, even if it seemed that Leigh-Mallory was possibly paying undue attention to the views of a junior officer. That junior officer was, in fact, proving himself, and if his over-enthusiastic manner was taken too seriously by some, Dowding felt that it was up to the A.O.C. to curb him.

'When I look back on it all now,' Dowding has said, 'it was asking a lot of any man to think of being able to curb Bader, particularly when he was doing so well in his own flying.'

But even Leigh-Mallory must have realised that some restraint was necessary. While the heavy raids on the airfields in the south of England and the attacks in the north of 15 August were in progress, and, as Bader's biographer has put it, '12 Group was held back to cover England's industrial heart north of London,' Bader was having to wait at his station at Coltishall in Norfolk, at readiness for any sudden call. 'Burning for the fight, Bader rang Leigh-Mallory and pleaded to be embroiled,' it is recorded.

'While agreeing that it was natural enough for all pilots to want to get into the fight, I cannot help feeling that it was curious that such a direct access should have been available in contacting the A.O.C.,' Dowding has commented, 'particularly from Coltishall, which was well away from the south.'

Bader's biographer credits Leigh-Mallory with replying: 'We can't put all our eggs in one basket, Bader. You've got to hang on and wait. No doubt the enemy would be delighted to draw our fighter cover away from the Midlands. In any case, I can't send you in until 11 Group calls for you.'

Douglas Bader seems to have failed to attach sufficient importance to the reasons behind the plans for Group coverage of the whole country. Right at this very time, on 15 August, when the Luftwaffe staged one of their greatest series of attacks of the entire battle and when No. 12 Group was engaged in the very task for which it was designed, there is this comment that 'it was 11 Group's battle and 12 Group was held back.'

'To begin with, No. 12 Group were never held back,' Dowding has commented. 'They were occupied that day with the raids coming in over the East Coast, and if they had come down into 11 Group I should have criticised them because they would have been intruding on the job that 11 Group were there to do. Secondly, they would have been wasting precious time and energy in going outside their own region, which was enough for them to protect at a time when it was actually under attack.'

In his work with the squadron at Coltishall, Bader went about 'expounding with the fervour of an evangelist the finer points of air fighting', it is stated, but, it is added, 'he was a dogmatist preaching dogma of a bygone day.' A further comment reads: 'Bader's sense of discipline was deep-rooted when it was a matter of obeying an order from Bader, or from anyone whom he respected; it was less predictable in some other circumstances.'

It was Douglas Bader's conduct in those 'other circumstances' which was coming to give Dowding cause for concern. 'In view of what was to happen later,' he has commented, 'I think that sums up pretty well the difficulties that Bader himself was having to face.'

Fighter pilots are by their very nature excessively individualistic. It is perhaps the outstanding trait in the characters of this breed of men. It is also the reason why so many of them appear all too often to be rebels. That was the spirit that was needed, and they had to be that way. But that spirit also needed to be kept under firm control, both by those in command and by the individual himself.

'. . . it was intolerable to Bader that others should be plunging into the fire of battle (not to mention honour),' Bader's biographer commented on his conduct a little later, 'while he was held impotently on the ground. Training had wrapped a cloak of correctness around the ebullient spirit, but now the spirit was bursting the seams again.'

'It was, in so many ways, such a splendid spirit,' Dowding has said. 'But it was so difficult to understand just why he should always be bursting at the seams.'

'Outwardly he exuded so much confidence that it was catching,' Bader's biographer wrote. There could be no question about that, and the reports that were finding their way to higher authority were leading to a keen appreciation of what Bader was achieving, and his name was attracting a great deal of attention. But always, it seemed, there was that 'little demon' that had to be taken into account.

Anyone who had any feeling of compassion could not fail to feel a little sad that this force should have been lurking there in the background of Douglas Bader's character. At times it made of him the extraordinarily gallant fighting pilot that he was and patriot that he is, and at other times it drove him to the voicing of opinions which were to many, including his Commander-in-Chief, of a doubtful validity, and which were expressed with an arrogance that amused some but all too often distressed others.

It also seemed to be overlooked at times by the younger pilots that all the senior commanders in the R.A.F. at this time had seen active service as pilots in the various theatres of the First World War, and most of them had served with squadrons on the Western Front. But for all their experiences during that earlier war, and some of them were very experienced, one seldom heard them refer to what they had known as young pilots.

'It was a different war,' Dowding once commented. 'We were pilots, and we worked on a sound foundation in having had that early experience of the beginning of war in the air. But it was all very elementary, and it was no use harking back to what had been done then. We still had a great deal to learn, but we had progressed far beyond those days of the war when we were young men.'

But for Douglas Bader his heroes of that earlier age were not mere pioneers. They were shining lights which attracted him and to a great extent bedazzled him. 'I'm certain Bishop and McCudden and the others were right,' he emphasised to his pilots in his squadron, repeating again the views that he had held throughout his flying career, old-fashioned though they may have been in the eyes of many of those with whom he was having to work.

'To think in such terms was out-of-date,' Dowding commented. 'Compared with what had been evolved and was in use in Fighter Command in 1940, there were really no fighter operations in the first war. There were fighter formations, and they flew in formations, but even they were on free-booting expeditions. There was none of the highly disciplined flying that had to be done in Fighter Command through the very nature of our strict ground to air control in 1940. That was the essence of the whole structure of Fighter Command: control on the ground, control in the air, and control between the ground and the air.'

From Dowding's point of view, the demands for almost any consideration of what had happened in the First World War was a retrograde step. It did not take into account the elaborate and intricate machinery of the control that had been evolved with such care over the years prior to the outbreak of war, and which was continuing to develop. But for a man of Douglas Bader's temperament it was extremely difficult to exercise the patience that was needed in fitting into such an overall system of control.

'This period is full of interest from a tactical point of view,' Johnnie Johnson wrote long afterwards, 'because the tactics developed by both sides formed the basis upon which our air battles were fought for the remainder of the war.'

In that development there was also further growth of the controversy that was to go far beyond the anterooms of the various messes and other centres of gossip, and was to embrace more than technical discussions; and it was to continue for such a long time to come. It was now becoming an issue between two schools of thought, and reputations were becoming involved in a distinctly unhealthy atmosphere.

The whole matter of tactics still called for a great deal of exploration. Since the outbreak of the war and during the early part of the battle it had been found that those who knew the most—from actual experience in the fighting at the moment—were advocating more flexibility, not less, in the formations that were to be used. The mustering of the forces in large formations for defence was, in this school of thought, a retrograde step, harking back to the First World War.

'I had no preconceived ideas about wings or anything like that,' Dowding said later. 'All I knew was that the experimental efforts to try them out had been failures. If the advocates of the big wings had only known it, the experience that had been gained was all against them.' However, in his despatch, he rightly called attention to the use made by Fighter Command at the time of the evacuation 'in the Dunkirk fighting' of wing formations of fighters. 'I am personally in favour of using Fighter formations in the greatest strength which circumstances will permit . . . where we could choose our time and build up our formations on the outward journey,' he wrote. 'I habitually employed four-Squadron formations as a preferable alternative to using two-Squadron formations at more frequent intervals; but, during the attacks on London, the available strength of Fighters did not admit of this policy, nor was time available.'

Of what would have happened if the larger wings had been used by No. 11 Group in the battle, Dowding added: '. . . in justice to Air Vice-Marshal Park, I think that, if the policy of big formations had been attempted at this time in No. 11 Group, many more Bombers would have reached their objectives without opposition.'

Of the many who have ventured to express their opinions about how the tactics in the fighting in the air in the defence of the country were, or should have been, handled in the Battle of Britain, none is sounder than Group Captain T. P. Gleave. Now retired from the Royal Air Force after a lifetime spent in the Service, most of which was in fighters, Gleave served on Dowding's staff at the Headquarters of Fighter Command right up to the time of the battle, then commanded a Hurricane squadron in the battle, and half-way through it was shot down and terribly burnt. He is now recognised for his work as a reputable historian, and an authority on the tactics used in the battle. Being one of those who was an actual participant in the fighting in the air as well as an historian who has made a penetrating study of the whole matter, Gleave's views are of particular importance. They are in complete agreement with all that Dowding believed at the time and holds to now.

'The prime purpose of a fighter defence is to prevent the enemy bombers reaching their targets,' Tom Gleave has pointed out. 'The essence in achieving this is time. To get a squadron off the ground took about three and three-quarter minutes with everything in its favour, the average possibly being four minutes.'

With those times as an established basis from which to work, and they are the generally accepted times, Gleave has pointed out that if a wing of two paired squadrons were to be sent off that would add another three or four minutes, and if three, four and five squadrons were ordered to operate as a wing the time taken to form up would stretch 'to twelve, fifteen and even twenty minutes or more'.

In its defence of the south-east of England, No. 11 Group did not have enough squadrons to be able 'to put more than one squadron against each raid until after the battle was virtually won,' Gleave continued. 'To have put paired squadrons or bigger wings against certain raids and none against others would not only have meant that the bombers would have been intercepted perilously close to their targets if not on top of them, but also that other raids would have been free to attack their targets as they wished.'

What came to be so gravely over-looked by those who were intent upon promoting the use of the big wings was that, as Tom Gleave pointed out, 'a wing is a defensive tactic for offensive purposes.' From that, it is obvious, the aim of the big wing has to be to provide a mutual protection in attacks over enemy territory, and in gaining this advantage, Gleave added, 'flexibility and power of manoeuvre have to be sacrificed, whereas the opposing fighter can attack in small formations from all angles and get clear, safe in the knowledge that they are over friendly territory.'

Since 'flexibility and power of manoeuvre' were essential in the fighting over England, it was, in Tom Gleave's view, 'folly' to try to meet the enemy raids in the Battle of Britain with wings.

The views held by Keith Park are now accepted by every authority and most of the pilots who were involved in the thick of the fighting. He has said, 'Owing to the very short warning received of enemy raids approaching England, or the south of England, it would have been quite impossible to intercept enemy formations with big wings before they bombed their targets such as the aerodromes and aircraft factories. At the very best, big wing formations from No. 11 Group, if we had used them, would have intercepted a few of the German raids after they had unloaded their bombs on vital targets, and were able to take evasive action by diving away in retreat under cover of their own fighter formations or escorts. The German escorting fighters, having the advantage of height and being freed from the need to escort their bombers, would have decimated our fighter squadrons.'

Park also had to rely on support being made available at any time that he might need it. 'It was with my consent that Park had to be free to ask for assistance from the two neighbouring Groups whenever such assistance, or support, was necessary,' Dowding explained. 'He did not have the aerodromes or the facilities to accomodate all the forces that we might have liked to have available in his Group in the south, and I thought that the right idea was that the Groups on his flanks should back him up. I expected that they would all work closely together in achieving that. Any reference to my Headquarters for decisions about that always meant delay, and since time was so pressing we could not have any delays.'

On the other hand, Park knew that he had to make the greatest use of what he had. 'Lord Dowding once told me quite clearly that I was not to call on the other Groups for support or for reinforcements until I had exhausted all my own resources,' he remarked many years later.

'It was unnecessary to expect that while Park still had resources of his own he should call on another Group for help,' Dowding added to that. 'The other Groups were either standing by, or should have been, or were actively engaged themselves.'

In comparing Park's position in No. 11 Group with that of the No. 12 Group Commander, Dowding commented: 'I cannot stress enough that the problems that faced Leigh-Mallory within his Group were quite different from the problems which were constantly facing Park in the need for quick response in his Group to the sudden enemy attacks. Park was in the front line.'

CHAPTER TEN

THE BATTLE

During the whole of the time of the heavy fighting in the latter part of August, it was natural that the squadrons of No. 12 Group should thirst for action. But Dowding had a broader view of what was happening than it was possible for anybody else to take, particularly out in the Groups, and there was the need for each of the Groups to fulfil their own roles: No. 11 bearing the brunt of the attack, with Nos. 10 and 12 Groups protecting their own areas and ready at any time to support No. 11 Group should that become necessary.

There had been no reason for Dowding to think that Park and Brand, the A.O.C. of No. 10 Group, were doing anything but playing their parts correctly and in the fashion that he expected of them. Park has fully acknowledged the support given him by Brand. But at the back of Dowding's mind there was continuing to develop the doubt about Leigh-Mallory's complete agreement with what was being expected of him; and part of the reason for his doubt was that he continued to hear about the attention that Leigh-Mallory was paying to what Dowding regarded as too free an expression of criticism by Douglas Bader.

By the last week in August, when the fighting was at an intense stage, No. 11 Group was very heavily engaged. 'Day after day while the fights raged Bader alternately sulked and stormed in the dispersal hut at Coltishall,' his biographer recorded. 'Ops ignored them ... he kept railing at the stupidity of keeping them on the ground while outnumbered squadrons had to engage a massed enemy.'

One cannot help but sympathise with a man of Bader's eager temperament finding himself in the position of being, as he thought, out of the battle; but he was not out of it. There was nothing 'stupid' about his squadron being kept on the ground at Coltishall. They were there as part of the overall plan for defence. They were not being ignored, and if anything had come their way they would have been ordered into the air.

'There were occasions when Park was so hard-pressed that all his squadrons were in the air at once,' Dowding commented. 'But was it for a squadron commander in Norfolk, in No. 12 Group, with a clearly defined task, to decide whether he should be drawn into some other task? Park could ask Leigh-Mallory to look after some of the north-eastern aerodromes of No. 11 Group if he felt it was necessary, and there were the squadrons standing by for that very purpose. Among them was Bader's own squadron, to be called upon when necessary.'

Friday, 30 August 1940, brought to Dowding all that he had feared might happen in the bombing of his aerodromes. Cautious husbanding of his resources through not putting up any unnecessary patrols, combined with the most careful controlling, had kept the situation within reasonable bounds. The course that was being followed had been wisely reviewed in the orders issued by Park on 19 August, and those orders had been scrupulously observed by No. 11 Group. This had been strengthened by Park's signal of 26 August about the necessity for Group and Sector controllers 'to put all squadrons in contact with the enemy . . .'

The information available to the controllers, the men who actually had to exercise the most careful and yet imaginative understanding of what was happening, was scanty enough, and there was the most alert appreciation of the necessity for exact information from the ground to the fighters in the air. It was fully realised that the Germans were now flying very large formations, or sweeps, of fighters in the hope that they would divert that control and attract the R.A.F. fighters to what could be nothing more than what has been described as slaughter. In the forward No. 11 Group, Park's orders were well understood. It was the German bombers that had to be watched for, and if no bombers were about the R.A.F. fighters were to be kept in the background. They were not to be sacrificed.

During the night before, there had been a fairly heavy raid on Liverpool, with smaller raids on the Midlands, and some activity over London. By morning the weather was fair, and it was generally a fine day with some cloud, which interfered at times with the Observer Corps visual plotting over land. By nine o'clock radar was picking up the first plots of the enemy forming up over Cap Gris Nez, and by half past ten there were indications of a heavy assault on the way. From then on it was a day of very great activity and the severest anxiety.

A comment has been made by the historian Ronald W. Clark that 'the fighting of August 30th was to have one very important affect on the rest of the Battle, since it crystallised the case for what was to become known as the "big wing" policy.' To that he added: 'The differing views were brought out into the open, as a result of the fighting on the 30th, by Squadron Leader Bader. On that one day the squadron shot down a dozen enemy planes without loss to itself, and the success convinced Bader that the concentration of larger numbers of fighters would pay dividends—that a Wing of fighters would be more effective than squadrons used separately.'

That evening, at Coltishall, Douglas Bader is reported by his biographer as saying to Leigh-Mallory: '. . . if we'd had more aircraft we could have knocked down a lot more. Other squadrons in the group have been standing by like us. Would it be possible for us all to take off together?'

In this one remark alone there is revealed yet again the grave misunderstanding, or misinterpretation, that existed of Dowding's whole conception of the way in which his command was to function. And to add to that it is further reported that Leigh-Mallory's reaction was to say to Bader: 'Sounds splendid.'

During the last week in August there were occasions when No. 12 Group failed in their duty to provide the protection that Park had asked for of his northern airfields and the Germans had got through and bombed them, while the squadrons of No. 11 Group were making the forward interceptions of the enemy to the south. Park had naturally lodged vigorous protests. On 30 August it happened again. The important airfield at Biggin Hill was hit very hard.

At a quarter to five in the afternoon of that day the long-awaited action came Douglas Bader's way, and he was presented with the opportunity for a full-blooded engagement with the enemy. His squadron had been ordered from Coltishall to

Duxford earlier in the day, and from there they were scrambled and ordered to cover at a height of fifteen thousand feet the No. 11 Group airfield at North Weald. Of what Bader thought as soon as he and his squadron were airborne, his biographer wrote: 'This was no damn' good. He wanted to be up-sun himself. Disregarding controller's words, he swung thirty degrees west. Might miss the enemy! One usually obeyed a controller.'

Under the tactical system upon which the whole defence was based, squadron commanders did not know the whereabouts of the enemy forces until they were airborne. Then they had to rely entirely upon the instructions passed to them by the controllers to bring about an effective interception. Any variation from the instructions given by the controllers could lead to the controllers themselves having their own planned interception thwarted.

The whole purpose of Bader's squadron being ordered into the air was to provide, in the plan agreed upon between Nos. 11 and 12 Groups, for the protection of the airfield at North Weald, and of an area around it into which they would be directed as the enemy's intention became clear. Already that day there had been the bombing of Biggin Hill by the Germans who were not seen by the No. 12 Group squadron which was specifically detailed to provide protection for it. Now, in the afternoon, the No. 11 Group squadrons were heavily committed to forward interception of the enemy. Park was relying on his request to Leigh-Mallory for the support, in protecting his airfields, that No. 12 Group were to provide.

Just about the time when Bader and his squadron got airborne at Duxford, a small force of German bombers flew up the Thames estuary as far as Sheppey and then, with no opposition, turned south and made, in the words of the official historian, 'an accurate and devastating attack' on Biggin Hill, the second of the day. It was one of the worst attacks suffered by a Fighter Command aerodrome. In the words of Wood and Dempster, 'the airfield was reduced to a shambles . . . with thirty-nine dead and twenty-six injured.'

During this attack on Biggin Hill, another enemy raid had come in, from over Sheppey. It was intercepted, but some of the bombers managed to get through to Luton, where the

Vauxhall motor works were hit, with over fifty people being killed.

'South-west of North Weald,' his biographer recorded, Bader and his squadron intercepted the enemy raid headed for that airfield. The single squadron waded into a large enemy force of bombers with its fighter escort, 'and not a bomb on North Weald'. When Bader and his squadron landed back at Duxford 'they totted up the score—twelve confirmed and several more damaged . . . not a single bullet hole in any of the Hurricanes.'

During the whole of that day, with so many of its squadrons involved, Fighter Command flew the second greatest number of sorties up to that time: 1,054. As a result of that massive effort the entire Command claimed thirty-six German aircraft destroyed, with a loss of twenty-five of its own fighters.

'Later Bader explained to Woodhall why he had disobeyed his R/T instructions,' it is stated, and he '. . . expounded his views with the usual vigour.' Making the perfectly sound observation that 'we've got to catch them before they get to their target,' Bader is then credited with saying: 'If the controller will tell us where they are in time—direction and height—we'll sort out the tactics in the air, get up-sun ourselves and beat hell out of them before they can bomb.'

Since that view, apart from the desire to catch the enemy before they could bomb, was in direct conflict with Dowding's whole concept of the control of his forces through the elaborate radar and radio warning and communications system which had been so carefully evolved, there was only one view that he could take of it. 'Monstrous!' he exclaimed.

The last day of August was one of the roughest for the R.A.F. in the whole course of the battle. Fighter Command lost thirty-nine fighters with fourteen pilots being killed, and the German losses were forty-one aircraft destroyed. It was the beginning of a week for Dowding that was to reach at the end of it a peak in his anxiety.

'Day after day the Luftwaffe pounded away at the airfields; day after day the same force of pilots held them off, split them up and shot them down,' Peter Wykeham wrote. 'Although the advantage in victories remained firmly on our side we were losing aircraft faster than the factories could replace them; the Command reserves were dropping, and with the bone-weary pilots flying four or more sorties a day it began to look as if the defences could be worn out by sheer weight of numbers. An average of a thousand enemy aircraft a day were coming over, the pilots were continually in the air, and the constant and desperate combats at odds were beginning to have their effect.'

A crisis was approaching, and for Dowding the problem was in the increasingly acute shortage of pilots. 'By the beginning of September the incidence of casualties became so serious that a fresh squadron would become depleted and exhausted before any of the resting and reforming squadrons was ready to take its place,' he wrote in his despatch. 'Fighter pilots were no longer being produced in numbers sufficient to fill the gaps in the fighting ranks.'

Long afterwards, Dowding made the comment: 'Knowing how critical the time was could only be put down to using one's common sense. Of course I had available all the intelligence, or what there was of it, which meant that I had information that was not generally known. There was the information about the build-up of the invasion forces across the Channel on the one hand, and on the other our own wretched chance of resisting if an attack were made.'

It was never easy for Dowding to express his own deep personal feeling about his pilots. 'But let there be no mistake about how he felt,' Francis Wilkinson once said. 'All along he had that immensely strong feeling for his fighter pilots. Every time he heard of casualties his heart bled. He really felt it.'

What appeared to be an aloofness in Dowding was something that struck many of those who served under his command; but the point made by Francis Wilkinson about Dowding's feeling for his air crews is one that must never be overlooked. Dowding was always very conscious of the grave dangers that all air crews encountered in any fighting in the air. He had flown and fought in the air in the First World War, and from first-hand experience he fully appreciated those dangers. In the Second World War, when he had control over the fates of so many men, Dowding was constantly aware of the violence of death, and, even if spared that, the pain and disfigurement from wounds that were such constant threats. He later made the comment: 'One of the worst features of the battle from my point of view was the continuous anxiety for the lives of my fighter boys and the wish that it might be possible in any way to ameliorate their lot.'

There are two R.A.F. organisations with which Dowding has always felt a particularly strong affinity. They are the Battle of Britain Fighter Association, which is made up of all those who flew in the battle, and the Guinea Pig Club. The latter has been described as the most exclusive club in the world: the club that nobody wants to belong to. It consists of those members of air crews who were burnt during the war and who came to be treated, under the late Sir Archibald McIndoe, at the Queen Victoria Hospital at East Grinstead.

As a result of being shot down on 31 August, Tom Gleave became one of the founder members of this club, and today he is known as the Chief Guinea Pig. He is also the historian of the Battle of Britain Fighter Association; and through these links a personal friend of Dowding's. The events that led to Gleave becoming a Guinea Pig provide a disturbing illustration of what happened to so many others in the course of the war.

Tom Gleave had arrived with his Hurricane squadron at the airfield at Kenley, in No. 11 Group, after having been in No. 12 and No. 13 Groups. He has spoken about 'how frustrating it was' to be in the north, and 'why the chaps were so maddeningly keen to get down to No. 11 Group'. Of his time at Kenley, he has further said: 'We were there during one of the most violent forty-eight hour periods of the whole battle, second only to 15-16 August, so far as we know, in German air force sorties flown and German aircraft lost, and the greatest of all in R.A.F. sorties flown and British aircraft lost.'

Less than a year after being shot down, Gleave wrote a telling description of the events that led, with such speed, to his becoming what he described as an 'R.A.F. Casualty' when the description was published. Part of it reads:

A large raid was coming in from the south . . . I glanced up to see what we were chasing. Right above us were rows of Hun bombers—

Ju.88s in line astern—and my aircraft was directly below one line of them and closing distance rapidly. I rocked my wings and then eased the nose up, taking a bead on No. 5 of the line of Huns and giving him a raking burst. I repeated the process on No. 3.

I was about to pull up to attack No. 1 ... when I heard a metallic click above the roar of my engine. A sudden burst of heat struck my face, and I looked down into the cockpit. A long spout of flame was issuing from the hollow starboard wing-root. The flames increased until the cockpit was like the centre of a blow-lamp nozzle. There was nothing left to do but bale out. The skin was already rising off my right wrist and hand, and my left hand was starting to blister, the glove being already partially burnt off. My shoes and slacks must have been burning all this time. I undid my harness and tried to raise myself, but found I had not the strength. I was comforted by the thought that I had my gun ready loaded if things came to the worst. I decided to pull off my helmet, open the cockpit cover and roll on my back so that I could drop out. My helmet came off after a determined tug: I opened the cockpit cover and that was the last effort I had to make. There was a blinding flash, I seemed to be travelling through yards of flame; then I found myself turning over and over in the air. ... My hand instinctively passed over the harness release and on to the rip-cord handle ... then came a gentle jerk as I was pulled into the vertical position. I felt my left hip and head strike the ground simultaneously and then all was still.

With an effort I stood up and surveyed the damage. My shoes still looked like shoes and I found that I could walk; why, I don't know, as my ankle and each side of my right foot were burnt and my left foot was scorched and had several small burns. My slacks had disappeared except for portions that had been covered by the parachute harness. The skin on my right leg, from the top of the thigh to just above the ankle, had lifted and draped my leg like outsize plus-fours. My left leg was in a similar condition except that the left thigh was only scorched ... Above each ankle I had a bracelet of unburnt skin: my socks, which were always wrinkled, had refused to burn properly. My Service gloves were almost burnt off, and the skin from my wrists and hands hung down like paper bags. The under side of my right arm and elbow were burnt and so was my face and neck. I could see all right, although it felt like looking through slits in a mass of swollen skin, and I came to the conclusion that the services of a doctor were necessary.

Those services were indeed necessary. Tom Gleave had to be given an almost entirely new face by the plastic surgeons in the work that was done for him under the care of Archie

McIndoe at East Grinstead. The effect that the sight of such injuries had on other people when they first saw them varied enormously. With Tom Gleave and his wife it was unique.

'What on earth have you been doing with yourself, darling?' Beryl Gleave asked when she arrived at the hospital and saw him for the first time. She is a woman of the same splendid metal as her husband. Gleave found it hard to give an immediate answer; and then he merely said: 'Had a row with a German.'

The first week of September brought to a climax the German onslaught on the airfields of Fighter Command. For Dowding it was to add yet more to the mounting strain, and then to bring relief. 'I naturally had to try to figure out what they were going to do next, and I had that on my mind all the time,' he has explained. 'And with the inexplicable changes of tactics they seemed to indulge in that was not at all easy.'

This was the worst period of strain for Dowding during the whole battle. Fortunately he was left in peace in his personal affairs, and he was able to devote himself unsparingly to the fighting; but by the end of that week it was noticed that he was showing more definite signs of the strain. By 6 September the situation so far as Fighter Command was concerned had become very, very grave, and Dowding was deeply concerned over just how much more his Command could take if the Germans went on with their heavy day attacks on his airfields. On that day, a Friday, King George VI and Queen Elizabeth paid a visit to the Headquarters of Fighter Command. They had lunch with Dowding in the officers' mess, and one of the visitors in the luncheon party that day has since commented on how strained and tired Dowding was looking.

It was small wonder. Fighter Command was stretched to the limit, and only the night before London had been subjected to a very heavy air raid that had in it an indication of much worse to come. If anybody knew the stark gravity of the hour it was Dowding. In his official history, Denis Richards wrote:

Not only was there very considerable damage to the ground organisation during this period, but the British losses in fighters so greatly exceeded the output from production that in three more weeks of activity on the same scale—if the Germans could have stood three more weeks—the fighter reserves would have been completely exhausted.

In his account of this visit made by the King and Queen to Bentley Priory, General Pile commented that Dowding had indulged on that occasion in one of his famous lectures in talking with the Queen. It is more likely that Dowding was trying to fill in the additional forty minutes beyond the scheduled time of their visit when he had to keep the King and Queen in the underground Operations Room because of one of the three heavy raids that were launched that day by the Germans, and which occurred while they were at Bentley Priory.

On 7 September there came into effect the big change in the German attack, and the weight of their onslaught by day was changed from the airfields of Fighter Command to heavy attacks on London by day and by night. With that change of tactics there came for Dowding a relief that was greater than he could then express. 'The command was literally wasting away under Dowding's eyes,' Wood and Dempster have stated, 'and there was nothing he could do about it if southern England was to continue as a defended area.'

'It brought an intense feeling of relief to me—intense relief,' Dowding commented much later and with great feeling about the change in the German plan. 'I could hardly believe that the Germans would have made such a mistake. From then on it was gradually borne upon me that it was a supernatural intervention at that particular time, and that that was really the crucial day.'

But all that Dowding could be certain about at the time was that across the Channel, such a short distance away, there was being assembled the great might of the German army. The spearhead of what was to come was in the skies; the warnings were out that invasion by the German army was a strong possibility; and on that day of 7 September the invasion became classified as imminent.

Hermann Goering himself was in command—for whatever that was worth—of the assault on London, and he stationed himself grandiosely at Cap Gris Nez to watch his air fleets go into the attack. It is impossible to resist wondering just how much Goering knew about, or understood, his two main opponents: Dowding the strategist, and Park the tactician. There was such a vast and complete difference between the German commander and his R.A.F. opponents, and the only point about which they could be said to have anything in common—it was a curiously close one in its own way—was that they had fought as pilots in their respective air forces, opposing each other in the air even then, on the old Western Front of so many years before.

While keenly aware of what the more indiscriminate German bombing meant to the civilian population of the country, Dowding was nevertheless heartfelt in his relief because he believed that it would give his Command just the chance that was needed to recover from the beating it had been taking. Being the humanitarian that he was he always felt acutely unhappy about the terrible plights into which civilians were plunged in the bombing. He remarked on that once to his sister, Hilda, saying how miserable he felt whenever he saw— and there was plenty of it to be seen—the bombed-out homes with all the privacy and dignity of human life, even of the simplest order, reduced to nothing more than a public display of so much wretched debris.

In his later despatch, Dowding referred in considerable detail to the work of the guns and the searchlights of Anti-Aircraft Command, treating all that work as an integral part of his whole report on the fighting of the battle. At one point in the despatch he wrote: 'The distribution of army units was, as a matter of fact, in a condition of perpetual change to meet new situations as they arose, and I must pay a very sincere tribute to the flexibility of the Army organisation, and to the tact, patience and loyalty of the Commander-in-Chief of the Anti-Aircraft Command, Lt-Gen. Sir Frederick A. Pile, Bart, K.C.B., D.S.O., M.C., which enabled these constant changes to be made without disorganisation.'

That was an official expression of Dowding's appreciation. There were other unofficial exchanges of views between Dowding and Pile on a more personal level that had in them expressions of considerable warmth on both sides. At one stage, in the middle of the battle, Pile's gunners had a particularly good day, at the end of which they claimed that they had shot down eight enemy aircraft and damaged another five. 'Dowding rang me up to congratulate us,' Pile wrote. 'I thanked him, but said that congratulations were really due entirely to Fighter Command and the man who had trained them.'

It was yet another generous comment for Pile to make, and it was then that there came from Dowding the more revealing expression of his relief. 'Pile, it's a miracle,' he replied, '—the miracle of the Marne over again. The pilots were wonderful, but it is a miracle.'

And when, a few days later, the claim was made by Fighter Command that they had had a particularly successful encounter with the enemy, Pile again generously commented that he 'did not feel in any way slighted' when Dowding spoke to him with feeling about his pilots, saying: 'England is being defended— saved by four hundred young men.'

There was reason enough for Dowding's great pride in these pilots of his because many of them were saving England and fighting to do that without the full training that they should have received. The reserve of pilots that Dowding had to call upon had dropped away alarmingly, and youngsters were being rushed to the squadrons in the line, some of them without even having had the chance to fire their guns in practice let alone in anger. The inevitable lower standard of the actual flying was very worrying, but there was nothing that Dowding could do about that. The squadrons had to be manned. The pilots were fine material and ready to give of their best, but that best fell short technically of the quality of those who were lost and whom they were replacing.

Half way through the battle, Dowding lived up to the promise that he had made to Francis Wilkinson, and without uttering a word about the inconvenience that it must have caused him, he granted permission for him to go back to flying. Wilkinson went through a refresher course, and then became an instructor at the Central Flying School.

'After the day battle was over and the boys used to be sent to us for their final polishing in actual flying,' Wilkinson recalled, 'I used to wonder how some of them had managed to survive. I had youngsters with D.F.C.'s who really couldn't fly, in the strict sense, the aircraft they had been fighting with. Some of them had hundreds of hours in those fighters, but the polish simply wasn't there. All the more credit is due to them for having done so well, and an awful lot of them must have been shot down in the battle because of that. But what else could be done at the time?'

It was an old problem in fighter operations in time of war, and it had been all too well-known during the First World War. From his experiences then, Dowding knew exactly what it was all about. But what could he do? As those weeks of the battle continued he went through an ever-mounting concern about this problem alone. On the one hand there was the shortage of pilots as a statistic that was a real fact of life; and on the other hand there was the emotional strain of knowing what the un-trained youngsters were having to face.

But if this was a crisis for the Royal Air Force, and for Dowding in particular, the Luftwaffe was also facing a crisis. The lead that the Germans had enjoyed in aircraft production was now lost to the British. For this achievement Dowding has always paid the highest tribute to Lord Beaverbrook, the Minister of Aircraft Production, and to Air Chief Marshal Sir Wilfrid Freeman, who had one of the best brains that the Royal Air Force ever had the good fortune to have guiding it. Freeman had been Dowding's deputy when he was Air Member for Research and Development, and had taken over from him when Dowding went to Fighter Command. Dowding always thought very highly of Freeman's great ability. After Beaver-brook became Minister, Dowding came to appreciate and understand the great driving force of this unique personality; and out of that there developed between these two men who were so different in almost every conceivable way a deep and lasting personal friendship.

Many years later, in commenting on the work that he did at the Headquarters of No. 11 Group, John Willoughby de

Broke said: 'How lucky it was for those of us who were doing the controlling that we did not fully realise at the time what a desperately serious battle for existence this country was fighting. If we had, we might have felt an undue sense of personal responsibility in our actions. We regarded all that we did and had to do as being part of our daily routine in life, and we carried out to the best of our ability our instructions as they were given to us by our A.O.C. But none of us on my level quite realised the seriousness of the situation. For one thing, we did not have access to the information that would have given us an overall picture.'

From late in August there was a steady decline in the relationship between No. 11 and No. 12 Group, and nobody seemed to know at the time the exact reason for that, other than that No. 12 Group had failed on occasions to provide the support that had been asked for by No. 11 Group. But in the early stages of that difference it was an internal, almost domestic affair.

'As 11 Group Controllers we believed that we had the right to ask No. 12 Group direct to intercept raids that we were unable to cover ourselves, to back us up,' Willoughby de Broke explained. 'I know that Park felt the same way. But the difficulties between the two Group commanders that developed over their differing views about how things should be done put a stop to that easy liaison. That was a pity because in the early days there was a good liaison and we were given great help by No. 12 Group when we asked for protection of our airfields in the north of our area. Then there came the time when they fell down, and our airfields were bombed, and that was when the trouble started.'

One of the bitterest memories that Willoughby de Broke has as a Controller at No. 11 Group was an occasion that, as he still speaks of it, causes him 'rage and indignation' over a failure in liaison between No. 11 and No. 12 Group.

'We could see on the table a large German raid flying straight up the Thames Estuary,' he recalled. 'We had all our own squadrons in the air tackling other raids. This big German raid was flying west, and the Duxford aircraft from No. 12 Group were steaming due east on a reciprocal course, about ten miles north of the incoming raid. It was impossible for us to intervene and get the 12 Group Controller to give the necessary orders because they were not under our control and communications were through Fighter Command Headquarters and at that time not directly between Group Headquarters. This took so much time that there was no interception. They passed what seemed to be so close to each other, and there could have been an easy and very good engagement.'

The root cause of the trouble was in the different thinking of the two Group Commanders and the break that that had brought about in their being able to communicate with each other. It was justifiable enough that they should have had their own views and opinions, but to what extent were those views and opinions in harmony with Dowding's orders? For the answer to that a study has to be made of their respective views on the use of the forces at their disposal. Which was it to be: at squadron strength, with the pairing of squadrons if possible, or in wings of squadrons?

When, towards the end of August, the north-eastern aerodromes of No. 11 Group were bombed because the squadrons from No. 12 Group were not in the right place, Dowding began to suspect that there was something more to it than a mistake. 'In fact, that wasn't the only instance of difference of opinions that came to my attention,' he said long afterwards. 'There were also the personal elements that came to be so deeply involved. But what I didn't know at the time was that the conduct of the No. 12 Group Commander as a whole amounted to a challenge to my orders.'

CHAPTER ELEVEN

DIFFERENCE OF OPINION

While the squadrons in No. 11 Group were fully occupied with countering the heavy enemy attacks that it was their lot to have to face, operating with swift and flexible action, further planning was going ahead in No. 12 Group with the idea of the use of larger formations. After the successful defence of North Weald by Douglas Bader's squadron on 30 August, Leigh-Mallory had 'said he would think about' Bader's plea to be allowed to use a larger number of aircraft working together as one unit.

Of the operations during 31 August, Douglas Bader's biographer wrote that it seemed that Bader's squadron 'were only sent up at lunch-time or tea-time to give 11 Group a spell when no German aircraft were about'. The next day Bader received instructions from Leigh-Mallory that he should 'try this large formation scheme of yours'. Bader went about practising taking off and leading in the air three squadrons, one of Spitfires and two, including his own, of Hurricanes.

'Farther south the Luftwaffe was still smashing at southern England and 11 Group seemed to be hogging the battle,' Bader's biographer wrote. 'Intolerable! Bader said so repeatedly.'

What was intolerable was that anybody in another Group should even think, let alone express, such views about the way in which 11 Group was being handled. It was an attitude taken in voicing criticism that could give rise to wholly unnecessary ill-feeling within the Command, and which could cause Dowding nothing but distress.

'It was an unfounded and most improper accusation to make,' he commented.

By 5 September, it has been recorded, Douglas Bader 'had the "scramble" time down to a little over three minutes in getting his thirty-six fighters off the ground.'

'All right, Bader,' Leigh-Mallory is reported to have said

after watching one of the practice scrambles. 'Next time 11 Group calls on you, take your whole team.'

The next time was the very next day, 7 September.

Of Douglas Bader's frame of mind on that important day, when the Germans started their heavy attack on London, his biographer wrote: 'All day he railed at Group, at Ops and the imperturbable Woodhall, demanding to be let off the leash.' But it was not until a quarter to five in the afternoon that the Duxford wing was ordered off, with instructions to 'orbit North Weald' at ten thousand feet.

'. . . Bader disobeyed instructions again,' his biographer recorded, 'going on past 10,000 feet to 15,000 in his eagerness to be well on top of anything that they sighted.' Even then, when they made contact with the enemy force—quoted as being made up of 'about seventy Dorniers and 110's mixed up' —it was still five thousand feet above them.

'Behind him the squadrons were trailing, unable to keep up,' Bader's biographer continued. It left Bader with the problem of 'attacking in a straggle from below with 109's on top. No chance to break them up. No time for tactics.'

After reading about that, Dowding commented: 'It doesn't sound to me like very good wing-leading.'

In the fighting that followed, with 'the other two squadrons . . . . so far behind that they had virtually missed the fight', Bader's squadron claimed eleven enemy aircraft destroyed. One pilot was lost, and his own aircraft was badly damaged.

'It didn't come off . . . we were too slow,' Bader is said to have reported to Leigh-Mallory the next day. 'If only we could get off earlier we could be on top and ready for them. Why can't we do that, sir?'

In answer to that—a question which reveals so clearly how little Bader seemed to understand the system of the inter-Group control—Leigh-Mallory had to explain to Bader the elementary planning of the structure of the groups in the Command and their dependence on each other. He pointed out that No. 11 Group did not have 'much chance to scramble big formations', but he added 'your score yesterday seems to justify the experiment, so carry on with the three squadrons.'

So far as Keith Park was concerned, his thoughts were on a more practical and less experimental level. John Willoughby de Broke has referred to that in a discussion that he had with Park at this time. It had to do with a matter about which Park felt very strongly. Both Park and Willoughby de Broke had had a great deal of first-hand experience in their time of casualties in action through having been pilots themselves in the earlier war. Park, in particular, had the additional experience to support his views of having, in his time, commanded fighter squadrons in war and in peace.

The point that Park wanted to make was that which must be forever uppermost in the minds of those who become responsible for fighting squadrons, all the way from the actual squadron commanders up. He believed so strongly that the squadron was the living unit, and its survival or death as a unit depended on the strength that it had in its composition. The degree of skill of each individual pilot was one thing, Park pointed out, but to the squadron it was a matter of how well that skill was incorporated in the squadron as a whole, and how thoroughly each pilot fulfilled his role in being an essential part of the squadron. The pilots had to be able to fly and fight, but they had to be able to do that as a whole and that whole, Park believed so strongly, was the squadron. He wanted to be sure that Willoughby de Broke and the other Controllers fully understood that.

'I assured him that he need not worry about that,' Willoughby de Broke said. 'We could not have agreed with him more.'

There was another point, Willoughby de Broke recalled, about which Park was equally certain, and it made such an impression on him that he was able to repeat Park's exact words.

'I know that you and the other Controllers must be getting very worried about our losses,' Park said.

Willoughby de Broke told Park that they certainly were concerned about that essential aspect of the fighting.

'Well . . . I've been looking into these casualty figures,' Park said, 'and I've come to the conclusion that at our present rate of losses we can just afford it. And I'm damned certain that the Bosch can't. If we can hang on as we're going I'm sure we shall win in the end.'

In a report to Headquarters, Fighter Command, on this first Duxford Wing operation of 7 September, Leigh-Mallory commented: '. . . the three squadrons were at a disadvantage through the loss of any element of surprise, through having to climb up to get at the enemy, and through the enemy fighters coming down on them from the sun.'

This so-called 'disadvantage' could be of no surprise to Dowding. 'The time provided for getting off was always a vexed question,' he said. 'But from what has been reported on this action it sounds as if the wing was either being badly led or it was incapable of being formed up as had been suggested was possible. In either case, on this occasion the whole idea of the use of the wing fell apart.'

Most of 9 September was, for Bader and the three squadrons at Duxford, 'another day of impatient waiting'. But about five o'clock in the afternoon radar information began to show enemy formations building up over the Pas de Calais. The Duxford wing was ordered off, and once they were in the air they were asked—Bader's biographer makes much of the way in which requests were made to him; orders were not given— to 'patrol between North Weald and Hornchurch' at twenty thousand feet.

Of what Bader thought of that, his biographer reported: 'Bader looked at the afternoon sun and thought: I know damn' well they'll swing west and come out of the sun. He forgot North Weald—Hornchurch and climbed his three squadrons south-west over the fringe of London; ignored the "angels twenty" too, climbing till they were specks at 22,000 feet over the reservoirs at Staines, still climbing.'

Bader then spotted an incoming raid: 'Two great swarms of them cutting across in front, heading for London . . . looked like sixty odd in each bunch . . . he wheeled to cut them off . . .'

'. . . the mathematics were good,' his biographer recorded of the fight that followed. 'Twenty enemy destroyed for the loss of four Hurricanes. But still Bader was not satisfied.'

In an interview with Leigh-Mallory immediately after-wards, Bader is credited with having said: '. . . if we'd only had more fighters we could have hacked the Huns down in scores.'

'I was going to talk to you about that,' Leigh-Mallory is reported as saying. 'If I gave you two more squadrons, could you handle them?'

It was in this manner that there came into being the big wing of five squadrons, and it was all done without Dowding being consulted.

In his report on this action which he put in to the Headquarters of Fighter Command, Leigh-Mallory stated that 'the Wing . . . left Duxford at 1700 hours . . . to patrol North Weald and Hornchurch.' He made no mention of the interception being made in the position claimed by Bader, which was quite some distance away from the area assigned to the Wing, but he referred to the engagement having taken place 'over the south-west suburbs of London', which was right across the other side of London from the North Weald—Hornchurch area. Leigh-Mallory concluded with the comment: 'The leader of the Wing considered that at least 20 further bombers could have been shot down if additional fighters had been available to renew the attack after the bomber formations had been broken up.'

While there was again an element of disobedience of orders in what Bader had done in not proceeding straight to the area he was told to patrol, it was a common enough practice for squadron commanders to use their own discretion about the height at which they would fly. Reliance on heights given by radar was risky because of its inaccuracy, and many squadron commanders preferred to add a few thousand feet to the height given them by the controllers.

In expressing his own views on this action, Johnnie Johnson has pointed out that Staines is 'thirty miles from Hornchurch', and that it is also 'well within 11 Group's preserves'. He then goes on to say about Douglas Bader: 'He was just in time to position his wing between the sun and two big shoals of bombers accompanied by the usual packs of 109s. Calling the Spitfire leader to cover their tails, he headed the two Hurricane squadrons at the bombers, hammered at the leading Dorniers, saw the bombers begin to break formation, watched sticks of bombs desperately jettisoned, and counted the burning bombers until the remants of one bomber formation withdrew, still hotly pursued by some of his pilots.'

It was unquestionably a most successful action, with the raiders being intercepted before they could do their bombing, broken up, and turned back with serious losses. 'Fortunately for Bader neither North Weald nor Hornchurch was attacked, otherwise Park might have lodged an official complaint with Dowding,' Johnson has commented.

After that engagement Bader 'took the plunge', his biographer recorded, and told Leigh-Mallory 'about disobeying controller's instructions'.

Leigh-Mallory apparently made light of that, and was more inclined to speak approvingly of Bader's views. 'I'll put this up to the right people,' he is credited with having told Bader after listening to him 'expounding his ideas' about a formation leader interpreting instructions from the ground 'as he saw fit', to use Johnnie Johnson's words.

'I wonder what Leigh-Mallory meant by such a curious expression?' Dowding has asked. 'Who were "the right people"?'

Even now, so long afterwards and with all the facts so well recorded, it is still difficult for Dowding to view with anything but regret this apparent disobedience of orders. Bader's biographer has said of Leigh-Mallory that 'he was also spreading Bader's gospel . . .'

'If the instructions given by the controller were for the squadrons to protect North Weald, that was where they should have been,' Dowding commented on Bader's behaviour on this occasion.

In a further comment, Johnnie Johnson wrote: 'Leigh-Mallory must have thought that a bit of occasional poaching like this was well justified . . .' It was this poaching—the word came to be used by other people also—on top of the lateness of some of the No. 12 Group responses to No. 11 Group requests for support—that began to incense Park, who was a stickler for the exact execution of orders.

'What I find very difficult to understand is the claim that Bader went so far in disobeying orders,' Dowding has commented. 'And his failure to challenge the statements in his biography only adds to my perplexity. With all Park's squadrons in the air and engaged, and with the northern aerodromes of 11 Group without defence, Bader was ordered into the air to provide it urgently. That was his function under the Group structure. If, as his biographer states, he did take it upon himself to act otherwise, and thus left these northern stations of Park's unguarded, he disobeyed orders and that, so far as I am concerned, would be insubordination.'

Even after all these years, Dowding still feels about Douglas Bader's actions as he felt about them at the time. He has described them as the outcome of 'a kind of attitude that so far as I was concerned was quite unacceptable.'

Harking back to his own time as a young officer, Dowding has commented: 'I know very well what it is to be rebellious about what one could consider is the dull lack of imagination in one's senior officers. But I felt that in Bader's case, at least as reported, it was different. He apparently seemed to think that we who were in command didn't seem to know what we were doing or talking about, and that if he disagreed with our policies he could make his own decisions. I don't think insubordination is an inaccurate description of the events portrayed in *Reach for the Sky* where he is presented as taking it upon himself to have a free hand about the war, his own conduct and his command of his squadron. If this is correct, it was very sad that he should behave like that, particularly when there was no need for it.'

Of Leigh-Mallory's appreciation of Douglas Bader at this time early in September, Bader's biographer states: '. . . Leigh-Mallory did not accept all that Bader said without reservations . . . he could be abysmally wrong or brilliantly right on any problem . . .' Nevertheless, by this time Leigh-Mallory was giving Bader full support, without consultation with Dowding about these new tactics, and it was becoming a matter of Bader's winning acclamation if he was right and running the risk of getting into a great deal of trouble if he was wrong. But such was his conviction that he was right— which some people regarded as stubbornness—that the only course that Bader could follow was to prosecute with the utmost vigour his views about the use of the big wing.

With that in mind, Dowding has asked: 'If he wanted a

compact wing of five squadrons how could he have all those pilots going off into individual dog-fights?' Trying to unravel what to him is a contradiction, in view of what Bader had said only a short time before in his condemnation of 'unwieldy processions' Dowding added: 'I suppose the answer from Bader's point of view would be that with these heavily escorted bomber raids you had to attack with a large wing in order to avoid being defeated by superior numbers. Or, as he has put it, inflict more damage yourself.'

In all the controlling from the ground, Dowding has himself pointed out, 'there are two points that one has to bear in mind.' They were points of the utmost importance to the pilots in the air. 'We all knew that there were inaccuracies in both height and the number of aircraft in the R.D.F. information,' he said. 'But we were working with the best information we could get, which was clearly a very great deal better than no information at all. Now we were all liable to make mistakes, but it was quite wrong to suggest that formation leaders could do better controlling in the air. It denied the value of the whole system of control that had been worked out and which was generally operating so well.'

Of the actions of Leigh-Mallory in so strongly supporting Douglas Bader, even at this early stage, Dowding feels an even greater perplexity. 'But I suppose it was what he wanted,' he said. 'He knew that I would only interfere in a matter of tactics employed by the Group if some very serious result ensued. In this case, he got away with it . . .' Commenting then on the suggestion that he might have exercised a firmer control over the actions of Leigh-Mallory than he did, Dowding said: 'It is possible that I should have known better, because it had always been my experience that if you didn't keep an eye on the course of events they were very often inclined to go backwards.'

After it was all over, and Dowding had a chance to view what had happened in a calmer atmosphere, he wrote in his despatch:

During this third phase the problem arose, in an acute form, of the strength of Fighter formations which we should employ. When time was the essence of the problem, two squadrons were generally used by A.V.M. Park in No. 11 Group. He had the responsibility of meeting attacks as far to the Eastward as possible, and the building up of a four-squadron formation involved the use of a rendezvous for aircraft from 2 or more aerodromes. This led to delay and lack of flexibility in leadership.

But Dowding nevertheless gave credit where credit was due. 'On the other hand, when No. 12 Group was asked to send down protective formations to guard the aerodromes on the Eastern fringe of London, it was often possible to build up big formations,' he continued in his despatch, 'and these had great success on some ocasions, though by no means always.'

It was in the reasons for the failure of certain elements of No. 12 Group to be there when needed that there are to be found the further difficulties which came to exacerbate the already strained relationship between Park and Leigh-Mallory. 'But what so many people seemed to forget, or to overlook,' Dowding commented, 'was that Park's whole position during the battle had to be one of defence. All that I had planned and built up in the structure of the Command was for the defence of the country. The big wings idea was for offensive tactics, not defensive, and it failed to prove its full worth in the defensive role.'

Among those who seemed to overlook this were some members of the Air Staff at the Air Ministry. Dowding was leaning over backwards, in some ways, to continue to give his Group Commanders a free hand to work out their own plans, provided that those plans were made known to him and that each Group Commander understood what the others were doing.

'They didn't seem to understand, or didn't want to understand, why I was allowing this great latitude to my Group Commanders,' Dowding has said. 'By that, I mean in how many squadrons they should send up to meet the different kinds of raids. That was the Group Commanders' problem, and it would depend on how many squadrons they had in the air and how many they had left on the ground. I did not want to tie their hands in any way, and I felt that they must be flexible in their own thinking. Also, it was because of the difficulty of full discussion with Headquarters in questions which demanded instant action on the part of the Groups that I left them with this free hand. On the other hand, I would not have been prepared to concede to my Group Commanders powers to go contrary to my views and wishes in important strategical issues.'

There was only one point about which Dowding has felt that Keith Park could possibly have acted a little differently. 'I wish he had kept me more personally informed about his difficulties with Leigh-Mallory,' he said. 'I know now that he tried to fight it out for himself. He would, and he deserves praise for that. But I might have been able to help him more. When the time came for me to intervene it was too late . . . too late for both of us.'

But the pressure at the time was such that it was impossible to get a clear view of what was happening. It also took a long time before it was in any way clear that there had been a confusion in the understanding of the conflicting claims. 'If I had known fully at that early stage what Leigh-Mallory was trying to do I would certainly have read him a lecture on the futility of trying to organise these big wings of five and more squadrons,' Dowding added. 'When, a little later, the day attacks were in the nature of tip and run raids, the use of big wings was even more futile, and they usually missed the Germans altogether. I purposely commented on that in my despatch.'

That comment refers to the results '. . . of the ten large formations ordered from Duxford into No. 11 Group in the last half of October, when the Germans were employing Fighter-types only'. Dowding pointed out that, 'nine of these sorties made no interception, and the tenth destroyed one Me 109.'

In comparison with the mounting conflict that was bedevilling the relationship between No. 11 and No. 12 Group during this latter stage of the battle, Keith Park has spoken of the good relationship that existed between No. 11 Group and the Group on his other flank, No. 10, which stood guard on his right. 'Brand adopted the same system of interception as practised by No. 11 Group,' he said. 'It was what I call the Forward Interception of enemy raids before they could drop their bombs on vital targets.'

In support of this forward interception technique of his, Keith Park has called attention to the views that were expressed by many German pilots after the battle. They were free with their comments that the fighters of the R.A.F. had harassed

the enemy bombers all the way from the coast in the efforts
that the Germans made to get to their target areas.

One of Dowding's most skilful and experienced pilots in the
battle, and as such is well-qualified to express an opinion, is
Group Captain J. A. Kent. He holds a view that has not been
sufficiently considered and which, when it was put to him,
won Dowding's firm approval. Kent pointed out that it was
quite wrong to think in terms of the squadrons belonging to
this or that group. 'The squadrons were changed around from
Group to Group and one did not simply belong to No. 10,
No. 11, No. 12 or No. 13 Group,' he said. 'The Groups were
static, but we belonged to the squadrons, and they were mobile,
being moved around the various Groups and sent out of the
line for a rest, with squadrons which had been on rest replacing
the ones that were operationally tired.'

This was the plan of Dowding's devising, and it was generally
well understood and accepted. 'Also, it is not true that No. 11
Group did not use wing formations,' Johnny Kent added. 'We
tried the wing formation but found that, in most cases, it was
unsuitable for our purposes.' First and foremost, he pointed
out, was the obvious fact that a wing could not possibly be as
manoeuverable as a squadron, and could not scramble and get
as readily as a squadron into position for an attack. And with
the radio sets then in use even the squadrons in large formations
could have been, and quite often were, on different frequencies,
and so could not speak to one another.

'Another point that seems to have been missed,' Kent added,
'is that usually when our squadrons operating from 11 Group
airfields met the enemy fighters the Germans had plenty of
fuel and could afford to fight. Being for the most part more
experienced, they inflicted a greater number of losses than they
did against the squadrons from the No. 12 Group wing whenever it came south to support us. By the time that wing arrived
in the battle zone the German fighters were usually running
short of fuel and could not afford to mix it. That, for one thing,
gave a false impression of the effectiveness of the Wing.'

That the squadrons when they were in No. 11 Group should
suffer greater losses was unquestionably due to their having to

fight the enemy when, as Johnny Kent has put it, 'they were most dangerous.' The casualties in pilots and losses in aircraft, and their sheer inability through those two features to form up in large formations at any moment that they might be ordered to do so, is illustrated in Kent's comment: 'On one occasion I was scrambled with orders to lead the Northolt wing of three squadrons. Between them the three squadrons could produce only nine aeroplanes.'

Another of those who spent practically the whole of the time of the battle in No. 11 Group was Ginger Lacey, who has said that he 'was proud and pleased to do so'. In offering his views on tactics, Lacey commented: 'I do not think there was any fighter pilot at that time with enough experience to handle and effectively operate a big wing, and the Battle of Britain was no place for anybody to be fooling around gaining it. But there was another side to this big wing business. The basic fighting unit was, and is, a section. Whether this was of two or three aircraft makes no difference.' The big wing was only a method of getting the maximum number of sections to the killing ground, Lacey pointed out. 'In the 11 Group pilots' view it was a cumbersome and time-wasting method of doing it. We also believed that if you did not get to the enemy bombers before they bombed you were only half doing your job.'

At the time when the biography of Douglas Bader was first published, in 1954, there were many points that the author made about outside influences which caused serious concern to those who had an interest in what happened, and were involved, in the big wings controversy. One of the influences that Dowding did not appreciate at the time was that which was exerted by the apparent standing of the adjutant of Bader's squadron, an officer named Peter Macdonald. He has been described by Bader's biographer as 'an industrious, imperturbable man who had been an M.P. for fourteen years and still managed to sandwich his parliamentary duties in between trying to pull the squadron together.'

It was not until the summer of 1968 that it was learnt by Lord Dowding, quite by chance, that a most illuminating and important paragraph had been added in a later edition of the book which had not appeared in it when it first came out. This additional paragraph appears immediately after the recording of Bader's success in the fighting with a big wing on 18 September. It reads:

The point was widely noted that it paid to scramble 12 Group Wing in good time. Peter Macdonald had had a hand in that. In the House of Commons one day he had spoken earnestly with the Under-Secretary of State for Air, who had suggested he see the Prime Minister. Macdonald had an hour and a half with Churchill, who was gruff at first, but then thawed, and next day began sending for various group commanders.

When that paragraph was examined by Lord Dowding and he realised its implications, his first response was to exclaim: 'It does rather take one's breath away.'

This categorical statement of a political interference going on behind Dowding's back without his knowledge in the running of his command has in it a clear indication of what was developing. 'At the time, I knew nothing whatsoever about it,' Dowding commented. 'Of course, so long as a squadron adjutant pays attention to his Service responsibilities there's no harm done. Those responsibilities are clearly defined. But it's another matter when a squadron adjutant, serving under my command, starts by-passing the correct procedure and chain of command in order to get the ear of the politicians. I think it was impertinent and quite extraordinary behaviour in engineering things in this way. And all done without my knowledge.'

It was then that Dowding raised the matter of the loyalty that he believed he had the right to expect from those serving under his command. 'It surely suggests some improper approaches were being made,' he commented. 'No one could deny a Member of Parliament the right to attend to matters that were in his political sphere. But was it right for him to introduce this purely technical matter of the tactical use that was being made of my command into such a political atmosphere?'

The weather at the outset of the memorable day of Sunday, 15 September 1940—Dowding did not get back from being away on tour until the afternoon—was 'misty but promised to be fine', Wood and Dempster have reported, adding that the day was 'remarkable for its ultimate change of German policy and not for its heavy losses, as the 185 German aircraft claimed would lead many to believe'.

The first wave of the enemy attack appeared on the scene at 11 o'clock in the morning. The No. 11 Group fighters intercepted, and the No. 12 Group wing of five squadrons was ordered off with instructions which Wood and Dempster describe as 'to patrol Debden—Hornchurch'. Bader's biographer gives the patrol line as 'Canterbury and Gravesend'. They made a good interception of the raiders over London.

Two hours later another heavy raid was launched by the Germans, and twenty-three No. 11 Group squadrons, three No. 10 Group squadrons and the wing of five squadrons from Duxford were ordered off. The No. 11 Group squadrons were heavily engaged in breaking up the enemy formations and turning them back. By the time that the Duxford wing got to the incoming raid they were, according to Bader's biographer, four thousand feet below the enemy bombers. 'Damn! Everything risked again because they were scrambled too late,' it is recorded of Bader's views.

'They found when they pieced that day's battle together,' this report on the Duxford wing's activity continues, 'that the 12 Group Wing had fully justified itself . . . in the two massed flights that day the pilots of the five squadrons of the Wing claimed 52 enemy destroyed and a further eight probables.'

That claim was out of a total of 185 made by the whole of the R.A.F. for that day. Bader's biographer wrote: 'After the war Luftwaffe figures stated that only 56 had been lost. R.A.F. pilots who fought in the battle flatly and vehemently disbelieve the German total. One might suspect that some of Goebbel's propaganda figures were discreetly promoted to official record status.'

Be that as it may, British historians accept the figure of fifty-six enemy aircraft destroyed that day by the R.A.F. and not the one hundred and eighty-five claimed at the time. Dowding himself was never impressed by, or paid much attention to, the rapidly compiled scores that were issued at the end of each day's operations. He knew that the machinery for sorting out all the information took longer than that to produce anything near a correct figure. And in any case, he also knew that it was well-nigh impossible to determine, in the heat of combat, just exactly how many aircraft were destroyed, probably destroyed, or damaged, as the categories were named for intelligence purposes.

It was over these scores that were issued with such alacrity that Dowding made a comment at one stage of the battle which illustrated clearly the caution with which he viewed them. The Secretary of State for Air phoned him about a report that had come in from the United States which, in view of the claims being made by the Germans, questioned the validity of the British claims. 'I told him that the Americans would soon find out the truth,' Dowding said. 'If the German figures were correct they would be in London in a week. Otherwise they would not.'

But there could never be any doubt about the success of the Duxford squadrons during the fighting on that day of 15 September, even if the score claimed is suspect. Leigh-Mallory is reported to have said to Bader: 'It's absolutely clear your big formations are paying dividends.'

Bader claimed that on the second occasion they were 'scrambled too late again' and then came—'warming to his theme', as his biographer puts it—Bader's summary of his view of what the overall Fighter Command tactics should have been.

'It doesn't make sense, Sir,' he is reported to have said to Leigh-Mallory. 'As soon as they start building up their formations over Calais we should get into the air and go south. We should be the ones to attack them first while 11 Group get off and get height.'

This view was another of the many that has given Dowding cause to wonder how such a lack of understanding could have been tolerated in officers serving in his command. 'It was contrary to the whole structure of the Command,' he has commented, 'and it takes into consideration only what was in the interests of the Duxford Wing.'

Even more perplexing for Dowding was the revelation that again Leigh-Mallory saw fit to tell Bader that 'the wing score today won't go unnoticed—I'll see to that myself . . .'

In the light of what was looming up on the horizon in his personal affairs, Dowding has since asked: 'By whom?'

With the launching by the Germans early in September of their full-scale night offensive—which came to be known by the British as the Blitz, as distinct from the day Battle of Britain, although in fact they overlapped—there was a new element introduced into the war in the air about which Dowding has always felt a deep anger. 'This idea of striking terror into the hearts and minds of the civilian population through this type of bombing is repulsive,' he has said. 'It is a political move, or attempt, to bring about an internal revolution. Our people had a lot to put up with during the war in the way of loss of life and property and so on, but did you ever hear so much as a breath of any idea that there should be a public revolution demanding peace?'

There could be asked a question about the British participation in the bombing of civilians later in the war, and it is a valid enough question. In case there might be one about where the responsibility for the introduction of this type of warfare on civilians rested, Dowding has added: 'It was, of course, in Hitler's mind—a belief in terror—and in the minds of those who worked with him. They were looking for an excuse to use it, and at the same time pretending, in 1940, to be so terribly upset over that little pip-squeak of a raid that we carried out on Berlin after he had bombed us, even though that was a German mistake. Is there any reason other than terror why he turned the whole of his air strength on to bombing London? He believed that he would attain his end by terrorising us. And being what we are that was what went a long way to saving the war for us.'

Of our ability to cope with the night attacks, Dowding has spoken of his own thoughts by explaining that 'we were in a promising position, but we had to be in much more than that.' There was a further anxiety for him in that which was an extension of all the earlier worries that he had had to face in the day fighting. 'We had to make every effort to expedite the work that we were doing in developing the radar-equipped night fighters,' he has said. 'Even before the end of the day battle I was spending a good many nights away at the airfield where the experiments in that work were going on. And all that had to come out of one's ration of sleep. There was precious little of that.'

For altogether too long, sleep for Dowding was at a premium, and there was nothing that he could do about it. Hilda Dowding has recalled occasions when she heard her brother arrive back at Montrose after those night expeditions, and she would know that he would be too tired to do anything but go straight to bed. She also knew that there was nothing she could do about trying to make conditions more comfortable for him. 'I often wished that he would have a hot bath when he got home to help him sleep,' she once said about the somewhat Spartan way that Dowding had of living. 'But he wouldn't, and I would know that he would not be able to get to sleep.'

Commenting on that long afterwards, Dowding chuckled and said: 'It was a matter of waiting for those phone calls from Downing Street.'

'I have always been of the opinion, perhaps somewhat naturally, that the Battle of Britain proper ended when Hitler cancelled the orders for the invasion which the Germans had been preparing to mount,' Dowding has said. 'At the time I couldn't know anything about that, and if anything the fighting in the air showed indications of intensifying. The first sign I saw that led me to feel sure that the invasion was off was at the end of September. And it was not a change in their tactics; it was a change in strategy.'

There the intensive day Battle of Britain ended, although the night Blitz went on unabated and with that end to the immediate possibility of invasion there came the first major defeat for Hitler. 'The fighting turned to those long night attacks,' Dowding recalled. 'The battle went on all right, but it wasn't the Battle of Britain. We knew that the barges, after the hammering that Bomber Command had given them, were dispersing, and that Hitler couldn't say "all right . . . off you go," and so the whole thing was off.'

There has been agreement that Dowding was the architect of that victory in that summer of 1940. Of those who built on the plans made for them by Dowding, Denis Richards has written: 'The public verdict... has rightly acclaimed Dowding's pilots as the foremost artisans of victory; and when the details of the fighting grow dim, and the names of its heroes are forgotten, men will still remember that in the summer of 1940 civilisation was saved by a thousand British boys.'

With the passing of time, and the dimming of those details, that agreement about the value of Dowding's work has become universal, and recently, going on for nearly thirty years later, the eminent military historian Sir Basil Liddell Hart, was able to write: 'Happily the Germans' bid to gain command of the air, as a preliminary to invasion, was frustrated by the superb efforts of the fifty odd squadrons of Fighter Command—under the masterly direction of Air Marshal Sir Hugh Dowding and Air Vice-Marshal Park. . .'

What would have happened if the German threat of invasion of Britain had not been averted as it was in the summer of 1940, and if Hitler had not turned his attention to the east instead of concentrating his effort in the west, is summed up by Liddell Hart in his further statement: 'If Hitler had concentrated on defeating Britain, her doom would have been almost certain. For, although he had missed his best chance of conquering her by invasion, he could have developed such a stranglehold, by combined air and submarine pressure, as to ensure her gradual starvation and ultimate collapse.'

But Hitler's thoughts and plans were turned and diverted towards the east, and so away from a further effort to starve Britain into a collapse; and it is now known, from all the evidence that has become available, that the situation became one which has been described by Liddell Hart in the words: 'When the Luftwaffe failed to drive the R.A.F. out of the sky in the "Battle of Britain", the army and the navy chiefs were glad of the excuse thus provided for suspending the invasion. More remarkable was Hitler's own readiness to accept excuses for its suspension.'

CHAPTER TWELVE

OPEN CONTROVERSY

With the slackening off of the German attacks by day there came the opportunity for Dowding to take a deep breath, and to pause, if only for a moment, to reflect on all that had happened in the past few weeks, and on what was likely to happen in the immediate future. No sooner was this pause taken, however, than the show-down that had to come between the two sides in 'the big wings controversy' broke into the open. With that it was inevitable that Leigh-Mallory and Park should meet in a head-on clash.

In the report that Leigh-Mallory had put up to Fighter Command on 17 September, which commented on 'wing patrols sent up by No. 12 Group . . . to protect North Weald and Hornchurch aerodromes,' the explanation was given that a wing was used because it was felt that single squadrons were 'wholly inadequate' to face the larger formations of enemy bombers coming over, formations which were protected by even larger fighter formations. Although a generally favourable comment had accompanied that report when it had been forwarded by Fighter Command to the Air Ministry, a very different situation in the nature of the enemy attack had developed by the last week in September, and that made out-of-date much of Leigh-Mallory's argument. From that time on the Germans were no longer using large bomber formations with large fighter escorts. Instead, they were sending over smaller and smaller bomber formations with larger numbers of fighters fitted with bombs, all of which were flung down by the enemy without much planning and quite often through being forced to jettison them. It was much more of a tip and run business on a very large scale, and the defending forces had to be prepared for even smarter responses over scattered areas at very short notice.

This wilder scramble was the tactical development in the day battle. At night, for which the Germans were now conserving their bombers, it was a long, hard test of endurance through hours of bombing which the enemy could go about with impunity. Dowding's concern in this change in German strategy was with the weakness of his defence under the cover of darkness. Now more than ever his thoughts and time were occupied with the problem of defence at night. There was still a great promise in the radar-equipped night fighters; but, for all the hard work that was being done, with a great deal of flying, there was no more than a promise.

But another problem was also presenting itself to Dowding. It was an internal one in the affairs of his Command, and was to a large extent personal, and he was finding it as unpleasant as it was difficult to resolve. It was the unhappy conclusion that he was having to come to that Leigh-Mallory was not conducting himself in the manner which Dowding felt he had the right to expect of one of his Group Commanders. The situation that was created by that caused him the gravest concern; but Dowding felt that he had to keep the whole matter to himself until he could reach a firm decision about it.

Not long after the battle was over, and writing while the memory of all that had happened was still fresh in his mind, Dowding referred to the clash with the comment: 'A somewhat unfortunate controversy grew up round the two points of view, and Air Vice-Marshal Park was subjected to some external criticism with which I did not agree. Fortunately, however, the disagreement did not become acute until mid-October, when the battle had been virtually won.'

There has been a criticism of Dowding that he should have intervened earlier in the disagreements that developed between Park and Leigh-Mallory. 'If I had,' Dowding has commented, 'the result would have been very different from what the Air Staff expected of me. But they got in first, and perhaps because of that there is something in the criticism that is made of me.'

In an effort to understand what it was that was expected of him, Dowding has searched for a suitable expression of his own views on the controversy that was, in the eyes of many of those who became involved, in some ways a contrived one of no great merit. 'At the time I thought that the whole business of intense discussion about whether we should use three, four or five squadron wings was so simple and inconsequential that it really hardly deserved a long statement being made,' Dowding said. 'But I must have been wrong there. Not about the principle of the thing or its importance. But about what people had in mind. It became obvious after a while that several people in responsible positions did hold opinions that were contrary to mine. And since, in their eyes, I seemed to be refusing to listen to what they had to say I was sentenced without trial. There's no doubt at all in my mind now that it was on that subject—the big wings—that Park and I were judged and condemned.'

In his official history, Denis Richards has written: 'The controversies, as opposed to the misconceptions, were fortunately limited to fairly narrow circles within the Royal Air Force; but they were concerned with matters so important as Park's tactics and Dowding's strategy.'

It is true that the unfortunate wrangling which was thrust upon Dowding and Park was limited to these narrow circles; but those circles were at the tip, and it was that which made of the controversy something that was so damaging to Dowding and Park. '. . . the unhappy truth was that the two commanders were largely at cross-purposes,' Denis Richards said of the disagreement between Park and Leigh-Mallory. But it went much deeper than that, as Dowding was to find when the quarrel came out into the open. '. . . Leigh-Mallory's tactical conceptions won a warm measure of approval from the authorities at Whitehall,' Richards added.

What Dowding did not realise, solely because he did not know about it at the time, was that Leigh-Mallory had won that 'approval' in the eyes of the Air Staff and the politicians. When he did come to realise it, later, he also had to assume that it had been won by Leigh-Mallory exerting an influence that could only be classified as coming into the category of a playing at politics.

'It was the only way he could have attained his end,' Dowding has said. 'He had to go behind my back in furthering his cause, and it is sad that he should have been driven so far in doing that.'

But there were forces that drove Leigh-Mallory to conduct himself in ways which other people also found extremely hard to understand, quite apart from being able to work with him in any harmony. He appeared to resent even the slightest hint of criticism, and on one occasion Lord Tedder had to rebuke him with the comment: 'A leader must be ready to take criticism.' There was also a curious lack of humour in his character.

One 'epic story', as it has been described by Group Captain Thomas Lang, who was another of the No. 11 Group controllers, and in this instance the one directly concerned, reveals this all too clearly. A lone enemy raider came in one day, in and out of cloud and rain as it made its way along what amounted to the dividing line between Nos. 11 and 12 Groups. Both Groups sent up fighters to intercept it, and a No. 11 Group fighter found it and shot it down. It crashed just over the boundary, and inside the No. 12 Group area.

Within a few minutes a signal from the A.O.C. of No. 12 Group appeared on the No. 11 Group Controller's desk. It read: 'Full explanation required why 11 Group fighters have shot down enemy aircraft into 12 Group area.'

There was a strong element of the inevitable in all that went on behind the scenes in the affairs of Dowding and Park during October and November 1940. It could not be recognised at the time but eventually the story of what went on had to come out into the open. For so long, and for reasons that were far from clear, it had been allowed to remain in the shadows in a way that only added to the speculation about just what happened. And then, in a book that he had published in 1964 but which did not come to my attention until some time afterwards, Johnnie Johnson let in a ray of light that brought me, for one, to the realisation that speculation was becoming even more confused, and that some of the accounts of those times which were regarded as being authoritative were, in fact, very misleading.

In a reference that he made to the situation that had developed, Johnnie Johnson referred to 'fighting talk,' and wrote: 'Throughout the Battle many high-ranking members of the Air Staff, senior civil servants, and politicians had visited the fighter stations, and some had encouraged the flight, squadron, and station commanders to talk freely about their problems. Visitors to Leigh-Mallory's airfields heard that since September the big Duxford Wing had not been given a chance because they never got enough early warning from 11 Group, but when the same people arrived at Park's airfields they were told that the slow, clumsy, conspicuous Duxford Wing could never get to 30,000 feet in time to take on the fighter-bombers. Unfortunately these discussions were not confined to healthy, frank arguments about fighting tactics, and there were some ugly accusations about poaching and morale. Upon their return to Whitehall some eminent men, who should have known better than to listen to junior officers denouncing their seniors, put pen to paper, and both Dowding and Park were called to the Air Ministry to discuss the size of fighter wings.'

That is a particularly good and reliable appreciation of the situation as it was developing, and it comes from a source that is beyond any questioning for authenticity. Johnnie Johnson then stated: 'The meeting was chaired by Air Vice-Marshal Sholto Douglas, Deputy Chief of the Air Staff. . . .' That came as a rude shock for me, and I began to understand why there had been comments from people whose opinions I respect, that in one particular aspect of my work in recent years I had been led badly astray, and had inadvertently added to the confusion.

During the course of the Second World War I served at various times in various Commands as Personal Assistant to Dowding, Keith Park, and Sholto Douglas, and out of that I came to know all three men very well. They also knew that I was keenly interested in their careers both through serving under them and, in a much more detached way, as a writer.

In the beginning, while still on Dowding's staff at the Headquarters of Fighter Command, I knew that in the structure at the Air Ministry the Air Staff officer responsible for the day-to-day operations of the whole of the Royal Air Force was the Deputy Chief of the Air Staff, who was then Sholto Douglas. In speaking of the time of the Battle of Britain, he has referred to himself as 'the senior member of the Air Staff most directly concerned. . .' Now, so many years later, it is with considerable embarrassment that I have found that in *Combat and Command* —Sholto Douglas's story, in the writing of which I was deeply involved—statements were made which present a questionable assessment of the extent to which Douglas was concerned in the controversy. This has since been commented upon unfavourably by several authorities, including senior officers in the Royal Air Force, who made a point of calling to my attention the inaccuracy of this presentation, and pointing out that by the very nature of his appointment the Deputy Chief of the Air Staff could not help becoming very closely associated with, and participating in, everything that happened.

In *Years of Command* Sholto Douglas stated: 'Although regrettably, as well as incorrectly over-stressed, there did occur during the course of the battle a difference of opinions over the way in which the fighters were being employed. It was this clash of personalities more than anything else which led to an unnecessarily heated argument one afternoon between Park and Leigh-Mallory at a meeting at the Air Ministry.' Elsewhere in this book he states: '. . . I heard Keith Park complain that No. 12 Group was, to use his word, "poaching". That sounded to me as if he was talking about his local shoot, and it struck me as rather surprising that he should look at what was happening in that way.' There is never any suggestion that the meeting which is referred to was the important one that was held on 17 October, and which needs to be discussed at some length.

It is sad for me that, despite all that was said in praise of Dowding in *Years of Command*, Sholto Douglas's handling of the situation at the time only added to the distress that was experienced by Dowding.

Quite apart from being Deputy Chief of the Air Staff, Sholto Douglas has said about the clash between Park and Leigh-Mallory that he 'naturally took the keenest interest in their differences of opinions. . .' There is added to that the statement: '. . . even if I was not then actually involved in the disagreement.' In summing up his position, Douglas comments: 'But from that time on, and certainly against my wish, I became drawn into their argument, and just as Dowding's name has since become linked in with Park's, so mine has become associated with Leigh-Mallory's. Neither Dowding nor I ever expected that that would ever happen, and we have never been at all happy about it.'

After he read that, Keith Park wrote to me and made the comment: 'I was surprised at the way Sholto Douglas shuffled out of his part in the controversy.' Dowding added to that by referring to it as 'wriggling out of it'; and he stressed that he has always been very happy over having his name associated with Keith Park's.

'It has since become clear that Dowding, also, was not as deeply involved in what has come to be called "the wings controversy" as many writers and historians would have us believe,' Sholto Douglas further stated.

When he was questioned about that, Dowding commented: 'After all that happened to me, both personally and professionally, I don't see how it would have been possible for me to have become more deeply involved.'

A careful examination has since revealed that Sholto Douglas was very deeply involved in this controversy. 'No matter what there may have been in the way of conflict between Dowding and other branches of the Air Ministry, so far as we on the Air Staff were concerned his relinquishment of his command was an honourable one in every conceivable way,' it is stated in *Years of Command.*

The passing of the responsibility for the difficulties that were caused Dowding to 'other branches' of the Air Ministry—and for that statement I must bear some responsibility—is entirely wrong. 'It was the Air Staff and only the Air Staff that caused me all those difficulties,' Dowding has since pointed out. The reminder of that led me to a deeper examination of the matter of honour in the manner of Dowding's relinquishment of his command.

In Sholto Douglas' assessment of the situation in *Years of Command* it is stated: 'I think Park was right to get his squadrons off the ground and at the enemy formations as soon as possible; but he should have had a better liaison with No. 12 Group so that they could have had their larger formations of fighters—which had had time to form up—ready to back up the early efforts of No. 11 Group. Leigh-Mallory should have been more understanding in that matter of liaison, and readier to give Park quick and effective support regardless of any theories about the way in which the battle should be fought.'

'That is a sensible enough appreciation in its way,' Dowding commented, 'but it was made with the value of hindsight, and it is not exactly what he thought at the time.'

That hindsight led Sholto Douglas to conclude: 'To some extent the responsibility for these lapses (in liaison) must rest on the shoulders of the staff at the Headquarters of Fighter Command. In the final analysis it was up to them to maintain the closest co-operation, through proper liaison, between the Groups which went to make up the Command.'

There is to some extent justification for this statement, Dowding has admitted, and even though, at the time, he was not fully aware of this failure in liaison, he has accepted the lapses as his responsibility. But in endeavouring to understand the position occupied by Sholto Douglas, it is necessary to examine several curious opinions that are attributed to him by the official historian. One of these was that he had 'never been very much in favour of the idea of trying to interpose fighter squadrons between enemy bombers and their objective' to which he added that he would rather shoot down fifty of the enemy when they had bombed their target than ten forward of it. Dowding has since commented that that was an extraordinary way of looking at the problem of the defence of the country.

'Every effort had to be made to stop the enemy before he bombed,' Dowding said, 'not afterwards. Surely that was a basic fact. I find incomprehensible the view that it would have been better to try to shoot down fifty of them after they'd done their bombing than ten before. Our job was to stop as much as we could of all the bombing before it took place, not to indulge in statistical studies.'

Of the situation that developed immediately after the battle was over, Denis Richards wrote: '. . . growing differences between the two Group Commanders eventually reached the point where the Air Staff felt obliged to consider the main tactical issue between them—the respective merits of the wing and squadron formations.'

It was in this that the Air Staff were, in Dowding's words, 'flogging a dead horse'. So far as he was concerned, the issue was an artificial one, and he could not take it as seriously as the Air Staff came to show that they were inclined to regard it. Dowding thoroughly approved of Park's tactics, and at first, even after receiving the agenda for the meeting called 'to consider the main tactical issue'—and to be held on 17 October —he could not fully appreciate what point there was in questioning the way that the battle had been fought.

The whole situation had already altered so much through the change of tactics being used by the Germans that any thought of using large, unwieldy fighter formations in defence was quite out of the question. For all that they might say about looking ahead, the Air Staff seemed, to Dowding, to be thinking only in terms of what was in the past.

In referring to the matter that was to be discussed, Denis Richards commented: 'This involved several very debatable factors.' He then went on to pose what Dowding has described as 'very good questions'. They were:

Should the successes of the Duxford wing be ascribed rather to the fact that the enemy formations had already been broken up by No. 11 Group? Had the wing neglected its appointed role of guarding No. 11 Group's northern airfields to chase the enemy all over the southern counties? Had No. 12 Group's keenness for battle resulted in perplexed controllers in No. 11 Group ordering up Spitfires and Hurricanes to investigate what was presumably a large hostile formation?

These were the questions put by Richards in the official history. 'What a pity it was that if it was a post-mortem they wanted, the Air Staff did not put those questions in that way,' Dowding commented. If they had, he would then have been better prepared for what was to happen, because he had already reached his own conclusions.

'It was just before that meeting that I came to feel that I had possibly made a mistake in allowing all my Group Commanders so much liberty in running their Groups in their own way,'

Dowding said. 'I suppose it was the rapidity of the development of that conflict that seemed to come about between 11 and 12 Group that brought it home to me.'

That it should have taken time for the development of the conflict to make any impact on Dowding was attributable to the way in which it developed. There was a strong personal element in it from the start, with the clash between Park and Leigh-Mallory on a personal rather than any official level; secondly, there was the personal anxiety of Douglas Bader to get to grips with the enemy, which was perfectly understandable in itself; and thirdly, there was the influence that Leigh-Mallory and his views were having on Air Staff thinking.

'I was entirely on Park's side without, up to that time, having had to say as much,' Dowding said. 'There was no need for me to say it. He was carrying out his assigned task, and there was no need for any comment from me. But I had come by then to realise that Leigh-Mallory was not conducting the affairs of his Group in the way I expected of him. I did not want to have to say you mustn't do this and you musn't do that. I expected more of my Group Commanders than that. And that was why, by mid-October, I had come to realise I would have to do something about what was going on and get rid of Leigh-Mallory.'

It would be easy to say that Dowding should have taken this very serious step as soon as he had reached such a conclusion; but he was loath to make such a radical change while the fighting was still going on. And then, before he could act, 'the trouble blew up', as he has put it, and the Air Staff brought about a situation that, instead of clarifying the position, only complicated everything.

'The Air Staff had already decided that fighter operations in the south had not been well co-ordinated,' Johnnie Johnson wrote of the situation that existed even before the meeting of 17 October was held, 'and that squadrons had fought independently and ineffectively.' But Dowding had no knowledge of that when he set off from his Headquarters to attend the meeting, which was held at the Air Ministry in Whitehall.

Among those present at this meeting were some of the most

important officers serving in the Royal Air Force. Dowding and three of his Group Commanders, Park, Brand, and Leigh-Mallory, represented the senior officers of Fighter Command. The Chief of the Air Staff, Cyril Newall, was indisposed, which was why his place as the chairman was taken by the Deputy Chief of the Air Staff, Sholto Douglas. Air Marshal Sir Charles Portal was there as the new Chief of the Air Staff designate. The Air Staff was represented by several other officers of air rank who were later to achieve distinction in the Service.

To the amazement of Dowding, Park, Brand, and others present, and there is no other word for their reaction, Squadron Leader Douglas Bader was brought to the meeting by Leigh-Mallory and allowed to take a place at the table. Much is made by his biographer of Bader's presence at this meeting. One well-known member of the Air Staff who was there has expressed his own 'astonishment and resentment' that Leigh-Mallory should have brought a young and junior officer to such a high-level meeting. It was subjecting Bader to the possible embarrassment of being out of place.

'. . . we're having a fighter conference at Air Ministry to thrash out all we've learned from the recent daylight battles,' Leigh-Mallory is credited with having said to Bader. 'I don't know whether I can get you in. It's rather high-level stuff, but I'm going to try because you're the only chap who's led the really big formations.'

Bader's biographer records that there were 'no fighter pilots', and that 'not a man below air vice-marshal' was present, and that Bader 'sat quietly, hands in lap'. There follows a somewhat fanciful description of what happened, with Bader, when called upon to speak, delivering himself of 'a good, terse homily to the effect that the chap in the air, not the controller, should decide when, where and how to meet the enemy.' That in itself was enough to suggest undoing all that Dowding had laid down and developed so painstakingly for fighter control. It is small wonder that Bader found that, in his biographer's words, 'Dowding seemed to be looking at him severely. . .'

'I should think I would have been,' Dowding commented, 'if that was what Bader found to be the most suitable way of running the Command.'

In that there is a key to much of the speculation over this meeting that has churned its way down the years. Johnnie Johnson said of Bader's position: 'It was a delicate business, and a mere Squadron Leader could not cast any reflections upon his commander-in-chief, for whom he had the greatest respect.' Johnson reported that Leigh-Mallory had told Bader that at this meeting he should 'hold his peace about the high-level control arrangements . . .' But Bader could not resist telling the meeting, Johnson also pointed out, 'how the wing leader, not the controller, ought to decide how, when and where to attack.'

To this day, neither Dowding nor Park has any knowledge of how the presence of Douglas Bader at this important Air Staff meeting at the Air Ministry was brought about; and Dowding, his Commander-in-Chief, still wonders why he should have been there without his permission, and why there was no representation of any other squadron commanders since it was apparently felt necessary to have expressions of opinions from those who were actually doing the fighting. Keith Park recently gave his views on this meeting when he said: 'Bader, for whose bravery and courage I have great admiration, was used . . . to make room for . . . Leigh-Mallory'.

Commenting on this statement by the former commander of No. 11 Group, and agreeing with him that, in his view, some people at the meeting were already committed to big wings, Dowding said; 'Leigh-Mallory had quite enough incentive of his own, without bringing Douglas Bader in.' Recalling what Leigh-Mallory had said so many months before about 'moving heaven and earth' to get rid of him, Dowding further remarked: 'I do not think Bader would ever have allowed himself consciously to become embroiled in such a move. It would probably have come to him as a shock to hear that Leigh-Mallory ever entertained such an idea. It was one thing to disagree with my views, and to express his criticisms forcibly, but it was another altogether to intrigue against his own Commander-in-Chief, which is why I think the latter was out of the question.'

Bader's biographer adds about the meeting: 'It went on for

another hour and a half before it broke up, and even then Bader felt that nothing definite had been decided.' He then states that Bader received a letter containing an 'Air Council' decision about 'recommended wing tactics', and added 'it was the stuff that Bader himself had found out and reported.'

For once in the whole affair, when that came to be mentioned to him, Dowding allowed himself a quiet chuckle over what is an obvious gaffe. 'It would indeed be a curious state of affairs when the Air Council start getting together and writing letters to a Squadron Leader,' he commented.

In his report on the meeting, Johnnie Johnson has been more factual and a great deal more correct, dealing with the whole matter in its true perspective. On that basis it is possible to look at the whole matter in a quieter way while at the same time trying to understand the position in which it placed Dowding and Park. It is of particular value, for instance, to note that the views of the Air Staff were made clear at the outset by Sholto Douglas when he spoke of the 'wish to outnumber the enemy formations when we meet them'. He admitted that it was an ideal not always easy to attain, and that 'the time factor might not allow us to do what we wanted.'

When asked to state his views, Park outlined the principle that he observed in No. 11 Group, which was often to use pairs of squadrons, but he pointed out that 'the factors of time, distance and cloud' made it difficult to lay down 'as a general principle that the "Wing" of fighters was the right formation with which to oppose attacks, even those made in mass.' It was his view that what success had been achieved by the use of the wing in No. 12 Group had been due to ideal conditions when the bombers of the enemy had become separated from their fighter escort and were in retreat. With the tip-and-run tactics now being employed by the enemy, Park said that he felt that the only safe system was the one that he had been employing all along.

As might have been expected, Dowding cast his views ahead when he was asked for his opinion, and spoke about the importance of the developments in radar equipment and techniques in gaining as much warning as possible of incoming raids, particularly in the matter of heights, and of the work of the night fighters. There could be no doubt that they all agreed that radar was of the greatest importance, and in this there was agreement with Dowding's views.

There was reason enough in the views that were expressed by Leigh-Mallory, when he was asked for them, for Park to become prickly. Leigh-Mallory said that he would welcome more opportunities to make use of the wing from Duxford, and of coming down to help No. 11 Group; and he told the meeting that he could get that wing into the air—a wing of five squadrons—in six minutes, and in position over Hornchurch at 20,000 feet in twenty-five minutes.

Long afterwards, Johnnie Johnson commented on that particular point with the statement: '. . . but the Duxford Wing had recently taken seventeen minutes to leave the ground and a further twenty minutes before it set course from base. Also, because it absorbed five squadrons from a relatively weak group, it left some highly important targets in the Midlands short of fighter cover. . .'

As the meeting progressed it became obvious that it was a post mortem and that all past tactics were in question. It was the intention to push through, no matter what might be said, the view that future fighter tactics should be in the use of wings, even to the extent of combining two wings into what the Air Staff had decided to call a 'balbo', after the famous Italian airman Italo Balbo, who had led with success long distance flights of formations of Italian aircraft before the war.

The exchange between Park and Leigh-Mallory became, in Sholto Douglas' words, 'unnecessarily heated'. But with each strongly pressing his own view, how could it have been otherwise? Dowding remarked that he felt that he 'could, with his Group Commanders, resolve any difficulties of control in sending' any support that might be required. But he had to listen to Bader express his opinion, 'from his practical experience', that the essence of the problem was time, and that if enough warning could be given to bring a large number of fighters into position he believed that 'they could get most effective results.'

For all that Dowding and Park believed, the views of that important meeting were summarised as being in favour of the employment of 'a large mass' of fighters, and that it would be of value to go even as far as operating two wings together as a 'balbo'. These views were recorded in the draft of the minutes, copies of which were sent to everyone concerned, including Dowding, Park, Brand and Leigh-Mallory, for comment.

The response from Keith Park was immediate. He sent in a lengthy paper in reply to the invitation to comment upon the minutes before they were finally placed on record. In it he referred to what he described as 'misinformed criticism' of the handling of the fighters by his Group, and he made 'the urgent request' that his views should be recorded more fully in the minutes. He said that he could not 'agree to the important statement which I made being omitted'.

In his reply Dowding objected to a statement in which he was said to have agreed on a point with which he was not in agreement. 'Please do not say that I agree, reluctantly or otherwise,' he wrote. 'I am carrying out orders which I believe to be dangerous and unsound with our present strength of fighter squadrons.'

There were also points raised by Quintin Brand about the minutes that he also asked should be corrected. Nothing was done about his requests, a matter that he commented upon in writing to Park. But Park had the same problem on his hands. The whole of his request was turned down.

So far as Park was concerned, he was now fighting to preserve the concept which he had formulated, with Dowding's entire agreement, in the use that should be made of his fighters in the battle. He willingly agreed to abide by the instructions that were issued that more use should be made of the Duxford wing, even though he questioned its value. At the end of October he wrote to Sholto Douglas about his views, and reported on the efforts that he was making to co-operate. He put on record the failure of the Duxford wing in the latest operations 'to make a single interception in No. 11 Group area on occasions when there were big raids of fighters proceeding towards London'.

In his view of the position in which Dowding was placed, Johnnie Johnson wrote: 'As commander-in-chief the question of how squadrons should fight was a domestic issue which he, and not the Air Staff, would resolve. The Air Staff, all of whom were much junior to him, had offered some advice, and whether or not he followed it was a matter for him. There the matter rested, but only for a short time. . .'

CHAPTER THIRTEEN

POST MORTEM

Out of the welter of all that it is claimed various people said and did at that time in November, 1940, there has come the fuel that has fed the steadily burning fires of a controversy that has been going on now for nearly thirty years. Being the realist that he is, Dowding has turned to the facts for his own assessment of what happened; and it is his contention that those facts speak for themselves and reveal a state of affairs that, while very few have known about it, must be considered in making any final decisions about his own position.

For longer than anybody has realised, the two influences that were to lead to Dowding's extraordinary experiences during that month of November, and which had started out quite independently of each other long before, were joined the moment he signed yet another letter of protest that he finally had to write to the Air Ministry early in that month. 'When one comes to study what happened then behind the scenes,' he has pointed out, 'the amazing thing is that so much of what has been published in the way of comment, quite apart from any historical record, seems to bear so little relationship to the facts.'

It has always been Dowding's view that 'looking at it from the opponents' point of view, if the Air Ministry had decided to back Leigh-Mallory and Sholto Douglas against Park and me they had no alternative but to get rid of me.' He has gone even further than that in his effort to understand the point of view of these opponents and has said that if they were to continue with that support of Leigh-Mallory and Sholto Douglas 'they were right to get rid of me.'

In that statement, as in almost everything that has had to be recorded in the telling of Dowding's story, there is an underlying element of sadness. That was never of Dowding's making, and it was no wish of his. But the shadow was cast, and it has remained, and in everything that Dowding now has to say it is said very much more in sorrow than in any anger. He has spoken of his awareness of his own failings, and that alone has made him gentler in his approach towards the evaluation that he has tried to make of the difficulty of the position that he found himself in at the end of the Battle of Britain.

At the time of the arguments over the use of big wings there was no reason for Dowding to feel that there might be yet another sudden change in the plans for his own future. The last firm date of the end of October as the time limit to his service at Fighter Command had been changed in August to no time limit being imposed, which left him feeling free to get on with the fighting of the night battle. The end of October came and was of no consequence so far as he was concerned. He still understood then that he was to be left in peace to get on with his work.

But looking back now on what he has come to feel is the most important aspect of that meeting of 17 October, Dowding commented: 'I feel that it was certain that the decision to get rid of Park and myself almost at once, that is to say within possibly a month's time, must have been taken as a result of that meeting. Of course, other important people at the Air Ministry would have had to be convinced of the need for that; but even then I was not told about it until the very last moment.'

On 3 November it suddenly became apparent to Dowding why there had been such 'sparse reports', as Strath Evill, his Senior Air Staff Officer commented, from No. 12 Group. Park had been pouring out reports and instructions from his No. 11 Group Headquarters, and writing long letters to Fighter Command Headquarters and to the Air Ministry. Leigh-Mallory, it suddenly became clear, had been working in an entirely different way, and that was made obvious to Dowding in a letter that he received that day from Sholto Douglas.

By this time Dowding was well past fifty-eight years of age, and in his rank of Air Chief Marshal, which he had held since the beginning of 1937, he was still the most senior officer on active service in the Royal Air Force. Sholto Douglas was forty-eight years of age, ten years younger than Dowding, and had been an Air Vice-Marshal since the beginning of 1938. He had a reputation for being a most capable and very forceful member of the Air Staff. The younger officers of air rank were beginning to overtake the older ones. Sir Charles Portal was of the same age as Douglas, and he was now Chief of the Air Staff in place of Newall, and had just been promoted to the rank of Air Chief Marshal. The passage of time alone was bringing about a situation in which it was inevitable that the younger men should press with increasing vigour as they made their way to the top.

In this letter, which has to be considered important because of the way in which it was to provoke Dowding, Sholto Douglas commented that it was clear that the differences between Nos. 11 and 12 Groups—'which were so patent at the conference' which was held on 17 October—had not been settled. He pointed out that No. 12 Group were complaining that the reason why their 'balbo' did not get to the scene of action in time to intercept was because they were not getting early enough warning from No. 11 Group.

Douglas also mentioned a letter he had received from Park in which there was Park's complaint that it was taking fifty-five minutes for the 12 Group 'balbo' to get to Sheerness, and that 'in consequence it never will be in time.' He quoted Park's views about 'the balbo idea' weakening the offensive spirit of individual squadrons of No. 12 Group, and Park's advocacy of pairs of squadrons rather than wings.

'I think that it is important that this difference of opinion should be resolved as quickly as possible, since it seems to be leading to a good deal of bitterness not only between the two A.Os.C. but between the squadrons,' Douglas commented. 'This obviously cannot be allowed to go on, and I think that it is for you to put the matter right by an authoritative statement of your views. This could be far more satisfactory than for the Air Ministry to try and act as referee.'

In defining his own position, Sholto Douglas stated that while he could appreciate Park's difficulties, 'I am inclined to support Leigh-Mallory's view.' Furthermore, he stated, in his view there was 'ever reason . . . to encourage No. 12 Group in their efforts to bring in superior numbers to intercept the enemy on the way home, even if they cannot get their "balbo" up in time to intercept him before he reaches his objectives.' It was to be noted that Douglas referred to 'No. 12 Group' and not to the Duxford wing.

Two points were raised in this letter by Sholto Douglas in support of views that were expressed in a report, a copy of which he attached to the letter, by the Under Secretary of State for Air, who had made an inquiry of his own on a visit to Duxford. They were related to technical details about giving No. 12 Group certain information 'so as to enable them to be in a better state of readiness when called upon to intervene.' Douglas added: 'Both these proposals seem reasonable to me.'

'They would have been reasonable but for the fact that there was no reason for them to be made,' Dowding later commented.

'I have a feeling—which may not be justified—that Park still has a sub-conscious aversion to another Group coming down and fighting in his area,' Sholto Douglas continued in his letter.

Keith Park was not the only one who had an 'aversion' to these intrusions, and it was not 'sub-conscious' on his part. Dowding had the strongest objection for the very simple reason that these intrusions upset the whole system of control, and he felt very strongly that they did little more, when they were un-coordinated, than confuse the controlling of aircraft by No. 11 Group Headquarters for their own vital area. 'It is not at all surprising that Park should object,' Dowding said. 'I also disapproved.'

In a final remark in his letter, Sholto Douglas asked: 'May I leave the matter in your hands?'

Since the airing of what Douglas had called 'the difference of opinion' had been so largely influenced, in Dowding's view, by the interference of the Air Staff, with a strong political backing from the Under Secretary of State for Air, Dowding could not help feeling perplexed over the request that he, the Commander-in-Chief, should now step in and do something about a situation which, he believed, had been created by these outside influences.

There was added to the letter a postscript which read: 'The U.S. of S. asks me to say that he hopes Bader will not get into trouble for having been so outspoken.'

For several reasons the letter from Sholto Douglas contained a distinct shock for Dowding. He felt that it was a further flogging of what he had believed for some time was a dead horse, and he wondered, yet again, what the Air Staff could be thinking about in making so much of what was to him a minor issue. Although he felt irritation that Sholto Douglas should have seen fit to write in the tone that he did, that was nothing more than a small point. But Dowding could not believe that the stage had been reached where there was, as Douglas had put it, '. . . a good deal of bitterness . . . between the squadrons of the two Groups.' He knew that there was rivalry. That was healthy, and only to be expected. But the allegation of 'bitterness' could not have been general, he felt, and such an allegation could have come from only one source.

That there was now a very strong difference of opinion between Park and Leigh-Mallory was only too apparent, but even then Dowding still believed that, though they were men of such forceful character, there was not a great deal to worry about. He still thought that they would keep those differences within the limits expected of them. That Park was doing all that was expected of him Dowding felt quite sure. Park was putting up a good case for a good cause, and Dowding was in agreement with him. But could the same be said, he began to wonder yet again, of Leigh-Mallory?

It had been impossible for Dowding to agree with Leigh-Mallory's views; and now it was becoming impossible for him to agree with the 12 Group Commander's ways of furthering those views. Dowding had gone on keeping his own counsel, feeling that, as Commander-in-Chief, it was for him alone to resolve the issue in his own way. He found Sholto Douglas's expression '. . . this cannot be allowed to go on,' somewhat aggressive, particularly when Douglas openly stated that he was 'inclined to support Leigh-Mallory's point of view'. Douglas could say what he liked, but that did not alter the fact that Dowding did not support Leigh-Mallory's views. He was not going to allow himself to be forced into any action that would support him; and, moreover, he was not prepared to accept Air Staff views which were based on incorrect information and assumptions.

But it was not the actual letter from Sholto Douglas that

caused Dowding to feel that he must make a protest so much
as the accompanying report by the Under Secretary of State
for Air, Harold Balfour, now Lord Balfour of Inchrye. It was
dated 2 November—the day before Douglas wrote to Dowding
—and it was indicated that a copy had gone to the Secretary
of State for Air as well as to other officials at the Air Ministry.

The report stated that a visit that day to Duxford had
confirmed the impression that had been made on the Secretary
of State when he had visited the station the week before. This
was that 'there is a conflict of operational views as between
No. 12 Group and No. 11 Group' which was felt acutely by the
units at Duxford. It was stated that the conflict had 'passed
from being confined to operational questions and has, in the
minds of those concerned, become a personal issue with the
pilots, who feel resentful against 11 Group and its A.O.C. as
well as the Air Ministry. . .' That allegation alone was a shock
for Dowding.

It was contended that the basis for this feeling was that they
were 'at the disposal of 11 Group' and 'are never called upon to
function, according to their new practised tactics of Wing
Formation, until too late', and that they were 'being denied
opportunities of shooting down Germans. . .' The view was
expressed that there was 'resistance by 11 Group to a point
which makes them—12 Group—so biased as to feel that 11
Group object to their poaching on that Group's territory and
are jealous of the Wing Formation being likely to shoot down
11 Group Germans.'

Referring to what was described as 'apparently needless
regulations', the report stated that 'Fighter Command Control
Room is not allowed to transmit' to No. 12 Group radar
information 'south of the Thames Estuary'. In a 'private
arrangement', it was reported, the Station Commander at
Duxford—Wing Commander A. B. Woodhall, who had been
working very closely all along with Bader in the formulation
of his wing tactics—had been obtaining information from the
Observer Corps, but he had now been told that orders had
been given that that was to be stopped. It was requested that
No. 12 Group should have 'improved' radar and Observer
Corps contacts.

The report went on to say that it was understood that certain officers 'in the units of 11 Group are entirely sympathetic to the Wing Formation viewpoint, that they are being ignored and wasted. Further, these 11 Group pilots are fine material but, as a result of constantly having to meet enemy forces in superior numbers, are becoming unnecessarily shaken in their morale while, of course, not succeeding in repelling the enemy in a way that a large formation can do.'

The gravity of the allegations made in this report was such that any personal feeling of indignation that Dowding might have had about its propriety, let alone its accuracy, would have to be controlled, he realised, if he was to make the assessment which was now so clearly necessary. It was also clear to him that the Air Staff had been prodded into feeling deeply about what they believed were severe internal dissensions within his Command. Dowding immediately passed both Sholto Douglas's letter and the Balfour report to his staff for detailed examination.

In the orders that had already been issued from his Headquarters, Dowding knew that the technical points raised in the Balfour report, including the passing of radar information, were well provided for. On 11 October—even before the conference at the Air Ministry—one such order had emphasised the importance of passing the earliest information possible to all Groups. And only four days after that conference a further instruction had been issued that No. 12 Group was to receive the same radar information as that given to No. 11 Group. In fact, the passing of such information had been going on for a long time. But Dowding wanted to be absolutely sure of all his facts before he made any reply. That was particularly necessary, he felt, since the Balfour report had been given a circulation which included the Secretary of State for Air and, automatically the Chief of the Air Staff.

'The only natural conclusion that I could come to was that the political branch of the Air Ministry was now concerning itself with the details of the running of my Command,' Dowding commented. 'It was becoming a political issue.'

After an intense and most careful examination made by his Headquarters' staff of both Sholto Douglas's letter and the report by Harold Balfour, Dowding received a detailed written assessment which he, in turn, examined with the greatest of care, and not a little grim annoyance.

'No matter how strongly I might feel about the Parliamentary Under-Secretary making inquiries in the way he did, and my disagreement with the facts produced, it was still my duty to reply to the Air Ministry letter,' Dowding later commented. 'It was my job, even it it was such a waste of everybody's time, to set them right.'

In speaking of Balfour, Douglas has described him as a 'shrewd' politician, adding: 'It was unquestionably Harold Balfour's first-hand experience through having been a pilot in the Royal Air Force which enabled him to serve us so well. Always an astute politician, Balfour was well aware of the value of making the right impression, and after he became Under-Secretary of State he handled his side of affairs with skill and imagination. Through our long friendship and knowledge of each other I never hesitated about discussing our problems with him, and he never failed to give me his full support.'

When it came to making a study again, many years later, of Sholto Douglas's letter to him and the copy of the Balfour report which accompanied it, Dowding commented: 'Their close association over such a long period of time and under such interesting and valuable circumstances explains, of course, a great deal that I did not then appreciate.' But while that explanation helped in his later studies, at the time Dowding could only feel that, as he has put it, 'the whole thing was getting out of hand.'

The time had now come, Dowding felt in preparing his reply to Sholto Douglas's letter, when he would have to place on record yet another protest. He did not mind doing that so far as it had to do with facts, but this time there was going to be an involvement of a personal element in what he was going to have to say which was acutely distasteful to him. It meant that he would have to express his views about two men who had shown great gallantry as pilots in their fighting in the air: one, Harold Balfour, in the First World War, and the second, Douglas Bader, right at the moment.

In all the long struggle over the years for what he believed was right for his Command, and through that the defence of the United Kingdom, Dowding had been dealing with hard facts, and there had never been, in his way of thinking, any need for an indulgence in any personal assessments, other than in routine matters affecting the officers under his command. But now, it seemed to him, the personal element had been allowed to intrude too far, and had even been forced upon him in such a way that he could not avoid taking note of it. In fact, so serious had it become that he knew that, much as he disliked having to do it, it was nevertheless his duty to make known just how he felt about the views that were being expressed by these two well-known individual-ists.

That there was room for improvement in some respects, Dowding did not want to deny, and right at the outset of his reply to Sholto Douglas he stated: 'I agree that this operation is causing so much friction and ill-feeling that I must withdraw the control of combined operations between Nos. 11 and 12 Groups from the Group Commanders themselves and issue the orders through my own Operations Room.'

Nevertheless, Dowding had to state, 'the story which Balfour has collected by his direct methods is wrong in its conclusions and in the facts on which these conclusions are based.' He then went on to deal with the claim about lack of radar information and pointed out that it was quite incorrect. No. 12 Group had always had passed to them by his Head-quarters all radar information 'down to the latitude of Dunge-ness—Gris-Nez', and they got it 'simultaneously with 11 Group'. Also, the claim that Duxford had been denied Observer Corps information was not true. They had been using 'an unauthorised system', which had interfered with the work of the Observer Corps, and that had been stopped 'at the request of the Southern Area Observer Corps Comman-dant'.

So far as the claim that the Duxford Wing was not being called for by No. 11 Group until too late was concerned, Dowding stated that 'my criticism is that the recent conference and all the fuss that has been made has resulted in 11 Group calling for assistance from 12 Group not only too early, but without the slightest excuse.' In support of that Dowding gave details of recent operations.

In the report that had been submitted to him by his staff, Dowding had been informed that the examination had to be based on information from No. 11 Group 'as No. 12 Group reports are sketchy'. He was informed that 'the Duxford Wing was called upon with great promptitude, in fact so promptly that it is clear that No. 11 Group could have had no grounds at the time for knowing whether the enemy attack was going to be large or small.'

Such was the effort made by No. 11 Group to co-operate, Dowding pointed out, that only the day before, on 5 November, the A.O.C. No. 11 Group had asked No. 12 Group 'to have the Wing on patrol' under conditions 'which could hardly have been related to any situation that he could positively foresee at that time'.

'. . . no-one will deny the advantages of a 3, 4 or 5 Squadron Wing against a determined enemy attack whether it be large or comparatively small, providing it can bring the enemy to action,' Dowding stated. But now the Germans were working with 'loosely formed high altitude fighter sweeps', and, he pointed out, 'there was less time for the Wing to come into action and less for it to bite on when it gets there.' He had come to the conclusion, he stated, that the 'continuous operation of this Wing of five Squadrons cannot be justified in existing circumstances'.

It should not have been necessary for Dowding to have to call attention to the bare facts of No. 12 Group's responsibilities, but since they seemed to have been overlooked, or were not appreciated, by the Air Staff, he referred to the way in which the use of the squadrons in building up the Wing 'diverts them from the normal tasks of No. 12 Group which are the defence of its own area, including some highly important industrial districts'.

Knowing far better than anybody else the problems faced by his Command in the defence of the whole country, Dowding stated: 'I am inclined to the conclusion that for the moment in this present phase, the use of the Duxford Wing is a misemployment of a valuable element of our very limited strength . . . it is probably no longer an economical or effective use of five squadrons.' In saying that he was also expressing the considered opinion of those of his staff, including his Senior Air Staff Officer, whose opinions were of the utmost importance.

In an effort to look towards the immediate future, an exercise in which Dowding had proved beyond all doubt during the entire term of his office that he was more far-sighted than was then realised, he offered the view: 'There is a growing tendency for the enemy to increase the frequency and weight of his attacks in the North and West; and, although it is perfectly obvious that his object is to weaken the London defence, the intensity of his attacks on London has fallen off recently and I may be compelled to make some redistribution of my force.'

The need for a further examination before he could take any 'precise action' was stressed by Dowding, and he stated that he would 'take counsel with my Group Commanders'.

In his report, Harold Balfour had made the statement: 'Squadron Leader Bader and his unit look forward to the time when the enemy may decide to renew their mass daylight raids.' Dowding has since said of that comment that while he appreciated such eagerness in his pilots to get to grips with the enemy, he could not agree with the way it was expressed, since no one could 'look forward to' more mass daylight raids, even though the possibility of that happening had to be kept in mind. At the time, he wrote: '. . . even now, these wings might, with luck, achieve a resounding success, but in this phase I think the odds are against that.'

What Dowding could not accept was the unfounded criticism which appeared in both Sholto Douglas' letter and the Balfour report. He felt that his whole position was being undermined; and there was the reminder for him that he had been offered by the Chief of the Air Staff back in July about the need 'to consider the retirement of the more senior officers in order to maintain an adequate flow of promotions in the higher positions in the Service. . .' But Dowding was the very last man ever to consider whether he should possibly protect his own position by a cautious indication that he might agree with Air Ministry views that were opposed to his own.

Having set the facts right, and corrected the statements

which had been made in the Balfour report, Dowding then turned his attention to the more personal aspects of the requests that had been made that he should intervene and set at rest the difficulties over morale which, it was alleged, existed in his Command. Dowding did not believe that these allegations were true; but he did believe, as he had for some time now, that there was a definite source which was causing disturbances.

Of the obvious part that was being played by Leigh-Mallory in all that was going on, Dowding could make only one comment. He had come to feel, with increasing conviction, that his No. 12 Group Commander was distinctly over-eager to further his own interests, and that he was exploiting every opportunity that he could to denigrate the work done by Keith Park in order to achieve that. 'Leigh-Mallory has many commitments of his own,' Dowding wrote in his reply to Sholto Douglas, 'and should "keep his eye in the boat".'

Of equal importance to Dowding, and linked with the actions of Leigh-Mallory in fostering within his Group the free expression of opinions by pilots to officials outside the Command, was the manner in which political leaders were being allowed to accept and then disseminate without his knowledge this same criticism. That, he considered, was most improper, and he reported his views to Sholto Douglas.

'There remains the question of an Under-Secretary of State listening to the accusations of a junior officer against the Air Officer Commanding Group, and putting them on paper with the pious hope that the officer will not get into trouble,' he wrote. 'Balfour has been in the Service and ought to know better.' He added his view that a great deal of the controversy had been initiated by Douglas Bader, 'who, whatever his other merits, suffers from over-development of the critical faculties.'

That rebuke was not made lightly. It was the result of Dowding's own distress over what had been reported to him. And when it came to speaking of the actions of Douglas Bader, Dowding was even more distressed, as he has continued to be ever since that time. Then, as he has stated so many times since, he felt an unbounded regard for Bader's great courage. But at this time of having to reply to the Air Ministry, Dowding had to place on record his opinion of actions that had been taken that had nothing to do with gallantry in the air, and the report could be only on that basis.

All that had been going on without Dowding's knowledge had now come to a head, and with a regret that was both deep and heart-felt, Dowding then wrote: 'This might give an opportunity of moving young Bader to another station where he would be kept in better control. His amazing gallantry will protect him from disciplinary action if it can possibly be avoided.'

So far as Dowding was concerned, there was now the grave question of what he regarded as disloyalty to him, as the Commander-in-Chief, added to the earlier views that he held about insubordination. The comment that Dowding made was expressed, as with his earlier views, with a full awareness of what he was saying. He indicated that he was doing everything that he could to avoid having to curb the impetuosity of a man whose gallantry as a fighting pilot was so great, but whose regard appeared to be so lacking when it came to the position that he placed other people in through that same impetuosity.

Little did Dowding realise what acute displeasure his perfectly justified comments were going to ignite in the minds of some, and what powder they were for use against him by those who were looking for an excuse to blast him out of office. Six months before, in May, he had put his signature to a letter that was hailed as a great declaration of the will and the right of our people to fight. When he signed the letter in November, 1940, he brought down on his head a political guillotine.

With the passing of time, and Keith Park's statements about his and Dowding's case, further examination is necessary of the claims that have been allowed to pass unchallenged for so long, even if this is largely an academic exercise. In 1968 Park wrote to Dowding about the vigorous statements he had made to the press, and he called attention to the value of the published views of Alan Deere. In these, Park pointed out, there was 'a crushing answer to Sholto Douglas and other supporters of the use of Big Wings during the Battle of Britain . . .'

'In two wars I have had grim opportunities of seeing human

endeavour stretched to its limits—and sometimes beyond,' Dowding once wrote. 'Alan Deere will always stand to me as an example of the best type of Fighter Pilot. . .'

As a pilot in the thick of the fighting in No. 11 Group, and as one of the most successful in the whole battle, Al Deere's experiences were second to none; and, because of all that he knew at first hand of what went on in Park's group, he wrote with an authority which matched in his support of No. 11 Group's tactics the views expressed by Douglas Bader in his support of the opposition. 'The Battle of Britain has been the subject of much misconception and not a little controversy,' Deere stated in his book published in 1959. 'The misconception arose over the extent to which Fighter Command's forces became depleted and the controversy centres mainly around the strategy of the Commander-in-Chief and the tactics employed by the Air Officer Commanding No. 11 Group, the principal commanders in the battle.'

One of the 'major problems' faced by Dowding in the battle was 'how and where to concentrate his squadrons', Deere has pointed out. 'His decision to concentrate only a portion of his available forces in the most threatened area—No. 11 Group— and to relieve tired squadrons as considered necessary from the less hard-pressed Groups has also been sniped at by many armchair critics, particularly those who supported the Leigh-Mallory concept of concentrating all the power in the threatened area.'

Certain people had made the serious allegation that morale was affected in No. 11 Group through the pilots 'having to meet enemy forces in superior numbers'. Al Deere spoke of 'the tremendous odds' that they had to face in fighting as Park directed, and about that he made the comment: '. . . I do not recall a single pilot saying other than that he thought it an excellent idea. I strongly support this view. . .'

Following that, Deere came to what Park described as the 'crushing answer'. 'It was over the question of mass formations —or wings of squadrons, as they later became known—that a really vital issue arose,' Deere wrote. 'Douglas Bader was the chief instigator of the use of wings in the Battle of Britain, and had sold the idea to Air Vice-Marshal Leigh-Mallory. Although concentration of force, which the mass formations implied, is a foremost principle of war, it did not apply under the conditions which affected the defence of these shores in the Battle of Britain, at least through the medium of wing formations. The sober truth is that, at this stage of the war, the information from the radar chain was neither sufficiently complete nor sufficiently reliable to permit the adoption of the policy with success. It would have been blind folly . . . to have hurled masses of defending fighters into the air on each and every occasion that a build-up occurred.'

After stressing that he was voicing opinions that came from his own personal experience—which was as all-embracing as any other pilots—Deere continued: '. . . there were very few occasions in the 11 Group area when it would have been possible to scramble and assemble two squadrons as a wing—let alone five as finally used from Duxford—in time to make an effective interception before the enemy bombers reached their target. Almost one hundred per cent of the interceptions by the Duxford Wing were over or just short of the target, and sometimes after the bombs had fallen, which supports the contention that much vital time was lost in forming up, and proceeding to the target, in mass formation.' Deere supported the statement that was made by Dowding in his despatch about the 'ten large formation sorties from Duxford into the 11 Group area': nine of these were unsuccessful, and only one Me 109 was destroyed by the tenth.

'From a fighter pilot's point of view, I hold that Bader's wing concept was wrong,' Al Deere stated. 'I know that most wing leaders agree with me, and certainly those who had the benefit of later experience.'

There has always been a particular appeal for Dowding in the view expressed by Al Deere in his statement:

In any discussion of the Battle of Britain it is important to remember that the aim of the Luftwaffe was to destroy Fighter Command in the air and on the ground and by so doing open the way for a seaborne invasion of England. Dowding's task was, therefore, twofold:
(1) to prevent the destruction of his forces, and
(2) in the process, inflict the maximum of destruction on the enemy air forces.
To achieve the second only was not in itself sufficient; he must also ensure that Fighter Command remained strong enough to influence

events should an invasion be launched. Park's tactics were, of necessity, based on the overall aim of his Commander-in-Chief and not, as some people fondly imagine, to destroy the German Air Force, a task beyond the slender resources of his Group and, for that matter, of the Command. That the strategy of Dowding and the tactics of Park were successful, is proven by the fact that by the end of August, when according to German estimates Fighter Command would be defeated, the 11 Group squadrons were still inflicting heavy losses on the enemy and all the Sector airfields were intact.

Deere also added that 'Dowding and Park won the Battle of Britain, but they lost the battle of words that followed. . .'

As might be expected, Al Deere is most outspoken in his objection to the allegation that was made about the state of morale among the pilots of No. 11 Group. In his forthright way, he exploded with a comment denying it that has to be left to the imagination. It was succinct, and of a brevity that would gladden the hearts of all the many pilots who agree with him.

On the question of morale in No. 11 Group, Ginger Lacey is another of those who is distinctly pointed in his view. His squadron suffered particularly heavy casualties during the battle, and his opinion is very clearly expressed in his statement: 'If anyone's morale should have been affected, it should have been ours, but it was not. We were tired, and frightened, and under strength, but we were never lacking in morale, and certainly not over the fact that we were not using big wings. Far from morale being affected by the lack of big wings, with the job we had to do in 11 Group we preferred to be without them.'

'Any suggestion that the fact that they were not operating in wings lowered the pilots' morale just does not stand up even to the slightest examination,' Johnny Kent has said. 'It is quite unacceptable to me or, I should have thought, to anyone who served in 11 Group in the battle.'

About the alleged feeling of resentment in No. 12 Group against No. 11 Group and its A.O.C. Tom Gleave commented: 'This is something I never heard of. It staggers me. I never even heard the slightest suggestion that the morale of No. 11 Group pilots was ever shaken by superior enemy forces. I have no doubt whatsoever that the boast made by our pilots in general that "three and four to one against is normal, and more than that is a little dangerous" was no idle one. That was symbolic of their terrific morale.'

One of the Controllers at No. 11 Group during the battle was Wing Commander (now Group Captain) E. A. Douglas-Jones, known to everybody as D-J. He had also commanded a squadron until just before the start of the battle. When he heard the allegation about morale among pilots who were fighting in No. 11 Group he was deeply shocked, particularly when this allegation was associated with the question of the use of wings. 'What a terrible thing for anybody to say!' he exclaimed.

The point has been made by Douglas-Jones that has been offered by others about the keenness of the pilots, which went so far that there was an almost universal complaint raised by the squadrons when orders were given for them to come out of the line and go north for a rest. No matter what was happening to them, no matter how severe the beating, they wanted to stay where they were and answer back. So far as the value of the use of big wings was concerned, Douglas-Jones associated himself entirely with his fellow controllers, John Willoughby de Broke and Thomas Lang, in stating categorically that the whole concept was quite wrong for use in No. 11 Group during the fighting in the Battle of Britain.

CHAPTER FOURTEEN

A QUESTION OF COMMAND

After sending his reply to the letter from Sholto Douglas, Dowding might have spent his days wondering about what was going to happen next. But there was no time to spare for any such idle thoughts. As before, his days and nights were fully occupied with work, and by now the night bombing offensive by the Germans, the Blitz, was in full fury.

That there was an undercurrent of speculation about what was going on did not altogether escape Dowding's attention, isolated though he had become, through no choice of his own, at his Headquarters at Bentley Priory. But the rumours that were circulating smacked too strongly of all that he had objected to so firmly in his letter to Newall of 7 July—when he had spoken of discourtesy and lack of consideration—for him to pay any attention to them.

So far as Dowding knew, he was still in the position of having no time limit imposed on his appointment. He had not been informed of any change in that, which had been made clear to him just under three months before. Common courtesy, which he had already asked should be observed, and which he had been assured would be observed, left him feeling that he would be given at least reasonable and adequate notice of the time for him to relinquish his Command. But there were these rumours.

Of what happened then, in the second week in November, Dowding stated: 'I received a sudden phone call at my Headquarters from the Secretary of State for Air. He told me that I was to relinquish my Command immediately. I asked what was meant by "immediately", and I was told that it would take effect within the next day or so. Since that was tantamount to my being given twenty-four hours' notice, and verbally at that, I pointed out that it was perfectly absurd that I should be relieved of my Command in this way unless it was thought that I had committed some major crime or something like that. But all that I could get in reply was that the decision had been reached, and that was that, with no explanation for such a precipitate step being taken.'

This was the last but one step taken in the long story of discourtesy, and even of common decency, that was shown Dowding by officialdom. But even that was not all. For some reason known only to those at the Air Ministry in whose hands there rested the handling of such matters, there was not even sent any sort of letter, either personal or official, informing the man who had just won the Battle of Britain that he was to give up his Command, and no mention was ever made of what he had achieved in his appointment and in the winning of the battle.

'They just got rid of me,' Dowding commented. Enlarging on that, he added: 'But I want it to be quite clear that I had no grievance on that score. It was the way it was done that hurt, when I was sent away as if I had been rather an indifferent sort of commander.'

Quite apart from the outcome of the battle, which had by then been decided, there were three events which, if it had not been for the actions that Dowding had taken at critical times, would have led to Britain losing the battle. The first was in the origin of the Hurricane and the Spitfire. The second was over the organisation of the whole system of control and getting it and all the fighter stations into operation and linked with radar throughout his Command. The third was when he argued with Churchill and won in the matter of sending more squadrons to France. There were not many people who would have been able to do that, and could present a record, even before the the battle came to be fought, as powerful and as distinguished as the one for which Dowding can so rightly take credit.

Twenty-eight years later, after an exhaustive search had been made, it was found that the crisp but thoroughly justified reply that Dowding had made to the criticisms advanced by those at the Air Ministry in finding fault with his handling of his Command was, in fact, the last document on record that dealt with this vexed subject. There were only two more short letters addressed to him, both hard on the heels of what was probably the most distressing and humiliating experience that Dowding was ever to experience.

After briefly, and so abruptly, telling Dowding on the phone that he was through, the Secretary of State for Air then informed him that he was not to take any disciplinary action against Douglas Bader over anything that he might have done. Despite the numbing shock of what was being said to him, Dowding did manage to make one reply.

'I answered on the spot and repeated what I had said in my letter,' Dowding has recalled. 'I paid what I considered was a fair tribute to Bader's extreme personal gallantry, and I said that that alone would protect him from any action on my part.'

That was all that was said on the phone, but for Dowding it was, as he put it, 'finally the end'. The hurt that was inflicted in those few moments was grievous.

The abruptness and curtness of the notification that he was through had in it an additional shock for Dowding because of the firm assurances of only four months before that he would be given plenty of notice when it came time for him to go. In his letter to Dowding of 5 July, Newall had said that if Dowding would continue in his appointment—'if you will again defer your retirement' was the expression that he had used—he would '. . . write to you regarding your successor'. No such information had been forthcoming about who was to take his place, even though there had been a further exchange of letters about the change in command. It was not until now, over four months later and with the great battle fought and won, that Dowding was abruptly given during that phone call the name of his successor, who was to take over in what was barely more than a few days' time. The officer was Sholto Douglas.

'After being told that, it was clear to me that there could be no more argument or any further discussion,' Dowding commented. 'Of course it was a shock to me, and yet in a way it seemed natural enough. The Air Council had been anxious to be rid of me since before the start of the war, and I suppose this was the appropriate moment, which I had supplied, in a way, by writing to them as I had. All said and done, there had been hanging over my head for a long time a whole shop-full of bowler hats.'

Whatever it was that induced the Air Council to make up their minds about Dowding's going, it led them to actions that were executed at a speed for which it is extremely hard to find any excuse. Dowding had placed a natural reliance on the Secretary of State for Air's assurance about 'the fairness of communicating with' him 'in good time', and he has never been able to understand why he should have been asked to disregard so completely that assurance.

But what is time and what is fairness and what are assurances in the political context? Dowding found out very quickly, so quickly that it seemed to come in the matter of only a few moments, and with as rude a shock as it is possible to imagine. But since those assurances, both personal and official, he had fought and won the Battle of Britain. Was that of no account? In certain aspects it could be said that the full realisation that the battle had been won could not be, or was not, fully appreciated; but that, even with every allowance being made for any doubts about the outcome of the battle, could be scarcely more than an unimaginative view of what had been happening. There was little excuse for any doubt by the middle of November as to the outcome of the day battle.

'Of course it wouldn't have been so easy for the politicians if they hadn't had that assistance from below,' Dowding once commented. And after a moment's thought he added: 'And it wouldn't have been so easy for those below if they hadn't had the assistance from those above.'

After he made his protest to Sholto Douglas in the letter that he wrote on 6 November, Dowding went on with his work which, as before, was all-absorbing, except that now his concern was with a battle at night, instead of by day. On 17 November, the day after the phone call from the Secretary of State for Air, Dowding signed the last of the very comprehensive reports on 'Night Interception' that he had been issuing to everybody to whom the subject was of any concern. It is indicative enough of his way of working that it should be, even in this very last moment, so thorough-going. In just over three pages of closely typed foolscap he covered the whole field, starting with a description of a visit that he had just made to the highly secret airborne radar unit working from the aerodrome at Tangmere, in Sussex.

In this report Dowding explained that he was present when the first attempt was made 'to work with the G.C.I-type apparatus' that had just been installed for a more exact and direct radar control of the night fighters from the ground. There was in this the origin of the world-wide radar watch that is now kept at all airfields on the movements of all aircraft. '. . . it suffers in its present state from several disabilities,' he commented. Dowding then went on to describe this first equipment—with its 'Plan Position Indicator' cathode ray tube—which was to develop so rapidly and so effectively into the complex network that is in use today.

From that, Dowding ranged over the whole field, reporting on matters that were highly technical, thereby revealing the grasp that he had on various aspects of electronics and the operational use that could be made of them; and, as one might expect, it was all written in the clear, terse style that was such a feature of Dowding's work.

Referring to it as 'the crux of the present situation', Dowding wrote about his hopes for the radar-equipped night fighter, but, he pointed out, '. . . the art of following an echo up to the stage of a successful interception is much more difficult than had been expected.'

After sending off copies of that report to all concerned, including one to the Secretary of State for Air, Dowding was away again that night from his headquarters on another visit to one of the aerodromes from which the night fighters were flying. When he got back to Montrose in the small hours of the morning he found waiting for him a letter from the Chief of the Air Staff.

'With reference to your recent correspondence with Douglas about a report made by Balfour after conversation with Woodhall and Bader,' it stated, 'the Secretary of State has directed that no reproof should be offered to either of the two officers on account of the conversations referred to.'

It would be an underestimate if one were to say that by this time Dowding was a little groggy from the two instructions that had now been given him about action that he must not take in the cases of two officers under his command. But even then, strongly though he felt about the extraordinary intervention that had been made in what he considered was a matter for him to decide upon, he replied briefly: 'With reference to your letter of November 17th, no reproof has been or will be offered by me to either Woodhall or Bader.'

There were these two blows that had rained down on Dowding's head: the personal one in the phone call from the Secretary of State for Air, and the one in the letter from the Chief of the Air Staff. To the sense of shock that had come with the first there was the added bewilderment caused by the second. Was this what a Commander-in-Chief was expected to accept when he was taking the initial steps to correct a situation, as he had been asked to do? He had replied to the request from the Air Ministry in a fashion that he considered was perfectly correct and proper, and he believed that he was thoroughly justified in what he had said. But, it seemed, because that did not suit the plans of the Air Staff, whatever they may have been, he was summarily dismissed without further discussion or a fully understood evaluation of his views.

'There was no way I could escape from the feeling that in making their decision the Air Ministry had weighed up the respective merits of the views held by me, the Commander-in-Chief, as opposed to those of one of my young squadron commanders,' Dowding commented. 'Those of the squadron commander prevailed. Even though I had presented my considered opinion about a matter concerning the running by me of my own Command, that opinion was held against me without any further word to me. Propriety alone, quite apart from everything else, seemed to have gone by the board.'

Many years later, in his effort to understand how it could all have happened as it did, Dowding said: 'It was contrary to the promise that had been made to me only a few months before, and it was contrary to all normal procedure in notifying a Commander-in-Chief about his relinquishment of his command. That is what I have never been able to understand. Everything seemed to go by the board: courtesy, good manners, the customary practices, the drill or procedure or whatever you like to call it. The whole way in which it was done was so hole-in-the-corner, just as if . . . well . . . as if something had to be hushed up. It has remained in my mind that the position was quite untenable. I do not want to appear to be making a song and dance and posing as an excessively aggrieved person. That is not in accordance with my views about the way one should live. But so many times I have asked myself why this extraordinary situation was forced upon me.'

What Dowding felt then, and what he still feels, is that it was quite correct for the Air Ministry to get rid of him if they were right and he was wrong. 'Apparently they had come to believe that they were right in advocating the use of big wings,' he once said. 'Since I believed that they were wrong, there was nothing else they could do but relieve me of my Command. I have no complaint on that score. The way in which I was told to go left a lot to be desired, but that is still not the whole point. But were they right over the use of big wings? What was the consensus of opinion within my Command among those who were most knowledgeable? And what were the results obtained by the big wing adherents when they had their own way?'

There have been over the years many expressions of opinion about whether the use of the big wings would have been the right way of handling the fighters in the Battle of Britain. Almost without exception opinion now is that the Air Staff were wrong and that Dowding was right. But that did not spare Dowding.

Nor did being right spare Keith Park. It was shortly after Dowding left Fighter Command that Park had to relinquish his command of No. 11 Group. He had been there only a bare ten months. 'I was notified that I was to go by the C.A.S.,' Park stated. 'At first I was offered a job on the Air Staff.' That would surely have been, so far as Park was concerned, the last straw. Instead he went to command a Training Group. His place at No. 11 Group was taken by Leigh-Mallory, who went there from No. 12 Group. 'He did not even bother to attend to the usual formality of taking over from me,' Park commented, 'so I handed over to my Senior Air Staff Officer.'

Attempts to explain what happened in the situation that developed at this time have been made by some historians, avoided by a few, and hinted at by many various writers. The

opinions of the pilots themselves are summed up in what Alan
Deere and Johnnie Johnson and Peter Wykeham have had to
say, to name only three of them. Group controllers, who directed the pilots in the air, and who were themselves pilots, have
also expressed their opinions from time to time, with those
from No. 11 Group presenting a unified front in denouncing the
use of the big wings.

'The advantage of hindsight makes it difficult to fault
Keith Park's record,' Johnnie Johnson commented. 'The size of
the fighting unit in 11 Group was conditioned by the time to
intercept before the bombing. It might well have been fatal
had Park always tried to get his squadrons into balbos, for not
only would they have taken longer to get their height but sixty
or seventy packed, climbing fighters could have been seen for
miles and would have been sitting ducks for higher 109s.'

Of particular value as an illustration of the general use of
the big wings that might have been made in No. 11 Group is
the evidence offered by Thomas Lang. He was a Controller
throughout the battle under Park, and also under Leigh-
Mallory after he took over. He now lives in Australia. Always
a staunch supporter of Keith Park, even today so many
years later, Lang recalls with near despair the grave lack of
understanding that Leigh-Mallory showed of the problems
faced by No. 11 Group during the course of the battle. Leigh-
Mallory would insist upon seeing everything only as he wanted
to see it, and Lang has called attention to Lord Tedder's
further criticism: 'Leigh-Mallory's weakness was his desire to
interfere with subordinate commanders.'

In the change of command of No. 11 Group, Thomas Lang,
for one, had good reason to feel the affect of that interference.
He has explained how Leigh-Mallory decided early in 1941,
shortly after becoming A.O.C. No. 11 Group, to conduct an
exercise using the conditions and circumstances of one of the
actual engagements in the battle during September, 1940.
The object was to prove his views about the effective use of
big wings.

'One of the operations was selected at random,' Lang
recalled, 'and L-M said he would take on the job of controlling.
He asked me to be the umpire as I had been in the group at
the time of the real thing.'

Everything was in order for the exercise, the state at each of the No. 11 Group stations being one squadron at readiness, one at fifteen minutes available, and the third, or more, at thirty minutes available. That state was clearly displayed, as it always was, on the boards in the Operations Room, being the essential guide to the Controller about the state of the squadrons of his whole Group.

Thomas Lang had this clearly displayed state well in mind, and he hoped that Leigh-Mallory fully understood it. In order to be quite sure about that, he put a direct question to him. 'I asked if he was satisfied with the displayed state, and he said that he was and was all ready to go,' Lang has recalled.

What then happened made history. 'The raid, a simulation of the actual thing, was a very rapid one in that the main attack came in without much weaving round over Pas de Calais, and within ten minutes was on its way over the coast off Gris Nez and flying fast towards London over Kent and Sussex,' Lang reported. 'L-M's first order shook the entire Ops. Room.'

The W.A.A.F. and R.A.F. plotters and staff on duty knew all about what had to be done and how to cope with it because most of them had been there through the actual battle. To their astonishment Leigh-Mallory ordered that a wing should 'patrol Maidstone at 30,000 feet'. The initial difficulty there, as everybody knew, was that no station was, as Lang put it, 'in a state of being fully alerted'. In other words the state of all the stations in the group so clearly displayed for use by the Controller was being completely ignored.

'I sent up a message to let L-M know that, even if the squadrons had all been at readiness, it would take the wing that he had ordered off at least fifteen, and probably more, minutes to get airborne,' Lang continued.

But that apparently had no affect on the A.O.C.'s idea of how the battle should be fought. 'He did exactly the same with another Spitfire station,' Lang explained. There had by then developed the situation where two Wings were supposed to be in the air whereas, in fact, the stations concerned were only able to alert the squadrons and bring them to a state which would enable them to become airborne within a reasonable time. And all this time the enemy raids were hurtling in over England.

'Believe it or not, but the same wing order went out to Kenley, North Weald and finally Northolt,' Lang recalled. 'By this time the raids were heading for the airfields to the south of London. Then came the plots showing that Kenley and Biggin Hill were being bombed. And still our wings of fighters were not even airborne. That ended that particular battle.'

When Thomas Lang reported to Leigh-Mallory on the result of the exercise he could do no more than explain that Kenley and Biggin Hill had been bombed while the fighters were still on the ground. 'After listening to me patiently enough,' Lang has explained, 'L-M merely said that the next time he would do better. The impression made on the Ops. Room staff was one of amazement that he could make so many mistakes with his "abominable wing" ideas.'

Shortly afterwards, in a talk with Thomas Lang in the Ops. Room, Leigh-Mallory suddenly announced: 'If there are any more major battles over England I shall control all of them.' And to Lang's astonishment he added that if a large-scale raid came in 'he would permit it to bomb its target', and that he would then intercept it on the way back to France. 'He said the enemy would be so badly mauled that he would never try it again,' Lang reported.

'Looking back on things now I believe that I ought to have been very much firmer, in fact stricter, with Leigh-Mallory,' Dowding once commented. 'He was not prepared to obey my orders, and I should have got rid of him.' Dowding has added to that the further view that 'it was all part of a pattern,' and no matter which way he looks at it he finds it impossible to come to any other conclusion than that. 'I don't feel that I have anything to repent, although in the light of after-events I do feel sorry that at the time I didn't take that firmer action.'

Although Dowding has remained silent for so long, Keith Park has not been so reticent about expressing his views. He has more reason, perhaps, to feel aggrieved. Dowding has clearly stated that it was not being relieved of his Command that disturbed him. But in Park's case, he was forced to give up his Command after having held it for such a short time. Many have asked down through the years—journalists, historians, biographers—in the many studies that have been published, just what happened, and just what it was that caused Dowding, and shortly afterwards Park, to be replaced under what appeared to be such curious circumstances.

In a statement that he made to the press in the summer of 1968, which was widely publicised in New Zealand, Keith Park could contain his anger no longer. He said that in his opinion the commander of the Group immediately to the rear of No. 11 Fighter Group created a political situation which he could manipulate to his own advantage. 'As a result of this,' Park said, 'just after the Battle of Britain was won the Air Ministry sacked Air Chief Marshal Dowding, and . . . I was relegated to command the flying training schools. I became a victim . . . only because I was subordinate to, and loyal to, Dowding.'

At the same time, in a letter to Dowding, Park wrote: 'I believe the specious argument in favour of the big wings in 1940 was used by the Air Staff and Leigh-Mallory to belittle our success in the Battle and as a pretext to remove you and me.'

The position of Douglas Bader in all this was, in Park's view, which he also expressed in writing to Dowding, that he 'was a brave and gallant Squadron Leader but was relatively inexperienced and may not have realised that he was being used.'

'. . . the Battle of Britain had, in fact, as the German High Command well knew, been won by the narrowest of margins,' General Pile said of the outcome of the battle in which he was himself so deeply involved. Having worked in such close association with Dowding throughout the battle, and having the direct access that he did to Dowding's office, he knew more than most about what happened. Of that he was later to write:

Perhaps the most astonishing outcome of this great battle, which today the Royal Air Force rank in their minds with Trafalgar, was that the Commander-in-Chief responsible for the victory was almost immediately transferred. Air Chief Marshal Sir Hugh Dowding had, of course, been a thorn in the side of the Air Ministry. I listened to many and lengthy arguments, first of all with the technical staff at the Air Ministry, and then, when he failed to budge them, with Sir Cyril Newall himself . . . it did not make him popular.

General Pile ventured to add to that the view that two of Dowding's supporters 'were Churchill and Beaverbrook'. While 'they gave him full credit for all he did,' Pile further stated: '. . . in the end they could not save him, and so, as he said somewhat sadly to me . . . he was sacked.'

At one time Pile made a comment about the way in which he and Dowding were able to reach agreements, and he credited Dowding with having said: 'The only two men in different Services who ever got on together are Pile and myself.' Many years later Dowding recalled: 'Tim Pile was a very good friend of mine, quite apart from our association while we were Commanders-in-Chief. We never had any difference of opinion during the time we worked together, and I knew that he was a very popular and efficient commander. It was always pleasant for me, personally, that we were such good friends.'

Because there was so much going on that was clamouring for attention, Dowding almost had to force himself to the realisation that the time had come for him finally to relinquish his Command. There had been so many postponements in the past, but now that it was all settled, and he was to go, he made his plans for that. Then, with those plans completed, he received a second letter from the Chief of the Air Staff. It read:

The Secretary of State has asked me to consult you about the announcement and date of Douglas's taking over from you. There has unfortunately been a slight leakage to the Press which we all much regret, and we therefore want to announce a list of appointments, of which this will be one, on Monday, 18th. Douglas cannot be made available to take over until Monday week the 25th, and what I am asking is whether you would agree to carry on in command until the latter date. In the announcement the date of the hand-over would be described as 'in the near future.'

This letter was waiting for Dowding when he arrived back at Montrose in the small hours of the morning after another visit to one of his aerodromes to see what progress was being made by the night fighters. He replied immediately, saying: 'I have been out on night operations and your letter reached me at 1.20 a.m.'

Of the feeling that was inspired in him over this further request for yet another postponement—short though it was—Dowding commented: 'Having been given a sharp notice to quit, the C.A.S. was now asking, in a perfectly natural and easy way, for yet another postponement. It was for only a few days, but it made me believe that he could not have known anything about the long history of all the other postponements. Had he known about that, and had he known, in fact, of the way in which I had been told to go, I doubt very much if he would have asked this of me. But he did, and there was nothing left for me to do but accept it.'

It was that which made Dowding merely add in his reply to the C.A.S.: 'Certainly I will carry on till the 25th if that will be convenient to you.'

By this time the rumour that Dowding was going was common gossip at his Headquarters. In my own diary I wrote: 'I do hope we are not up to our usual muddling game. My heartfelt sympathies are with the Old Man.' In some unaccountable way it had also become known at Headquarters that Dowding was to make a visit to the United States of America.

In the face of all this, Dowding was completely withdrawn. He gave very little sign, even to those who were in closest contact with him, of what he was feeling. But to the more observant, or to those who, perhaps, knew him better than he realised, it was obvious that he was unhappy and bewildered. It has always been my belief that he was in a state of shock. To that there was added the news of the change that was to take place that appeared in the newspapers. The *Daily Telegraph* had it on the front page in its issue of 20 November, with a photograph of Sholto Douglas as 'Fighter Command New Chief'.

This abrupt upheaval in all his affairs was to cause difficulties even in Dowding's domestic life. He had to consider his sister's position and future. 'I naturally had to tell her right away what had happened,' he said. 'We had been living for a long time in the official residence that was provided for the Commander-in-Chief, and it had become our home. We had to get out in a hurry and make way for the new C.-in-C. Even under normal circumstances my sister would have needed all the notice she could possibly have to settle everything and arrange to move out.'

'It was all a terrific rush,' Hilda Dowding recalled. 'I had to make my own arrangements for where I was going to live. And I had to plan for the servants we had who had been working for us. We were working against time, and up to the very last moment we were still packing things up in order to get out as quickly as possible. And then, for all the rush, when the new man arrived he decided not to live there.'

In British military history there is to be found one established custom that has always met with approval in the eyes of the public. It is that of promptly recognising the military commanders—the admirals of the fleets at sea, and the generals of the armies on the land—of successful campaigns and battles. That recognition has always taken the form of various honours and awards, and promotions in rank. Those honours and awards have meant something to everybody concerned: they were the public recognition of successfully fought campaigns.

But what happened after the success of the Royal Air Force in the Battle of Britain? This was the first and only battle fought exclusively in the air. It is accepted and recognised as a very great victory, comparable in every respect with the other great victories won by our armies and our fleets, and it rightly takes its place as such in our history.

Many of those who served under Dowding during the battle have wondered why, as soon as it became apparent that the battle had been won, the achievement was not recognised in the customary fashion by immediate awards to their Commander-in-Chief. But Dowding has always been very reluctant to express any opinions about the fact that he and his Group Commanders, received no immediate recognition for all that had been achieved in this great victory.

One of those who has felt very strongly about this curious departure from the recognised and established custom is Lord Willoughby de Broke. 'Those of us who worked under Dowding's command were astonished when the only award that he got from a grateful country for winning the Battle of Britain was to be given a bowler hat,' he commented. 'Although he was given a peerage much later on, we all felt that that peerage ought to have been given at the time. Failing that, he at least deserved the honour of being promoted to the rank of Marshal of the Royal Air Force. All of us in Fighter Command felt that he was ill-rewarded for his outstanding services to the country.'

The views that were held by Dowding at the time about any personal recognition that might be made of his achievements may be inferred from his reaction when, in September 1940, he was created a Knight Grand Cross of the Order of the Bath. Harold Balfour had written a letter of congratulation, to which Dowding replied: 'Very many thanks for your letter of congratulations which I very much appreciate. If I could, I would like to cut the Decoration up into a thousand pieces and distribute it to the Fighter Boys who are the ones who have really earned it.'

Peter Wykeham has offered a shrewd comment on that, and its relationship to a more appropriate recognition, with the statement: 'These were the words that any one would have expected who knew the real Dowding. They were sincerely and strongly felt. But there was something very matter-of-fact about this award, coming when it did. As a very senior officer, in fact the most senior officer in the Royal Air Force, close to the time when he must expect to retire, he might normally have hoped for some such distinction, even if there had been no war at all. Many officers have been awarded it, before and since, as an expression of satisfaction for a routine job well done. It was the first of the indications that Dowding was going to escape the plaudits ordinarily extended to a victor, and the squadrons were to feel the omission as a reflection on themselves.'

There are on record innumerable accounts of the way in which Winston Churchill took a keen personal interest in the appointments of the senior officers of all three Services, and of the bruises and scars that various admirals and generals came to bear as a result of that interest, which many thought of as interference. In his book on Wavell, Dowding's contemporary and old friend, John Connell has written of Churchill's tactics in his dealings with his military commanders: 'Churchill used every weapon of aggressive debate—mordant sarcasm, prosecuting counsel's bullying, extravagant rhetorical flourishes, urchin abuse, Ciceronian irony and sledgehammer brutality.'

Winston Churchill disliked Wavell, and that dislike was unquestionably based on Churchill's lack of understanding of the man. 'General Wavell, who was inarticulate to the verge of dumbness . . . failed to get on terms with him,' Sir Ian Jacob has written, adding, in his assessment of Churchill, that '. . . he was a poor judge of character . . . brought up in an atmosphere of political controversy, and thought nothing of rows and discussion.'

Since Wavell and Dowding were cast in the same mould, and they had so much in common, it could all too easily be assumed that Churchill might have felt about Dowding as he did about Wavell. What were Dowding's experiences in the political cauldron in which his old friend Wavell had found himself only a few months before, and in which he was placed himself in November? Maurice Ashley has written: 'The victorious commander of the fighters in the Battle of Britain was Air Marshal Dowding. Immediately after the battle was won he was retired, to Churchill's displeasure. . .'

At the time when Dowding's whole future was thrown into such a serious state of uncertainty by the sudden order to him from the Secretary of State for Air that he was to relinquish his appointment as Commander-in-Chief, Fighter Command, a suggestion was made by Lord Beaverbrook, the Minister of Aircraft Production, that Dowding should go on a tour of the United States of America. At the Prime Minister's request, Dowding went to see him, and of what was said at their meeting Dowding wrote: 'Churchill told me how he felt about my being replaced as Commander-in-Chief of Fighter Command. He expressed to me his surprise that this should have been done "in the moment of victory".'

If Winston Churchill kept the very tight control that he is known to have exercised over the senior appointments in the Services, how did it come about, it must be asked, that he knew nothing about Dowding being relieved of his command? There is a particular urgency in this question when one notes that Churchill made a point of referring to Dowding's going in 'the moment of victory'.

'If it was done without reference to Churchill, and he had reacted true to form,' Dowding has since commented, 'he'd have gone through the roof. But he didn't. Moreover, he did not indicate to me that he had made any personal opposition to it. There is something about what was said to me that I have always found difficult to reconcile with what was known of the way things were done.'

In the book *Action This Day*, which is a joint account by several very well known men of their personal experiences of 'working with Churchill', the point is stressed time and time again that Churchill always insisted on everything being in writing. But, there is no record on file of any written instruction from Churchill to the Air Ministry about Dowding's appointment or his having to relinquish it. That would appear to support all that Churchill had said to Dowding; but one cannot help asking if Dowding was among the first of the Air Marshals to have to bear the dubious distinction of Churchillian disfavour.

To what extent that disfavour, if it did exist, was an outcome of any personal intervention on Churchill's part in the wings controversy, and how much that weighed against Dowding, is very difficult to assess. There is the allegation that through the political intervention of the adjutant of Douglas Bader's squadron, and the interest taken in that by senior politicians, the Prime Minister made enquiries. If he did that in the manner that is credited to him, Churchill must have been fully acquainted with what had been going on behind the scenes, and with the views of the Air Ministry.

It would then seem, if that allegation is true that, from the time of his lone stand against Churchill at the Cabinet meeting of 15 May until the moment in November when the ill-advised support was given by authority to Dowding's opponents in their conception of the big wings tactics, Dowding must have been a marked man. And if that is true, then Wavell's prediction about what would happen to Dowding, as a result of his opposition to Churchill, had come true with politics winning the day.

During the morning of 20 November, Dowding compiled a list of officers serving at his Headquarters whom he wished to have invited to a farewell cocktail party that he was to give at his home at Montrose. It was obviously a trying chore for him. I had the task of issuing the invitations by telephone. Of that I wrote in my diary: 'Some accepting gracefully, some enthusiastically, some volubly—but all accepting.'

In addition to the routine work of the office that day there were also several phone calls that had to be dealt with from officials of the Ministry of Aircraft Production. They were stressing the wish for Dowding to be on his way to the United States as quickly as possible. 'Still no indication from the Old Man as to how he feels about that,' I wrote.

In the afternoon Dowding wrote on a quarto sheet of plain paper, still using his old pen to do it, his farewell message to those men of his command about whom he felt so deeply. If outwardly he showed no sign of how he felt, there was a full enough expression in that message, which he instructed should be sent as a signal to all units under his command. He addressed it to 'My dear Fighter Boys,' and it read:

In sending you this my last message I wish I could say all that is in my heart.

I cannot hope to surpass the simple eloquence of the Prime Minister's words 'Never before has so much been owed by so many to so few.' That debt remains and will increase.

In saying goodbye to you I want you to know how continually you have been in my thoughts, and that, though our direct connection may be severed, I may yet be able to help you in your gallant fight.

Goodbye to you and God bless you all.

CHAPTER FIFTEEN

ANOTHER WORLD

With the sudden coming to an end of all that Dowding had worked so hard for, and had lived for with such devotion over a long period of time, and the culmination of all that in the intense experience of the battle which had been fought so hard and won so splendidly, it would have been both natural and proper for the whole of our people to look to the Commander-in-Chief of Fighter Command and to pay him due homage. So far as those who served under him were concerned, there had always been the utmost respect, and after the battle they had added to that a pride that they felt in him as their leader. But from the country as a whole, from those outside his Command, there could be only silence. The world's attention was rightly focused on the achievements of those who had done the actual fighting—Dowding's 'chicks'—and their leader, who had always been an aloof figure, was allowed to remain at first in, and then very quickly to disappear into, the shadows.

Any homage that may have been, and was due, meant nothing watsoever to Dowding. It is only now, with time placing the events in the correct perspective, that it can be seen how strangely his great service was allowed to go at the time quite unacknowledged, and how callously those who could have been kinder saw fit to brush him aside. Because of the deeply rooted reticence that is so much a part of his character, Dowding allowed that to happen without giving it a thought. Such recognition meant nothing to him.

Right to the end, despite all that happened and the unhappy way in which his conception of Manners had been so violated, Dowding remained the thorough-going professional airman: cool, objective, and, for all his distress over the personal unhappiness caused him, entirely decorous in his manner. That he was tired was beyond doubt; that he was hurt was very understandable, though he showed no sign of it; that he was as considerate as ever in his personal relationships with other people I have particular reason to recall through having been a first-hand witness of those last hours of Dowding's at Bentley Priory.

During the meeting that Dowding had with Winston Churchill he was told by the Prime Minister more about Lord Beaverbrook's suggestion and their joint wish that he should go to the United States of America on the technical mission on behalf of the Air Ministry.

'I replied that I did not wish to accept such an appointment under the Air Ministry, about which I said some rather rude things,' Dowding recalled.

'I have the right to demand that you should accept this appointment,' Churchill replied.

'So I went,' Dowding added.

In the course of the tour that he made of the United States and parts of Canada, Dowding visited aircraft factories and military bases and establishments, and he talked with a vast number of people, including important discussions with the President. In the itinerary of that tour, which extended over a period of nearly five months—from 18 December 1940 to 5 May 1941—there was sufficient rigour to have given any presidential candidate cause to shudder. Of the results achieved, only histories dealing with technical matters can provide an adequate answer. Dowding had not wanted to go, and there was agreement later that he was not exactly the right man for the demands that were made upon him. He was a great military commander. He was not a businessman, and he was very far from being a politician.

The only outcome of that tour that has lingered in Dowding's mind was the position that he found himself in as the result of help that he tried to give in easing a difficult situation that had developed for British subjects living in the United States. The regulations imposed by the British Government in their effort to conserve precious dollars were such that the income of these people from British sources could not be converted into the dollars which they needed for bare living, and there were situations of outright hardship that were entirely unjust.

When Dowding had this state of affairs brought to his attention during the course of his tour he gave vigorous support to help ease the stringency of the regulations. But all that bounced smartly back on him, to his astonishment, when he saw the Prime Minister on his return to England. Winston Churchill expressed his anger to Dowding about what he had done, accusing him of interfering in something that was none of his business.

Towards the end of June 1941, an official letter arrived for Dowding from the Air Ministry stating that it was the Air Council's wish 'that you will be good enough to write a despatch on the Battle of Britain, which was fought under your Command during July, August and September last. . .'

That in itself, Dowding felt, was a pleasant enough task to look forward to, and he gladly accepted it. But the very next paragraph of that letter, for all its official coolness, had about it an all too familiar ring.

'I am at the same time to inform you that the Council greatly regret that, with the conclusion of your work on this despatch, they will have no further employment to offer you,' it was stated. 'You will accordingly be placed on the retired list with effect from 1st October next . . . and the requisite notice will appear in the London Gazette in due course.'

Dowding had three months in which to write his despatch. 'This suited me very well,' he recorded in his notes at the time. He set to work, in a willing mood, and he has commented on the very material help that was given him in this important undertaking by the well-known John Nerney, who was then the Head of the Air Historical Branch of the Air Ministry, and who was particularly knowledgeable about the history of the Royal Air Force. Out of Dowding's work there came the document which bears the introductory note: 'The following despatch was submitted to the Secretary of State for Air on August 20th, 1941, by Air Chief Marshal Sir Hugh C. T. Dowding, G.C.B., G.C.V.O., C.M.G., A.D.C., Air Officer Commanding-in-Chief, Fighter Command, Royal Air Force.'

On 27 September 1941, a year to the day when, it was later realised, the Germans must have known, by their change in tactics, that they had failed in the day Battle of Britain, Dowding finally received from the Air Ministry an official notification about his retirement from the Royal Air Force. Signed by Sir Arthur Street, the highly respected Permanent Under-Secretary of State for Air, the letter read: 'I am commanded by the Air Council to state that, on the occasion of your retirement from the active list, they desire to place on record their high apprecia- tion of the valuable services which you have rendered during your long and distinguished career in the Royal Flying Corps and the Royal Air Force. The Air Council have most particu- larly in mind the ability and tenacity with which, over a period of more than four years, you discharged the onerous responsi- bilities, both in peace and war, of Air Officer Commanding- in-Chief, Fighter Command.'

Notice must be taken of the fact that no direct mention was made even in this official document of Dowding's success in the Battle of Britain. There was only the stilted reference to his having 'discharged the onerous responsibilities' of a Com- mander-in-Chief 'both in peace and war', without any reference at all being made to the greatest feat that has ever been achieved by any air commander. It was well known by then that the R.A.F. had won that great battle—there was publicity enough about it propagated even by the Air Ministry—and yet there was still a reluctance by officialdom to give appropriate credit for that. It is correct that modesty should be shown in speaking about one's achievements. But Dowding was an essential part of the Royal Air Force, and why, one has to ask yet again, did the Air Ministry go on so persistently avoiding mention of his name in the context of the Battle of Britain?

On the same day that Dowding received that letter he had an interview with the Secretary of State for Air during which Sinclair told him that it was the wish of the Prime Minister that he should 'take on the job of looking for possible economies in the Air Force'.

'This I was most reluctant to do,' Dowding stated, and the next day he wrote, from his home in Wimbledon, to Sinclair. Referring to all the letters that had been exchanged before and during the Battle of Britain, Dowding pointed out that on 29 June, only four months before, he 'was informed for the eighth time in my service (for I was twice told that I should have to leave the R.A.F. in Lord Trenchard's time shortly after the last war) that I should be placed on the retired list.'

After pointing out 'this event took place in due course,' Dowding added: '. . . I readjusted my whole life and ideas; took this house and furnished it; brought my sister up from the country to keep house for me; and wrote a small book. I have in fact been completely happy as my own master for the first time in my life.'

The strength of Dowding's feeling about what was now being suggested is revealed in the next paragraph, which reads: 'You may imagine then with what distaste I view the prospect of returning to harness under the same yoke which has galled me so deeply. If I thought that the Country needed my services and that this need did not exist a month ago and could not have been foreseen, if I were convinced that this was the case, I should not hesitate to put all personal considerations aside and to do what you ask. But I do not think that this is necessary.'

Instead of asking him to do this work, there were other retired officers who were suitable and who would be happy to do it, Dowding suggested. He added: 'If you will do me the honour of reading the latter part of my book when it is published, you will understand me when I say that I believe that my energies may perhaps be better employed outside rather than inside the service.'

Only two days before, one responsible newspaper, the *Observer*, had posed a question about Dowding's retirement from the R.A.F. with the statement: 'It is the more astonishing to those who are in touch with aviation that it should have been found possible to place Sir Hugh Dowding on the retired list at the present time. No Air Force officer has done greater things than he, and it can hardly be believed that the country has, at this critical moment, no further need of his services in the Royal Air Force.'

No one could know how Dowding felt about that, and how embarrassing, while still being well-intentioned, it was for him to have people asking such questions. What had happened was, in fact, something that he wanted to have happen, so that, once and for all, he could sever all links with a past that he felt, for his own peace of mind, he must forget.

This subject of the critical comments that had been appearing in the press about his retirement was mentioned by Dowding in his letter to the Secretary of State. 'You probably know me well enough to need no assurance that I have nothing directly or indirectly to do with any sort of press campaign, but these criticisms may possibly be the cause of some embarrassment to you,' he wrote. 'If you would like me to do so, I will make a public statement, written or broadcast, saying that I am well content with the situation as it exists and asking my unknown friends to desist from their well-meant efforts. If you don't like the suggestion, please forget that I have made it.'

But Dowding was not to be let off. A summons came for him from the Prime Minister, and at 5 o'clock on the afternoon of 30 October he found himself facing Winston Churchill yet again in the Cabinet Room at No. 10 Downing Street.

'He told me that he had personally selected me for the duties proposed,' Dowding recorded in his notes at the time. 'He said that he had seen my letter to Sinclair.' Dowding asked why someone like Salmond or some other Marshal of the R.A.F. could not do the work.

'Because I want you to do it,' Churchill replied.

To Dowding's surprise, Churchill told him that he had known nothing about his being retired from the R.A.F. Dowding has said that he was 'so astonished' at this that he could only put a direct question about it to the Prime Minister.

'Do you mean to say that you were never told about my retirement?' he asked.

'I knew nothing about it until I saw it in the papers,' Churchill replied.

Dowding felt compelled to tell the Prime Minister that it was with the utmost reluctance that he would agree to work under Sir Archibald Sinclair, 'whom I disliked and distrusted'.

'He is one of my oldest friends,' the Prime Minister replied. 'I don't think he has ever spoken badly of you, though others may have.'

Now that he was finally on the retired list, Dowding explained to the Prime Minister, he wanted to publish the small book— it was a long essay—that he had just written, adding that part of it had to do with the air. He could not have done that while he was still a serving officer. Realising that Churchill was determined to have his own way, Dowding said that he would start work in the appointment 'as soon as the book was published'. The Prime Minister then agreed that there should not be any announcement about the 'impending employment', as Dowding called it, until after the publication of the book.

'He told me that the C.A.S. had already assured him that no further economies were possible,' Dowding recorded in his notes, 'and I felt then that the appointment was certain to revive all the smouldering animosity which had existed between the Ministry and myself during the past five years. However, the P.M. was so insistent that, much against my will, I finally accepted the appointment.'

Dowding left a copy of the manuscript of his book with Churchill. It had been in the hands of the Air Ministry officials for over a fortnight, he explained, and Churchill assured him that he would read it over the week-end and 'be my censor'.

After this somewhat prickly meeting with the Prime Minister, Dowding wrote to Sir Archibald Sinclair and to Lord Beaverbrook, explaining to them that Winston Churchill 'had overridden my refusal'. He received an immediate reply from Beaverbrook, who wrote: 'The Prime Minister told me about it today. He said that immense responsibility now develops upon you, and believes you will discharge your job with such spirit that immeasurable benefits will flow. Perhaps in the future in the battlefront we will be together again. That is my hope. Heaven knows, you were a tough master.'

The next move that Dowding made was to see Sir Arthur Street at the Air Ministry. Street was in many ways the father confessor of many of the Air Marshals of his time. Dowding told Street that pending the Prime Minister's agreement to his book being published, he would start work unofficially on the preliminary papers having to do with the work that was being asked of him.

The choice had been given Dowding by both the Prime Minister and by Sir Archibald Sinclair about the conditions of his service, and Dowding asked Street to see to it that there should be a cancellation of the gazetting of his retirement. He did not wish to be employed as a retired officer, and the Prime Minister had already agreed to that cancellation.

'You would get more as a retired officer,' Street advised him. 'I'm not doing this for the money,' Dowding replied.

That rejoinder to Arthur Street's well-intentioned advice was not intended to be as unappreciative as it might have sounded. Dowding was far from being a man of any wealth, and there was a stern need for him to husband his somewhat slender resources; but he genuinely felt that in this instance it was not a matter of what money he could make out of the work. It was the work that was to be done, if he was to do it, that was of importance.

The very next day a file marked secret, the first of the papers, was delivered to Dowding at his home. Three days later Dowding returned the papers to Arthur Street; and the next day Dowding wrote to the Prime Minister and told him that he thought that the project was being tackled 'from the wrong end'. He also reminded Churchill that he was awaiting his decision about permission to publish his book.

An immediate reply to this reminder was made by the Prime Minister. 'I have looked through some parts of your proofs (sic) and have had the book carefully read for me by Brendan Bracken,' Churchill stated. 'We both agreed that for various reasons it would not be a good thing for you to publish the book at this time. The Air Ministry are moreover anxious about the technical aspects. I have asked you to do a very important work which will be a real service to the country, and for which I believe you are specially fitted. I would suggest to you that this duty should come first, and that you should defer the publication till after you have discharged it.'

This rejection, for that was what it amounted to, would have been a discouraging enough one for any author to have to accept. For Dowding there was in it yet further disregard for what he wanted to say about matters which concerned him very deeply; and favour was being shown by officialdom in getting from him what they wanted regardless of his own feelings. A few days later he had a talk with Brendan Bracken about the ban that had now been placed on his book. In addition to being the Minister of Information, Bracken was one of Churchill's closest personal friends. He told Dowding that he would speak to the officials at the Air Ministry about the book, and see what he could do about getting it cleared for publication.

The next day Dowding wrote to Bracken about that. 'The Air Ministry, so far as my knowledge goes, have not opposed publication in toto,' Dowding wrote, 'but they are anxious about the technical aspects. Of course I could delete or amend passages to which reasonable objection could be taken, if the book were not thereby eviscerated; but, if in the discussion of the principles of modern air warfare I should arrive at an unorthodox conclusion, I think that I should be allowed to state a case for thoughtful people to get their teeth into. There is no fact in the book which the Germans do not know, or if there is I will excise it.'

The issue over whether or not he was to be allowed to publish what he had come to feel so strongly about, was a very grave one to Dowding, and, as always, he did not give up without a fight. 'It is difficult to know exactly where duty lies in this sort of dilemma,' Dowding continued in his letter to Bracken; 'but, on thinking things over, I feel that in surrendering my liberty I have yielded too easily to the appeal to the military habit of obedience in which my life has been spent. The book was written under a compelling urge, and I think it would do good in making people think about the war, and still more good in making them think about after the war.'

Through his own long experience of the ways of officialdom, Dowding felt that there were several influences at work trying to silence him. But he also knew that whereas with the Air Staff he could make firm statements, as he had done so often in the past, now he had to exercise more caution. He concluded his letter to Bracken with the statement: 'The decision was the Prime Minister's, but you are his responsible Minister. If, therefore, you were able to advise the Prime Minister to modify his decision I should be very happy. If publication is delayed till after the war, it will be too late for the book to serve its purpose.'

Two days after writing to Brendan Bracken, Dowding was asked 'to dine and sleep at Chequers'. Over dinner that night there was a discussion about the work that Dowding was to do in finding possible methods of saving man-power. After it, in the customary fashion, there was the showing of a film. In this case, it was a Russian one. 'Everybody raved,' Dowding recorded in his notes, 'but I thought it crude.'

It was not until 'late at night' that Churchill finally got around to speaking to Dowding about his book. 'He mentioned the passage in which I had expressed views about our policy of the Balance of Power,' Dowding wrote, 'and he said that he thought it would be quoted by our enemies.'

To Dowding's astonishment, Churchill then went on to say, in Dowding's words, that he 'did not believe in world harmony', and he compared it 'with the result of mixing together all the paints in a child's paint box'. Dowding's notes continue: 'He thought the English Speaking Nations might work four hours a day after the war and have a good time during the other twenty.' On top of that there came for Dowding the disturbing impression from the way the Prime Minister was speaking that he 'didn't seem to believe in working for peace', and that he believed an 'atmosphere of struggle necessary to avoid decadence'.

As might be expected, it was impossible for Dowding to remain silent about that. 'I said that was all very well in the old days when all that was necessary was for men to keep their bodies fit and their weapons handy,' Dowding recorded. But Churchill merely commented that he was not interested in the remote future.

So far as Dowding was concerned it was a 'perambulating conversation' to the accompaniment of the playing of gramophone records, with the Prime Minister breaking off from time to time to join in the chorus. It was an 'occasion not suitable for serious or intelligent discussion', was the only comment that Dowding could make in summing up his unsatisfactory visit to Chequers.

After that discouraging experience, Dowding wrote again to Brendan Bracken. He said that it was clear to him that the Prime Minister would not change his mind about the ban that had been placed on the publication of his book. In his notes, Dowding wrote: 'I was glad that B.B. should know my views.'

Three days later Bracken replied: 'This seems to settle the

matter for the present, but in any case I suppose that your return to the active list would have affected the question of immediate publication.' To Dowding's surprise, Bracken added: 'I always shared the Prime Minister's indignation at your having been placed on the Retired List, and I was more pleased than I can say to read of your new duties.'

The official notification that was issued to Dowding about the nature of these duties in what was to him a thoroughly unpleasant task read: 'To examine the Establishments of the Royal Air Force in the United Kingdom and to report to what extent and in what particulars they can be reduced without prejudice to operational efficiency.'

As a result of his intensive inquiries, Dowding made a number of proposals about economies in man power. 'Most of them were hotly opposed by the Air Ministry,' he wrote some years later, 'and I resumed my position as Public Enemy No. 1. It was an extremely unpleasant situation and there was no reason why I should tolerate it after six months, when I could find none but minor extravagances to criticise.'

Into this unpleasant atmosphere there seeped one day a rumour that Dowding was to be sent to the Middle East to continue with what he described as 'my witch hunt' out there. 'This prospect was quite intolerable,' he commented, 'so I made an offensive minute by a Member of the Air Council an excuse for a show of injured dignity and asked to be placed on the retired list at my own request.'

Under these circumstances, Dowding made a comment in his own notes on the close of his military career that said no more than 'so ended my forty-two years of Service.'

With his first retirement in October 1941, one of the earliest of the many articles that Dowding was to write over the years that lay ahead appeared in the *Sunday Chronicle*. It was on the Battle of Britain. Dowding sent a copy of it to Keith Park, who replied from the Headquarters of No. 23 Training Group, which he was now commanding, in the quiet depths of Gloucestershire.

'Your article is the more gratifying,' Park commented, 'as I heard last week that the present A.O.C. 11 Group is still relating with relish his own account of a certain Air Council Meeting after the Battle was won. According to that account, the S. of S. decided that the A.O.C. 12 Group was correct in his claim that he could have won the "Battle of Britain" more easily etc. etc., than was done by H.Q. 11 Group. Your article is not only interesting reading, but should counteract false tales that are apparently being put about.'

In a second reference in this letter to these 'false tales that are very unfair to H.Q. Fighter Command as well as H.Q. 11 Group,' Park added that under his command 11 Group had 'put into practice so effectively the policy laid down by the Commander-in-Chief'.

That was said only a year after the Battle of Britain had been fought and won, and questions with sound reasoning to them had not yet been asked in any broad sense about the treatment that had been accorded the two men who had led Fighter Command in the Battle. It was too soon after the event to be able to appreciate that in any general sense. Moreover, those who were in the ascendancy after their successful manoeuvring in opposition to Dowding and Park were seeing to it that, as Park had pointed out, the truth of what had happened was not being allowed breathing space.

Ten months after Dowding's last appeal to be allowed to publish his book, he wrote again to Brendan Bracken about it, on 27 September 1942, referring to his last letter of the previous November. 'Nearly a year has lapsed, and I am again and finally on the retired list,' he explained, 'so I want to ask you if publication may now be permitted.'

Mentioning that official permission to publish the book in the United States had been sought in April through the British Ambassador in Washington, Dowding explained that 'the proposal was negatived by the Air Ministry.' He went on to state: 'The book is bound to be published some day, and I don't want to lay myself open to the criticism that delay in publication was due to any inertia in my part.'

But official permission to publish was still withheld, and the book—*Twelve Legions of Angels*, subtitled An Essay in Straight Thinking—was not finally published until 1946, after the war. All that Dowding had feared about this delay possibly ruining the chances of his gaining a public hearing were then realised, and the book was, in his own words, 'a resounding flop'. That was a great pity because, slight though the book is in size, it is, as he has described it, 'pure Hugh Dowding'.

In the early summer of 1942, Dowding discovered, with a feeling of perplexity that was strongly tinged with an understandable anger that his completed despatch was being withheld from the correct circulation which he believed should have been given to it. He well appreciated that it was a highly secret document, but why it should have been witheld from some of those who were most intimately concerned with its contents he had no way of knowing. In writing to the Prime Minister on another subject, Dowding mentioned that. He spoke of what struck him as a refusal at the Air Ministry to accept his opinion, and, in support of that, he pointed out that 'my despatch on the Battle of Britain has been withheld even from Commanders-in-Chief and Service Members of the Air Council.'

This comment on such an extraordinary state of affairs about a document as important as this despatch reached Winston Churchill in Cairo, where he was on a visit after travelling to Moscow for his first meeting with Stalin. Churchill was not exactly in a happy mood. For one thing, the disastrous raid at Dieppe had taken place only a few days before. And there were difficulties being reported to him in the planning with the Americans for the future. Churchill had more than enough to worry about.

The only bright spot on his horizon at that moment was the lifting of the siege of Malta, where several ships out of a convoy of fourteen managed to fight their way through to the relief of the island; and curiously enough the recently appointed Air Officer Commanding in Malta was Keith Park. He had immediately started using in the defence of the island the very same tactics that he had used with such distinction in the Battle of Britain. Park went on using them in Malta with such marked success that they proved yet again how right he had been in the tactics that he had used during the summer of 1940.

'This vigorous, skilful, and very experienced commander was appointed to Malta because the defence of the island

seemed for the time being even more important that its offensive against enemy shipping,' the official historians Richards
and Saunders have stated; 'and what Park did not know about
fighter defence was not worth knowing.'

In the reply that Winston Churchill made from Cairo to
Dowding's letter, he wrote that he was 'enquiring into how it
was that your despatch on the Battle of Britain was not published. I understood more than a year ago from the Chief of
the Air Staff that it would be published.'

This was not the point that Dowding was trying to make, and
he replied immediately to the Prime Minister, stating: 'I did
not suggest that my despatch on the Battle of Britain should be
published. I don't think it is suitable for general publication
until after the war. But I do think that it ought to be sent to
senior and responsible officers in the services, so that my
opinions may at least serve as a basis for discussion by individuals outside the inner circle of the Air Ministry.'

On 6 September 1942, back in London, the Prime Minister
wrote to Dowding about 'a full report from the Chief of the Air
Staff about the publication and circulation of your despatch on
the Battle of Britain'. Churchill stated that 'it was agreed that
your despatch should not be published now because of the
secret material which it contains. But copies of it were sent to
all concerned in the Air Ministry, including Service Members
of Council, and to the Air Officers Commanding-in-Chief of
the Home Command. Copies were also sent to other Service
Departments, who would no doubt bring them to the notice
of the officers concerned.'

The extent to which official interest was being shown in the
despatch was revealed in Churchill's further statement: 'I may
add that early this year, the American Ambassador asked me
whether the President could be shown a copy of your despatch
and said that it would be most useful if the information in it
could be made available to the American military authorities.
Both these things were done.'

There was a certain element of satisfaction for Dowding in
knowing that the Americans were showing such an alert
interest in his despatch, but the details given in Churchill's
letter about the alleged full circulation still did not tally with
the first-hand information that he had received. He wrote to

Churchill again to inform him of the position. He named the senior commanders, and even a Member of the Air Council, who had told him that they had not seen the despatch.

'I told Sinclair that Pile had not had a copy, and he expressed concern and made a note,' Dowding reported, 'but nothing happened, so I gave Pile my copy. Gossage, when commanding the Balloon Command, asked for a copy and he told me that his request was refused. Besides being an ex-member of Council he was commanding 11 Fighter Group for the first months of the war, and his work was mentioned in the despatch. All this is quite unimportant, but I should like you to know that I had reasonable evidence for my statement to you.'

But the Prime Minister did not think that it was 'quite unimportant', and only five days later, on 13 September, he wrote to Dowding stating: 'I am now informed that, although the circulation list, including Service Members of Council and Commanders-in-Chief, was approved in September 1941, owing to an oversight copies of your despatch on the Battle of Britain were in fact circulated only within the Air Staff.'

It was as Dowding had suspected, and there had been yet another gaffe on the part of somebody at the Air Ministry. Churchill continued: 'Instructions have now been given to remedy this, and copies of the report have been sent to the Service Members of Council, Commanders-in-Chief at home, and the other Service Departments. The Chief of the Air Staff himself is seeing that copies go to General Pile and Air Marshal Gossage. While regretting this error should have occurred, the Chief of the Air Staff assures me that your despatch was most carefully studied in the Air Staff and that many of the views expressed in it have long since been incorporated in the corpus of Air Force doctrine on matters of Air defence.'

Into the quiet of the other world—it could almost be described as a seclusion in which Dowding was living after his final retirement—there came on 12 May 1943, going on for three years after the Battle of Britain had been fought and won, the long overdue recognition of all that he had achieved. In the post that day, addressed to him at his home in Wimbledon, an envelope arrived that was marked 'Urgent Personal and

Confidential', with 'Prime Minister' stamped on the front and '10 Downing Street, Whitehall' on the back.

Opening the letter with an understandable apprehension, Dowding found that it was from Winston Churchill. It was to tell him that it had been proposed that his name should be put forward for the honour of a Barony, 'in view of your ever-memorable services to this country during the Battle of Britain'. Churchill added the comment: 'I should like you to know that when I first mooted this proposal it received the warm acclamation of your colleagues in the Royal Air Force and in the Air Ministry.'

Although he naturally appreciated this gesture, delayed though it was, Dowding had become interested, by then, in other matters. When he had finally been retired from the R.A.F., he had, in his own words, 'to decide what I should do with the rest of my life'. He was much too alert to be able to sit back, and too active both by inclination and by temperament to want to vegetate in the manner that might have been expected of a retired and very senior officer. 'I did not want to go in for "guinea-pigging" in City directorships, even if such positions should be offered to me,' he commented. 'I wanted to do something useful with the rest of my life.'

At the time he thought of what he called 'three alternatives' for further study and work that might appeal to him. The first was 'to brush up my mathematics so that I might be qualified to understand something about nuclear physics'. In *Twelve Legions of Angels*, which was written, it must be remembered, in 1941, he had offered the comment: 'I shudder to think what may happen if and when the energy locked up in the atom becomes available to the human race.'

The second alternative was 'to join in the investigation of those mysterious phenomena which come under the generic name of radiesthesia'. The third was 'to delve into the mysteries of spiritualism'. This third alternative had first attracted Dowding's attention during the First World War when he had read *The Life Beyond the Veil*, by Vale Owen, but he had not given it much thought since then. An official alternative for an entirely different way of life had come to him with the offer of the Governorship of Southern Rhodesia. 'I had no hesitation in declining,' he said of that. 'I had seen too many

Governors and High Commissioners in action to covet their jobs.'

It was in spiritualism that Dowding found a keen interest and stimulation, and in the years that lay ahead he did a great deal of work studying and examining 'the very voluminous evidence which existed on the subject'. He then succeeded, as he has explained, 'in thoroughly convincing myself of the fact of the conscious survival of death and the possibility of communicating with dead people in certain circumstances'.

In the course of this work, Dowding met Mrs Muriel Whiting, a young widow whose husband, Max, had been a flight engineer in Bomber Command—as with so many others he was in the R.A.F. Volunteer Reserve—and had been killed in 1944 when the Lancaster in which he was flying was destroyed during a special mission over enemy occupied territory. She also had an intense interest in spiritualism and theosophy, and these interests which they shared brought them close together. Out of a deep understanding of each other and a compassion that led them both to feel a need to help those in distress, there also developed other interests, one of which has been their intense desire to further the prevention of cruelty to animals. They were married in 1950, and together they became recognised leaders in the spheres in which they worked as both pioneers and authorities.

After some twelve years of keen activity in this work, Dowding was suddenly afflicted with arthritis of a particularly wide-spread nature and rapidity in development. It became for him a most severe handicap, and it has increased in its severity since then; but, as would have been expected of such a man, in the restrictions that have come to be placed on his life there has never been a word of complaint. He has much to thank his wife for in the help that she has given him, and Dowding makes a point of happily acknowledging that.

On 24 September 1946, a Sunday which was marked as one of remembrance before the Sunday nearest to 15 September became the recognised day for such national observance, Dowding made a broadcast for the B.B.C. He spoke about how slowly the full importance of the Battle of Britain had dawned on the people of this country, which, he observed, seemed strange to him.

'My memories take me back to a period of almost intolerable stress and anxiety which is, nevertheless, now very precious to me,' he said. He suggested that people should not think too much of individuals and personalities, adding: 'Think of us as a Battle of Britain team in which everyone from Prime Minister to aircraft hand played an allotted part. Think especially and with eternal gratitude of the pilots—those who returned to base and those who did not.' Thought should be given to the wounded and the bereaved, he suggested, and, 'in days when material values loom so large remember too that illimitable power which upheld our arms in those dark but glorious days . . . which we poor mortals know as God.'

Those pilots and other air crews to whom Dowding referred in that broadcast who had survived the war banded together immediately afterwards and formed The Battle of Britain Fighter Association. Dowding became the President of the Association, and Keith Park the Vice-President; and among the aims of the Association were the welfare of its members and their dependants, and 'to preserve the memory of fighter aircrew who died in the Battle of Britain'.

The date of 15 September was selected as the day for a national annual remembrance of the Battle of Britain. It has continued in that fashion, and each year on that day there is held a reunion of the members of the Fighter Association whose qualification is that they should have flown at least one operational sortie during the battle in one of the fighter or Coastal Command or Fleet Air Arm squadrons which took part in the battle. Dowding became associated with these reunions, which, after a time, came to be held at the Headquarters of Fighter Command at Bentley Priory, and he made a point of attending them right from the start and up until his illness made that impossible.

In the minds and the hearts of those of the Fighter Association there has always been, despite the little that they knew of Dowding, or even saw of him, during the battle, a feeling of the utmost loyalty and a great pride in having served under him. On the occasion, in 1969, of his eighty-seventh birthday, Dowding received from the Association a telegram which read:

'Many happy returns and affectionate greetings from your chicks.'

Among those chicks in this year, twenty-nine years after the battle, were men such as the Chief of the Air Staff, Air Chief Marshal Sir John Grandy. In the battle he had been a Squadron Leader commanding a Hurricane squadron. A member of the Air Council, the Air Member for Personnel, Air Marshal Sir Andrew Humphrey, had been a young Pilot Officer in the battle. There were others who had come to positions of high command in the Service; and there were others who had made their way in distinguished careers in civilian life; and there were those who had been content to live their lives without the necessity of having to achieve any particular public distinction. All of them shared in the one great experience which gave them the right to wear the golden rosette on the ribbon of the medal of the 1939–45 Star which indicates participation in the fighting of the Battle of Britain.

CHAPTER SIXTEEN

'WHERE WOULD WE HAVE BEEN . . .?'

There was a great deal about the Battle of Britain that has given Dowding cause to feel a pride that has never dimmed in the men who served under his command. That has always been uppermost in his mind. There were also, as was perhaps only to be expected, some aspects of the battle that have caused him to feel a hurt that has lingered, and which has attached to it an inevitable sorrow. Being of the reserved nature that he is he has never been given to expressing himself openly or in force about his own personal feelings. To some extent that could be regarded as a pity. If he had been able to explode, the sorrow over the actions of some of those who served under his command might not have lingered on in his mind. For too long he remained silent; but it is small wonder that he did because, whether it was intentional or unintentional, the infliction of the damage that was done was of a nature that brought to him a very deep personal distress.

'Why were they all so opposed to Dowding, and why did so many people go out of their way to deny him what he was entitled to?' a former member of Leigh-Mallory's staff once asked, and without waiting for a reply added: 'Was it because they could not stand it when Dowding was proved so right and they were proved so wrong?'

It could never be said of Dowding that he ever tried to force a conclusive proof that he was right. He has always tried to arrive at a fair assessment of what he had attempted to do, believing in what he was doing, and he always fought hard for that. But the last effort that he would ever make would be to try to score off anybody at their expense, or dismiss lightly the efforts of other people, even though he might not agree with them. Everyone, in his view, was entitled to some position of attention, and no one should ever have to endure sheer neglect.

After the war, when at last it was all over and the cheering was at its height and the honours and awards to the successful commanders were being passed out thick and fast, what thought was given to the man who, nearly five years before, had laid the foundations for the great victory that was being celebrated? Two years before Winston Churchill had written to him about his acceptance of a peerage and his 'ever-memorable services to this country during the Battle of Britain'. Dowding had accepted that, and had quietly gone on his own way.

Now, when the huzzas where loud and those who had led us to victory were rightly being accorded acclamation, there was no mention of the name of Dowding in any of the official honours and awards and promotions. It was in the last, in the promotions, that there was a curious oversight. Many times it had been asked, even during the war, why Dowding had not been made a Marshal of the Royal Air Force. Now others were promoted to that highest rank in the Service. There was sufficient reason, and a precedent was now established, for this reward. But Dowding remained an Air Chief Marshal.

That Dowding's name was remembered in official circles, even if not in public recognition, is revealed in a letter that the Secretary of State for Air wrote to Dowding on 9 May 1945, the day after the VE Day which marked the ending of the war in Europe. 'On this historic day, I send you on behalf of the Air Council a message of cordial greeting,' Sir Archibald Sinclair stated. 'It was under your inspiring leadership that the Battle of Britain was won and our island citadel was saved. The whole nation, indeed freedom-loving men and women the world over, will always gratefully remember you and the gallant "few" who fought and flew under your command.'

Down through the years there have been repeated questions asked about the reason why Dowding has never received this important promotion to the highest rank in the Royal Air Force. But for all the lip-service that has been paid to the suitability of such recognition of what Dowding had achieved, twenty-eight years had to pass before a firm public statement about that was made by one of his fellow Air Marshals.

In a letter in the *Daily Telegraph*, Air Marshal Sir Robert Saundby, who had been Deputy Commander-in-Chief of Bomber Command, described himself as 'no uncritical admirer of Dowding's'; but he nevertheless saw fit, quite voluntarily, to make about Dowding the statement: 'No one can deny that he led Fighter Command with determination and ability in the

Battle of Britain, one of the decisive battles of the world. Even at this late hour it would be a very proper act of grace and justice if Lord Dowding were to be promoted to the rank of Marshal of the Royal Air Force.'

That was the expression of the opinion of a distinguished officer of air rank. It is echoed in the minds of the many who have wondered about this matter. Foremost among them are those who served under Dowding's command, and particularly his pilots. 'The treatment he received after the battle still baffles me,' Ginger Lacey once said. 'I cannot understand how the authorities were able to talk about the fate of civilisation hanging on the outcome of the Battle of Britain, and yet discard the victor.' And then Lacey asked the question that has been for so long in the minds of so many of Dowding's supporters. 'Where would we have been if Stuffy had lost the battle?'

In speaking about the resurgence of interest that has developed in what happened in the summer of 1940, Dowding had in mind the effect of the film *Battle of Britain* which was released in the summer of 1969. This contains an authentic portrayal by Sir Laurence Olivier of the part of Dowding as Commander-in-Chief of Fighter Command in that crucial time of nearly thirty years ago. But the film is more than just a story about Dowding's achievements: it is the story of the whole battle, as seen from both sides and at all levels.

Along with Tom Gleave, Robert Stanford-Tuck, 'Ginger' Lacey, and Claire Legge of the W.A.A.F. at the time of the Battle of Britain, I was asked to help with advice in the making of the film; and at the same time it became my responsibility to keep Dowding fully informed about what was being done. The producers of the film were extremely anxious that the mammoth task that they had embarked upon should meet with Dowding's approval. He was consulted, and the plans for how he was to be presented were discussed at length; and the enthusiasm of Harry Saltzman and Ben Fisz, the co-producers, and the director, Guy Hamilton, more than satisfied Dowding that they were intent upon doing full justice to the overall story.

So keen did Dowding's own interest become in the actual

making of the film that he visited the studios at Pinewood and the sites on location at the actual airfields which had been used in the battle. He watched some of the shooting of parts of the film, including those with Laurence Olivier at work in a reproduction at the studios of his office as it used to be at the Headquarters of Fighter Command at Bentley Priory; and he was able to see some of the results of that work on film as it was put together.

One afternoon in the summer of 1968, on the airfield at Hawkinge, which lies above Folkestone, and from which some of Keith Park's squadrons of No. 11 Group used to take off during the battle, Dowding talked with Trevor Howard, who plays the part of Park in the film. They were sitting beside one of the Hurricanes which was being used, and filming was going on only a short distance away. The weather was just as it had been in that September of twenty-eight years before: a sparklingly clear, hot, sunny day.

From the direction of the Channel, no distance away, two of the Spitfires which appear in the film came hurtling in, the singing of their Merlin engines awakening strong memories in the minds of those who had known what it had all been like. The two fighters, of that slim beauty that no fashion can decry, slid easily through the air over the airfield, turned, and came in and landed on the grass in a style that marked them as part of a golden age of flying.

Although Dowding watched the aircraft with intense interest, his thoughts were on the subject that we had only just been talking about. He turned to Trevor Howard, and he said: 'If it hadn't been for Keith Park's conduct in the battle, and his loyalty to me as his Commander-in-Chief, we should not be here today.'

At this moment in what we call time, nearly thirty years after the fighting of the Battle of Britain, when we stand with a threat constantly in our minds and we are so beset by fear, it is worth considering, if only for a moment, the views that were expressed by Dowding only two years after he had fought that great battle, and while the Second World War was still in full spate. We have become accustomed to military leaders expounding their views on what should have, or might have, been done, and many of them have been as tiresome as the politicians with their glib excuses and self-adulation. The airman Dowding was a military leader in every sense; but what was his outlook on the future in its relation to the bearing of arms?

'The views that I held then are the same today,' he has said. And because of what we have become those views are of interest, and value today.

'Is war a Good Thing, or not?' Dowding wrote in December 1942. '. . . there are those who think that war and training for war are necessary for the virility of the race, and that periods of continuous peace lead to softness, luxury and decadence. The abstract thought that war is a useful safety-valve for over-population may even be in the minds of some, although it rarely finds expression. If we think that war is good, we are in a happy position; all we have to do is refrain from action and we are assured of an indefinite continuance of this benificent institution.'

But Dowding could never accept that. 'I venture to think, however, that the exponents of this theory constitute an altogether insignificant minority,' he continued; 'we have suffered too much individually and collectively. We look past the flapping of the flags, the blare of the bands, and the cheering of the crowds, and see war as a hateful remedy for worse evils, into which we have been driven with extreme reluctance.' As with everybody else, Dowding asked the age-old question: 'How is it going to be possible to stop war?' His answers rested in 'three possibilities, long, medium and short-term'.

The long term view, Dowding suggested, would be found 'if and when the standard of morality and unselfishness of the individual improves (and) this improvement will be reflected in the moral behaviour of the State'. But he could not see 'that human nature will undergo any such transformation in a period which is within the horizon of our vision today'.

The short-term measure for the control of war could be found, Dowding suggested, 'in the operation of an International Police.' He did not like that, feeling that it 'is not very practical unless the nations contributing to the upkeep of the police force think alike, and continue to do so amid the stresses and strains. . .' He thought of it 'at best' as amounting to 'half the world being kept in subjection by the other half', and he felt that 'it can be expected to do little more than to give us a breathing space to set our house in order.'

'Is there a medium-term policy?' he asked, for it is to the medium-term that we must look for hope and help. For that he turned to a subject which always held for him the greatest interest, and it is a strictly practical one. '. . . an essential step in the creating of contact between nations, and the enlargement of the political unit,' he wrote, 'must be the creation of a common language in some shape or form.' With his never-failing appreciation of reality, Dowding admitted in his further consideration that 'it is idle to discuss the question in the abstract;' but, he stressed, 'the solution depends upon what the nations can be persuaded to accept, and that is essentially a political problem.'

Immediately after any reading of the views of Dowding's, and even after re-reading and studying them many times, there is an inclination towards allowing a slick question to leap into one's mind. Is this not all so very idealistic? The only answer that can be made to that is that it is, of course, idealistic. But only a cynic would belittle on those grounds these thoughts of Dowding's. Where would we be, for all the troubles that beset us today, and for all the disillusionment and bitterness which are so rife, without those whose belief in their ideals give them the courage to work for them? In his fighting of the Battle of Britain, Dowding was both a practical airman and an idealist. It is a relief to find a military leader of such stature thinking, after his time in actual service has ended, in terms of the humanities rather than sheer physical deterrents as a way to the future.

But then, Dowding, the man of simple faith and such great integrity, will always be known above all else as a profound and fearless humanitarian. In this troubled world of today, torn as it is with greed and strife and near despair over man's inability to control himself and to work with any semblance of pride in self and Service and Manners, this airman has always pointed a way, steep though it is, to hope, and warned us of the one great danger that now so gravely besets us.

'Is it really too much to hope that . . . mankind may be induced to eschew the use of force in international relations and that he should do so from motives of altruism and brother-hood, and not from the low motive of fear?' he wrote shortly after the end of the Second World War. 'For fear is the last enemy, fear is the basis of hatred and jealousy and suspicion and cruelty; nothing good or stable was ever built on a foundation of fear.'

INDEX